DATE DUE

WITHDRAWN

D1648329

The Role of Private Placements in Corporate Finance

The Role of Private Placements
in Corporate Finance

ELI SHAPIRO

Sylvan C. Coleman Professor of Financial Management
Harvard University

CHARLES R. WOLF

Associate Professor of Business
Columbia University

Harvard University
Graduate School of Business Administration
Division of Research
Boston 1972

Library of Congress Catalog Card No. 72-87769
ISBN 0-87584-099-X

Printed in the United States of America

Acknowledgments

THIS MANUSCRIPT had its origins in an abortive attempt to produce a manuscript on the Corporate Bond Market as a part of the National Bureau of Economic Research Study of the Post-War Capital Markets. As such, the project was financed by a grant from the Life Insurance Association of America. We wish to acknowledge our indebtedness to both organizations for their financial assistance. In addition, the Sloan Research Fund at the Sloan School of Management at M.I.T. and the Ford Foundation Grant for Research in Finance to the Harvard Business School were generous in their assistance.

Dr. James J. O'Leary, former Director of Research of the Life Insurance Association of America, and Dr. Kenneth M. Wright, currently Director of Research, were continuous sources of encouragement and help. Professor Raymond Goldsmith of Yale University, Director of the Post-War Capital Market Project, was a constant source of help, encouragement, and constructive criticism. Professor Bertrand Fox of the Harvard Business School, formerly Director of Research, was helpful both by his knowledge of the corporate bond market and by his persistent needling to complete this manuscript. A special note of thanks is owed to Professor Victor L. Andrews of the Georgia State University who contributed to the original version of this manuscript many years ago.

Many people were helpful in all or parts of the review process as the successive drafts appeared. Mr. Sidney Homer, retired Partner of Salomon Brothers, was both a source of extremely useful information and a very constructive critic. Professors Maurice Wilkinson, Stanley Diller, and Roger Murray of Columbia University commented on some or all of the manuscript. Professors John Lintner, William L. White, and Warren Law at the Harvard Business School provided us with helpful insights which are incorporated in this manuscript. Mrs. Elizabeth Bancala of the LIAA Staff and Mr. Robert Menke of the SEC gave unstintingly of their knowledge of the relevant data. Messrs. Richard Fisher of Morgan Stanley and P. R. Reynolds and J. H. Bloodgood of The Travelers Insurance Companies supplied useful criticism of our manuscript.

Numerous businesses were helpful in their cooperation. These include Lehman Brothers, Salomon Brothers, Kidder Peabody, Morgan Stanley, Goldman Sachs, and the Robert Morris Associates. The Pension Fund Departments of Morgan Guaranty, Bankers Trust, First National City Bank, and the U. S. Steel Corporation deserve our thanks for the time they gave us. In addition, the Prudential Insurance Company, the New England Mutual Life Insurance Company, and the John Hancock Life Insurance Company gave us both the time of their staffs and valuable data series. Many state and local retirement funds and corporate treasurers responded to our requests for information.

Mrs. Marion Buhagiar of *Fortune Magazine* was very helpful in editing a diffuse manuscript. Last, but not least, are the helpful contributions made by Mrs. Rowena White, Mrs. Crystal Rousos, Mrs. Sheila Burnham, and Mrs. Pat Beckman in preparing various drafts. Needless to add, the errors are the authors alone.

ELI SHAPIRO
CHARLES R. WOLF

August 1972

Table of Contents

List of Tables

Exhibits

List of Figures

Introduction

FOR TWENTY YEARS following World War II there was little doubt about the increasing importance of private placements in corporate financing. The growing institutionalization of savings and the development of the private placement market seemed inextricably linked. Indeed, by 1964 two-thirds of all corporate bonds were privately placed, and the belief in the dominance of private placements was vindicated, or so it seemed. Subsequent events in the financial markets, with conditions sometimes bordering on chaos, were paralleled by a sharp decline in the relative importance of private placements. This decline raised considerable uncertainty about the future role of private placements in corporate finance. In order to assess this role, we set forth in an attempt to explain postwar developments in the private placement market and in particular to identify the factors which contributed to the changing importance of private placements as a source of corporate financing. This book presents a report of this study.

A new corporate bond issue can be distributed in two ways. The issue can be sold to a syndicate of investment bankers who in turn resell it to the public. The issue can also be sold directly to one or a small group of investors. The first method is a public offering; the second, a private or direct placement.

The private placement market became an important source of funds for corporations beginning in the 1930s as a result of the institutionalization of savings and a shift in the acquisition of corporate bonds from individuals to life insurance companies. The private placement market was recognized legally in the Securities Act of 1933. This act, which was designed to protect the uninformed investor, required all issues sold publicly to be registered with the Securities and Exchange Commission before the time of sale.[1] The act exempted private placements from the registration requirement because the issues pre-

---

[1] Issuers which are exempt from the registration process include the U.S. Government and U.S. Government agencies, state and local governments, commercial banks, savings and loan associations, railroads, and charitable institutions. Issues which are exempt include commercial paper, issues of less than $300,000, and issues sold completely within one state.

sumably would be sold to a small number of institutional investors who had the capacity to investigate the security and the issuer before purchasing. The private placement market was also strengthened by tax laws which encouraged the purchase of tax-exempt municipal bonds by individuals and taxable corporate bonds by almost or wholly tax-exempt institutions such as life insurance companies and pension funds.

During 1933–1945 one-quarter of all corporate bond offerings were sold privately. This increased to 42% during the postwar period (1946–1970). In response to the growth of private financing in the early postwar years, a number of studies appeared which analyzed the private placement market, particularly the relative advantages to borrowers and lenders in participating in this market. Since the early 1950s, however, the private placement market has received only cursory attention in the literature on the financial markets. The purpose of this study, then, is to describe and analyze developments in the private placement market which have occurred during the postwar period, particularly during the past decade. In the process we hope to provide the reader with some insights into the future role of private placements in corporate finance.

The most important characteristic of the private placement market is that it serves as the major source of long-term debt financing for smaller, less financially secure companies. One reason is that small borrowers tend to sell small issues; there are simply more of them. But there are other reasons such firms are attracted to this form of financing. The distribution costs for privately placed issues are significantly less as a percentage of the proceeds for small issues. The underwriting fees and other expenses incurred in preparing a registration statement are eliminated. Borrowers in the private market are able to tailor the terms and provisions of the loan agreement to meet particular needs; this is especially important to the less financially secure borrower. Lenders in this market are willing to accept somewhat unusual features because they usually obtain fairly close control over the operations of a company in a private placement. Furthermore, these lenders are not disturbed by the fact that these unusual provisions reduce marketability; private placements have limited marketability anyway.

Moreover, the small borrower is virtually excluded from selling issues in the public market which is confined to the larger, high quality issues. Floating an issue publicly is expensive, and small borrowers also find it prohibitively expensive to provide a standardized set of terms and provisions. The standard contract, which appears with little variation in most straight-debt public issues, is a prerequisite for successful public distribution. It enables securities to be traded in both the new issues and the secondary markets solely on the basis of the borrower's credit rating.

The concentration of small issues sold in the private placement market distinguishes this market in a number of ways. To begin with, the private market is much less impersonal than the public market. In tailoring the terms and provisions of the loan agreement to the needs of individual borrowers, the borrowers and lenders come into close personal contact. In a public offering, on the other hand, an issue passes directly via underwriters to investors scattered throughout the country. The terms and provisions are decided on by the borrower and his underwriters to satisfy the standard contract requirements prevailing at the time, and the issue is then offered to investors on a take-it or leave-it basis.

Renegotiations of a private placement loan agreement frequently occur in the issues of smaller companies, and these too bring the borrower and lender into contact. As a result, customer relationships can develop that are similar to those between commercial banks and their customers. When privately placed loans have been brought to a successful conclusion, it is common for the borrower and the lender to continue the relationship and for the lender to accommodate the borrower in preference to others when the money supply is tight. Financial advice and assistance frequently may be offered by the lender to the small borrower who typically is less sophisticated in financial matters.

The distribution role of investment bankers is quite different in the private placement market from the market for publicly offered securities. In the public market the investment banker performs two functions, both underwriting and distributing new issues. In the distribution of privately placed securities the investment banker acts *only* as an agent for the borrower in placing the securities; he avoids the risk of temporary ownership. Moreover, since the supply of funds to the private market is concentrated in the hands of a relatively small number of buyers and the private placement method of sale limits the number of buyers to which an issue may be shown, the role of the investment banker as a distributor in this market is also special. Instead of attempting to reach as many potential buyers as possible, the investment banker attempts to minimize the number of buyers. This requires a knowledge of the particular preferences of the individual investors with respect to the yield, quality, and contract provisions of an issue. The investment banker must also keep informed about the availability of funds at these institutions. Although such knowledge is helpful in the distribution of publicly offered securities, it is not critical to a successful distribution.

In the early history of private placements, the supply side of the market was completely dominated by life insurance companies. During the past two decades both private pension funds and state and local retirement systems at times have become active lenders in the private market. The entry of state and local retirement systems as lenders in the private market, in turn, contributed to the development of a market for private placements which consisted of issues sold by large, financially secure industrial corporations. In most cases the terms and provisions of these issues duplicated those of the issues sold publicly by these companies.

Like the larger life insurance companies, the investments of most private pension funds have been concentrated in the lower quality, higher return segment of the private placement market. Most state and local retirement systems, in contrast, have been required by law to lend only to issuers with higher credit ratings. Moreover, they seldom have had the personnel experienced in acquiring issues with nonstandard features. There is, of course, an investment group composed of medium-sized insurance companies and some private pension funds that have broad quality tastes and tend to buy along the entire quality spectrum if the yield and loan provisions are acceptable. The resources of this group, however, do not appear to represent a significant fraction of the total resources available for investment in private placements.

During the postwar period the supply of funds to the private market grew at a relatively steady rate until recent years. These few years were characterized by rapid monetary expansion followed by severe monetary restraint. The latter produced a substantial curtailment of funds available for investment on the part of life insurance companies. In addition, both private pension funds and state and local retirement systems reduced their acquisition of private placements in favor of common stocks and publicly offered corporate bonds. Fluctuations in the percentage of corporate debt sold privately, however, have resulted chiefly from changes in the demand for long-term financing on the part of corporations. During years of modest corporate long-term borrowing, such as 1964, private placements accounted for as much as two-thirds of corporate bond sales, but private sales accounted for only 16% of the bond market in 1970, a year of heavy financing.

When the demand for long-term funds on the part of corporations has been modest in comparison with the supply available in the private market, many large, financially secure corporations have sold their debt privately. Since the opportunity to negotiate the terms and provisions of the issues was usually quite unimportant, these companies were attracted to the private market chiefly by the narrow interest rate differentials (net of distribution expenses) between the two markets. These issues contained standard terms and provisions which encouraged the use of agents in the distribution and negotiation process. State and local retirement systems were the major buyers of these issues. Since the number of such buyers was comparatively large and the contracts were standardized, the relation between borrowers and lenders was much less personal and therefore was similar to that evident in the market for publicly offered corporate bonds. The high percentage of corporate bonds sold in the private market in 1964 to a large extent resulted from the sale of private placements by these larger corporations.

During periods of heavy financing demands, in response to an increase in the yield differentials between the public and private markets and a deterioration of the terms on which funds are available in the private market, financially secure corporations that are able to borrow in either market have shifted their financing to the public market. Regardless of market conditions, however, smaller, less financially secure companies have satisfied the major fraction of their long-term financing needs in the private market. It is true, however, that in periods of shortages of long-term funds, lenders in the private market have insisted on so-called incentive features or "equity kickers" as a condition for making many of the private placements. During such periods less financially secure corporations have also acquired funds in the public market through the sale of convertible bond issues for which the standard contract requirements are less severe or through the use of special financing arrangements such as equipment trust certificates.

Recent changes in the investment policies of life insurance companies and pension funds toward greater participation in the stock market have not as yet signaled any significant reduction in the volume of private financing available to small borrowers. If these institutions continue to expand their portfolios of equities in the future, however, there may be smaller sums of money available in the private placement market relative to the demand for such funds by corporate issuers. A probable result of this is that there will be fewer private placements sold by financially secure corporations than there have been at times in the past.

In the chapter that follows we discuss the terms and provisions of corporate bonds which are sold privately. Then the relative use of the public and private markets by different borrower categories are documented and explained. The third chapter examines the investment policies of the major lenders in the private market and their participation in this market during the postwar period. A discussion of the distribution process of private placements in the market for new and outstanding issues follows. Finally, in the last chapter we attempt to explain the cyclical patterns in the division of financing between the public and private markets through an analysis of the structure of supply of and demand for financing in these two markets.

CHAPTER 1

Characteristics of the Private Placement

PRIVATE PLACEMENT AGREEMENTS are far more heterogeneous than publicly offered loan agreements. In part this stems from the flexibility of the negotiation process involved and the opportunity available to both parties to the agreement to tailor provisions to meet particular needs and preferences. The less secure financial standing of the typical borrower in the private placement market also makes it more difficult to satisfy a standard set of requirements.

A distinguishing characteristic of the private placement, however, relates to the protection of the lender; generally the agreement is more restrictive than a public offering. This reflects in part the lower credit standing of the average borrower in the private placement market. But it also reflects the fact that restrictions in a private placement can be amended quite simply with the lender's consent. Apart from offering greater protection, a tighter set of provisions enables the lender to remain in closer touch with developments in a company—an important advantage according to most investors in this market.

In the remainder of this chapter we discuss the more important provisions of the private placement loan agreement and draw some comparisons with those found on a publicly offered issue.

Repayment Provisions

Three repayment provisions are usually included in a private placement agreement. The first requires the borrower to repay a certain portion of the loan annually after a certain time has elapsed from the date of the issue. This is known as the mandatory sinking fund requirement. A second provision relates to repayments from earnings which can be made at the option of the borrower. The third repayment provision deals with funds obtained through the sale of other debt. This last provision is better known as the "call provi-

7

EXHIBIT 1–1

Private Placement Loan Agreement Repayment Provisions

9. **Fixed and Optional Prepayments Without Premium.** (a) The Company covenants and agrees that on January 15, 1970, and each January 15 thereafter to and including January 15, 1989, the Company will prepay $5,000,000 principal amount of Notes (or the then unpaid principal amount of the Notes if less than such amount). On each such date the pro rata portion of such required prepayment allocable to any Note pursuant to Section 11 shall become due and payable thereon by the Company.

(b) In addition to prepayment as provided in paragraph (a) of this Section 9, the Company may at its option, on January 15, 1970, and on each January 15 thereafter to and including January 15, 1989, prepay Notes, as provided in this paragraph (b) in an aggregate principal amount equal to not more than $5,000,000 (or the then unpaid principal amount of the Notes if less than such amount). The right of prepayment contained in this paragraph (b) shall be non-cumulative. The exercise of the right of prepayment contained in this paragraph (b) shall not relieve the Company to any extent from its obligation then or thereafter to make the prepayments required by paragraph (a) of this Section 9.

(c) All Notes or portions thereof prepaid pursuant to paragraph (a) or (b) of this Section 9 shall be prepaid at their principal amount, plus accrued interest thereon to the date fixed for prepayment, but without premium.

(d) Designation of the Notes or portions thereof to be prepaid by the Company pursuant to paragraph (a) or (b) of this Section 9 shall be made by the Company as in Section 11 provided, and the Company shall give notice, in the manner and to the extent in Section 12 provided, of the Notes or portions thereof so to be prepaid.

10. **Optional Prepayments at Premium.** (a) In addition to the prepayments provided for in Section 9, the Company may at its option, at any time, or from time to time, prior to maturity, prepay Notes as in this paragraph (a) provided, either in whole or in part, at the principal amount so to be prepaid plus accrued interest thereon to the date fixed for such prepayment, and plus a premium equal to the applicable percentage of the principal amount so being prepaid set forth below:

If Prepaid During the Twelve Month Period Ending January 14	Applicable Percentage	If Prepaid During the Twelve Month Period Ending January 14	Applicable Percentage
1966	4.50%	1978	2.10%
1967	4.30	1979	1.90
1968	4.10	1980	1.70
1969	3.90	1981	1.50
1970	3.70	1982	1.30
1971	3.50	1983	1.10
1972	3.30	1984	0.90
1973	3.10	1985	0.70
1974	2.90	1986	0.50
1975	2.70	1987	0.30
1976	2.50	1988	0.10
1977	2.30	1989	0.00
		1990	0.00

EXHIBIT 1-1 (Continued)

provided, however, that the Company shall not be entitled to exercise prior to January 15, 1970, the foregoing right of prepayment, directly or indirectly, from the proceeds of, or in anticipation of the creation by the Company or any Subsidiary of, any indebtedness for moneys borrowed having an interest cost (computed in accordance with generally accepted financial practice) to the Company or such Subsidiary of less than 4.50% per annum.

The aggregate principal amount of Notes and portions of Notes at the time being called for prepayment pursuant to this paragraph (a) shall be at least $5,000,000 or a multiple thereof or shall constitute the aggregate principal amount of all Notes at the time outstanding and not theretofor called for prepayment. The exercise of the right of prepayment contained in this paragraph (a) shall not relieve the Company to any extent from its obligations to make the prepayments required by paragraph (a) of Section 9.

(b) Designation of the Notes or portions thereof to be prepaid by the Company pursuant to this Section 10 shall be made by the Company as in Section 11 provided, and the Company shall give notice in the manner and to the extent in Section 12 provided, of the Notes or portions thereof so to be prepaid.

SOURCE: Extracted from the private placement loan agreement of a large corporation.

sion"; the whole issue is typically called when the borrower repays the outstanding obligation with funds obtained from another security issue.

While the borrower is required to repay some portion of the loan, both the optional repayment and call provisions restrict or penalize him when he repays more than the required amount. This is done by having him pay a premium above par when he elects optional prepayment or calls the issue. Sinking fund payments are presumably designed to reduce the risk of principal loss. The optional prepayments and call provisions attempt to prevent a reduction in interest return at the possible expense of increased risk of default. Through these provisions, the lender attempts to steer a middle course in his trade-offs between risk and return. These kinds of arrangements make sense for borrowers with poor credit standings. A sinking fund requirement for a large and financially secure company, however, provides at best little additional assurance to the lender; and it could well result in the loss of interest return which the other two repayment provisions are attempting to prevent.

A sample of these provisions taken from the private placement loan agreement of a large, top-rated company is shown in Exhibit 1-1. Each repayment provision is discussed at greater length below.

Required Repayments—The Sinking Fund

The sinking fund provides for an annual payment on the loan—usually starting five or ten years after the date of issue and ending at maturity. The sinking fund payments may be designed to amortize the whole issue or to leave a balloon (a substantial payment) at maturity. The purpose of the sinking fund is to improve the quality of an issue by periodically reducing the size of the outstanding loan and to minimize the risk of lending large sums to a single borrower, a problem particularly acute in direct acquisitions. In addition, the annual payment requirement assures that the borrower has been able to meet a series of small hurdles in his financing. The degree of flexibility afforded the borrower in meeting this requirement, however, is quite wide in a direct placement. For example, sinking fund payments on directly placed issues can be waived, with the lender's consent, in years of depressed sales or when the borrower's need for internal funds for other useful purposes is great. Sometimes the sinking fund payments are contingent on earnings. This flexibility is in sharp contrast with what happens in a publicly sold issue; in public sales an issuer who is also trustee of the issue must enforce indentures of the debt contract literally.

Optional Repayments

There are two kinds of optional repayments open to the borrower:

(1) Repayment from excess cash flows without penalty.
(2) Repayment from excess cash flows with penalty.

Typically, the borrower has the option to double the mandatory sinking fund payment in any year provided his earnings are sufficient. However, for any repayments above this amount or for any repayments which are made before the first year of the mandatory sinking fund, the borrower must pay a penalty. The size of this penalty depends on the year of payment (as shown in Exhibit 1–1).

The optional repayment provision provides the borrower with greater flexibility in the repayment of an issue when there is a legitimate economic reason for such a payment. It also serves to reduce the risk to both the borrower and the lender, especially if the former is in a cyclical business where earnings from one year to the next might be insufficient to cover sinking fund requirements and still leave the borrower with enough funds for normal operations. Although he is not legally required to do so, the lender is more likely to let required payments be skipped in times of cash tightness if optional repayments have been made in the past.

The Call Provision

The call provision of a private placement specifies (1) the period of deferment during which an issue may not be refunded through borrowing at a lower interest rate and (2) the schedule of premiums which must be paid to the lender when the issue is called.[1, 2]

The premium schedule is fairly standard: beginning at one year's interest and progressively decreasing to 0% premium near the maturity of the issue.

The period of deferment is, next to the interest rate, the most important item in the loan agreement. The deferred call feature is also found in loan agreements for public offerings, but it is usually more restrictive in a private placement. The reason for this is that the buyers of private placement issues are more sophisticated and experienced in the value of the deferred call feature. Large life insurance companies and private pension funds that buy private placements bargain more forcefully for call protection or, more often, simply will not buy issues which do not meet their minimum call provision requirements. Smaller insurance companies, private pension funds, state and local retirement systems, and individuals who buy publicly offered issues appear willing to accept less protective call provisions. Their inexperience in the valuation process probably accounts for their behavior.

The call protection provided on public offerings and private placements was virtually the same during the high interest rate periods of 1966 and 1969-1970. It is too early to determine whether this development signals a change in the awareness of lenders in the public market of the value of call deferment. More likely it reflected reluctance on the part of borrowers to pay the higher interest rates demanded by lenders for limited call protection.

Large institutional investors value call protection highly because it prevents the borrowing company from refunding an issue during periods of low interest rates and thus helps to maintain the lender's investment return. Evidence of life insurance companies' preference for issues with restrictive call protection, for example, is provided by the decline in their holdings of utility issues during the postwar period. Until 1969 the Securities and Exchange

---

[1] A company might also repay the issue from the sale of a new issue at an interest rate which is higher than the rate on the original issue. Under these circumstances, the company would still have to pay the appropriate premium penalty but it could call the issue during the period of deferment applicable to refundings at interest rates below the original coupon. A company might undertake such a refunding to modify the maturity structure of its debt or, if its credit standing has improved, to obtain more liberal indenture provisions. Refundings of this type occur infrequently.

[2] In the financial markets the terms "nonredeemable" and "noncallable" are used interchangeably to refer to an issue which may not be retired for any reason or under any circumstances until a specified number of years have passed. The term "nonrefundable" is used to indicate an issue which may not be refunded through the sale of another debt issue at a lower rate for a specified number of years, but which may be retired before this time with other sources of funds such as excess earnings. "Nonrefundable" issues are usually sold by commercial banks and appear infrequently in the issues of other borrowers.

Commission refused permission to public utility holding companies under its jurisdiction to incorporate nonrefunding provisions in their debt issues.[3] Some state regulatory commissions have been similarly adamant. The absence of restrictive call provisions on utility issues was, in part, responsible for their declining popularity among life insurance companies beginning in the early 1950s.[4] As a percentage of life insurance companies' total assets, public utility issues increased from 11.6% in 1945 to 16.5% in 1950 but progressively declined thereafter to 9.1% in 1969. During the same 22 years, industrial and miscellaneous issues held by life companies increased from 4.3% to 25.4% of their total assets.[5]

Additional evidence of the growing importance of call protection to life insurance companies is provided in a 1958 survey of their acquisitions.[6] Between 1953 and 1957 corporate bonds which provided some call protection rose from 45% to 84% of acquisitions. The period of protection against refunding was also lengthened. Bonds bearing no-call provisions for their entire life rose from less than 20% of acquisitions in 1953 to 30% in 1957. Issues protected against refunding for at least one year increased from 25% in 1953 to 55% of the total in 1957. Some of these issues bore additional protection in the form of an initial call premium greater than the coupon rate. No similar study has been made since 1958. Industry observers agree, however, that life insurance companies as well as other lenders increased their insistence on restrictive call provisions during the 1960s.

SEC data suggest that borrowers usually take advantage of the opportunity to call their issues during periods when interest rates are declining (see Table 1–1). Since interest rates have generally risen during the postwar years, these periods occurred infrequently and were of short duration. The proportion of new issues used to retire outstanding securities, for example, was relatively high in 1954, 1958, and again in the early 1960s when interest rates were low in comparison with the years preceding and following them. The

---

[3] The SEC's position was set forth in two cases: *Indiana and Michigan Electric Company* (35 SEC 321, 326) and *Arkansas Louisiana Gas Company* (35 SEC 313). In 1969 the SEC first allowed public utility holding companies to issue 5-year deferred call issues (35 SEC 16369).

[4] In addition, a desire to diversify their security portfolios contributed to the decrease in life insurance companies' investment in public utility issues in the early 1950s. In later years the desire to increase portfolio return contributed to the decline. Beginning in the late 1950s state and local retirement systems became large investors in the corporate bond market. This group concentrated their purchases of corporate bonds in utility issues and reduced their relative yields and in turn their attractiveness to insurance companies still further.

[5] Institute of Life Insurance, *Life Insurance Fact Book,* 1970.

[6] Life Insurance Association of America, "Survey of Life Insurance Company Investment Policies Toward Refunding Protection on Corporate Bonds," 1958. Sample data covered 47 life insurance companies with 50.7% of the assets of all life insurance companies at the end of 1957. Acquisition figures covered all corporate bonds except railroad issues.

TABLE 1-1
Purpose of Corporate Financing by Volume and Percent
1954-1967
(Dollar amounts in millions)

| Year | Purpose | | Total | Retirement as a % of Total | Moody's New Issue Corporate Bonds |
	New Investment	Retirement			
1954	$ 7,490	$ 1,875	$ 9,365	20.0%	3.22%
1955	8,821	1,227	10,049	12.2	3.56
1956	10,384	364	10,749	3.4	3.88
1957	12,447	214	12,661	1.7	4.71
1958	10,823	549	11,372	4.8	4.26
1959	9,392	135	9,527	1.4	4.94
1960	9,653	271	9,924	2.7	4.82
1961	12,017	868	12,885	6.7	4.70
1962	9,747	754	10,501	7.2	4.46
1963	10,523	1,526	12,049	12.7	4.41
1964	13,038	754	13,792	5.5	4.54
1965	14,805	996	15,801	6.3	4.71
1966	17,601	241	17,841	1.4	5.59
1967	24,097	312	24,409	1.3	5.91

NOTE: These data were not compiled after 1967.
SOURCE: Securities and Exchange Commission.

fraction of new financing used for retirements was low during 1957, 1959, and 1966–1967 when interest rates were comparatively high.

The importance of call protection to investors can be inferred from the spread in interest rates between callable and deferred callable issues sold in the public market. Figure 1–1 shows the interest rates on new issue public utility callable and 5-year deferred callable issues as compiled by Salomon Brothers, Inc. Although the spread was virtually zero during periods of stable, relatively low interest rates, most noticeably the early 1960s, it widened to as much as 28 basis points during quarters of relatively high interest rates. Investors obviously attached little importance to the deferred call feature when rates were already low and call protection was of little value. The deferred call feature acquired considerable value, however, during high interest rate periods such as 1959, 1966, and 1969–1970 when rates were expected to fall and the probability and cost of an early call was thought to be substantial.

In a study of these spread on issues sold during the 1950s Hess and Winn discovered little evidence that investors in corporate bonds required higher returns on callable issues.[7] It seems likely, however, that this stemmed from the particular period which Hess and Winn examined. During that period, in-

---

[7] *The Value of the Call Privilege.*

FIGURE 1–1

Yields on Callable and 5-year Deferred Call Issues
New Public Utilities
1957-3/1970-4

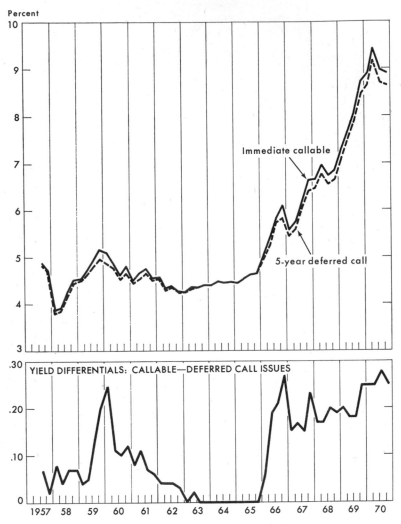

SOURCE: Salomon Brothers, "An Analytic Record of Yields and Yield Spreads," various issues.

vestors were just beginning to acquire some experience concerning the importance of the deferred call feature and had not yet attached a measurable value to it. Moreover, during most of the 1950s interest rates were rising so that investors probably assigned a small probability to interest rate declines of the magnitude which would trigger the refunding of callable issues. The subsequent data indicate that investors have at times attached considerable value to the deferred call feature.[8]

No comparable data on yields in the private placement market are available. In theory one might expect that since the call provision and the interest rate are both part of the package which the investor buys there would be a trade-off between them; that is, if the borrower desired a less restrictive call feature, he would have to pay for it with a higher interest cost on the loan. In practice, however, the data necessary to establish this trade-off rate are not available. Little direct bargaining between the borrower and the lender appears to take place over the call provision. The borrower is chiefly interested in the cost of the loan, and he is usually willing to meet the lender's terms on the call feature rather than to pay a higher interest rate. As a result a consensus is generally formed by different investing groups around a particular call provision or set of provisions which are acceptable to them.[9]

To attract the desired amount of funds, a borrower would have to compensate for a liberal call feature by increasing the interest rate on the issue by an unacceptably large proportion. It is also likely that a borrower could obtain only a small reduction in his interest rate by offering a call provision which is more restrictive than the one required by the potential buyers of the issue. In sum, the shape of the demand curve for the issue as a function of the call feature no doubt encourages the borrower to include a call feature which just meets, but does not exceed, the prevailing minimum requirement of potential investors.

It seems clear, moreover, that in the lower quality private market where insurance companies and private pension funds supply the major portion of funds, the cost of attempting to reduce call protection would be quite expensive and might possibly deny the borrower access to funds. In contrast, in the higher quality segment of the private placement market the increase in the interest rate that resulted from a liberal call feature would probably be somewhat smaller, since borrowers have the option of issuing in the public market.

Both direct evidence and deductive inference suggests that the consensus

---

[8] See, for example, Jen and Wert, "The Value of the Deferred Call Privilege." Jen and Wert measure yield differentials between issues with different call protection periods as a function of interest rate levels. However, they do not explicitly relate these differentials to investors' expectations. As Pye and others have suggested, this can be accomplished only within the context of an optimum bond refunding model. See Pye, "The Value of the Call Option on a Bond," *Journal of Political Economy*; Pye, "The Value of Call Deferment on a Bond: Some Empirical Results"; and Weingartner, "Optimal Timing of Bond Refunding."

[9] A study of the call features of issues bought by the corporate pension department of a commercial bank during 1962 and 1963, for example, revealed that all 20 real estate issues, all 6 finance company issues, and 8 of 10 industrial issues had 10-year deferred call features. In contrast all 20 public utility issues had 5-year deferred call features.

call feature in both the high and low quality sectors of the private market (as well as in the public market) changes over the business cycle. When interest rates are low and the supply of funds is plentiful, investors accept reduced protection. Not only has the borrower better bargaining position, but the probability of a call is also less since interest rates are likely to be higher during the life of the issue. When interest rates are high, however, and funds are in scarce supply, the deferred call period probably increases. Lenders are not only in the superior bargaining position; the probability that the issue will be called before maturity is also somewhat greater.

Incentive Features

Incentive or equity features—familiarly known as "kickers"—attached to debt issues provide the lender with an option to acquire the common stock of the borrowing company. One type, the convertible bond, enables the lender to exchange the bond for common stock at a price stated in the agreement. When the market price of the company's stock has risen above the conversion price, borrowers typically force lenders to convert by calling the issue at a stated price below conversion value. A second type of incentive feature, the warrant, is an option to buy for cash the common stock at a stated price which may remain the same or increase over time. There may or may not be a termination date for exercising the warrant. Warrants are usually detachable from the debt issue itself so that the lender may sell them in the market at his option without buying the common stock.[10]

After a long period of limited popularity, the use of incentive features in debt financing has increased rapidly since 1965 (see Table 1–2). The growth of incentive financing accelerated during the 1968–1970 period to account for as much as 28% of the annual commitments of major life insurance companies (see Table 3–7). The rapid growth in incentive financing in the private market can be attributed, in part, to the high interest rates prevailing during the latter half of the 1960s. Some companies, no doubt, were unable to obtain funds unless they provided an incentive feature. However, the choice of this particular method to allocate a limited supply of funds—the use of incentive features rather than higher interest rates—reflects a fundamental change in the attitudes and policies of borrowers and lenders.

Institutional lenders such as life insurance companies and corporate pension funds have become increasingly performance-conscious in recent years. They have also become aware of the limited contribution fixed-income securities can make to their investment performance. Furthermore, borrowers

---

[10] For a discussion of convertible bonds and warrants, see Van Horne, *Financial Management and Policy*, pp. 321–328, 351–375.

TABLE 1-2

Incentive and Total Corporate Borrowing in
the Public and Private Markets
1956-1967

(Dollar amounts in millions)

	Public Offerings				Private Placements			
Year	Convert-ibles	Debentures -with- Warrants	Total P.O.	% Incentive Financing	Convert-ibles	Debentures -with- Warrants	Total P.P.	% Incentive Financing
1956	$ 763	N.A.	$ 4,225	18.1%	$ 163	N.A.	$ 3,777	4.3%
1957	995	"	6,118	16.3	69	"	3,839	1.8
1958	1,071	"	6,332	16.9	77	"	3,320	2.3
1959	536	"	3,557	15.1	92	"	3,632	2.5
1960	356	"	4,806	7.4	105	"	3,275	3.2
1961	625	"	4,700	13.3	84	"	4,720	1.8
1962	346	"	4,440	7.8	99	"	4,579	2.2
1963	234	"	4,714	5.0	122	"	6,158	2.0
1964	366	$ 54	3,623	11.6	59	$ 81	7,243	1.9
1965	1,181	38	5,570	21.9	83	164	8,150	3.0
1966	1,764	122	8,018	23.5	109	277	7,543	5.1
1967	4,108	304	14,991	29.4	367	278	6,964	9.3
Total	$12,345	$518	$71,094	18.1%	$1,429	$800	$63,200	3.5%

SOURCES: Convertible Financing and Total Financing: Securities and Exchange Commission. Warrant Financing: Hayes and Reiling, "Sophisticated Financing Tool: The Warrant," Exhibit 1, p. 139, compiled from "Corporate Financing Directories," *Investment Dealers' Digest.*

have become increasingly willing to provide incentive features with their debt issues.[11] This increased willingness can be traced to the progressive relaxation of traditional debt/equity guidelines during the past decade. The debt/equity ratios of corporations increased from 16% to 20% from 1958 to 1967. During the same period the equity/asset ratios of corporations fell from 66.7% to 58.7%.[12] Borrowers have used incentive financing to increase their debt capacity. And lenders have been willing to accept greater financial risk in return for the higher expected returns available on issues with incentive features. Other lenders have in turn become willing to provide more senior capital to such borrowers because of the protection afforded by junior debt issues with equity options.[13] Finally, incentive financing accelerated during the latter part of the 1960s because borrowers wished to avoid the high interest rates lenders demanded on straight-debt issues; borrowers frequently were con-

[11] Hayes and Reiling, "Sophisticated Financing Tool: The Warrant."

[12] *Ibid.,* p. 139. For a discussion of the changes in the debt/equity ratios of the Fortune 500 companies during the 1960s, see Loomis, "The Lesson of the Credit Crisis."

[13] *Ibid.,* p. 141.

cerned that the investing public might interpret high rates as a sign of deteriorating credit worthiness.

The volume of convertible financing has substantially exceeded the volume of warrant financing as incentive features have proliferated in recent years. The heavy volume of convertible issues was sold largely in the public market, however. In the private market the volume of warrant financing exceeded the volume of convertible financing during 1964–1970 (Tables 1–2 and 3–7).

When issuing convertible securities, borrowers can obtain relatively more favorable price and credit terms by selling the securities to individuals rather than institutional investors because individuals appear willing to accept a lower rate of immediate returns. Until 1968 individuals were also influenced, in part, by the relatively low margins required to purchase convertible issues. They were able to borrow up to 85% of the market value of listed convertibles but only 20% to 30% on common stock. This differential has been almost completely eliminated. In addition, individuals undoubtedly have been attracted to convertible issues by the protection against substantial capital losses provided by the debt portion of the package. Because individuals can buy only publicly offered securities, companies have relied primarily on the public market when issuing convertible securities.

When issuing debenture-with-warrant issues, however, borrowers have been able to obtain relatively more favorable prices and terms on private placements with institutional investors. Institutional investors prefer warrants to convertible issues because the warrants give them greater control over the realization of the equity portion of the issue. Warrants are typically detachable from the debenture. Investors can realize the equity portion at any time without waiting, as in the case of convertible issues, until the market price of the common stock has risen above the conversion price. Moreover, a warrant option usually sells at a larger premium than a convertible option.[14] Finally, in the case of debenture-with-warrant issues, the lender can retain the debt portion of the issue and continue to receive interest income after he has sold the equity portion. This is not possible with a convertible issue.

The weighted average size of issues with incentive features sold in the private market (Table 1–3) is close to the average size of all straight-debt issues sold in this market. One would infer from this that the use of incentive financing has not been limited to a particular size category of corporate borrowers. The average size of publicly offered convertibles, however, was substantially larger than the average size of privately placed convertible issues. As discussed more fully in subsequent chapters, differences in the distribution

---

14 *Ibid.*, p. 148.

TABLE 1–3
Average Size of Corporate Issues
by Type and Market
1964–1967
(In millions of dollars)

| Year | Public Offerings | | Private Placements | | |
	Convertibles	Debentures-with-Warrants	Straight-Debt Industrial	Convertibles	Debentures-with-Warrants
1964	$ 7.3	$ 3.9	$6.2	$2.8	$ 4.8
1965	19.4	4.8	5.7	3.9	5.5
1966	18.3	11.1	N.A.	3.7	11.5
1967	17.7	11.7	N.A.	4.7	6.6
Average	$16.9	$ 8.8	$5.6*	$4.1	$ 7.1

* Annual average of 1951–1965.
SOURCES: Convertibles and Debentures-with-Warrants: Hayes and Reiling, Exhibit 1, p. 139. Straight-Debt Industrial Issues: Cohan, *Yields on Corporate Debt Directly Placed*, p. 15, compiled from the *Investment Dealers' Digest*.

costs of public offerings and private placements are a decreasing function of issue size. Thus, large borrowers tend to borrow in the public market and small borrowers, in the private market.

Forward Commitments

A forward commitment is a firm agreement on the part of a lender to supply a specified amount of money at a specified interest rate within an agreed-upon time period. Forward commitments have been used by life insurance companies, corporate pension funds, and state and local retirement systems in their lending operations in the private placement market. Life insurance companies, mutual savings banks, and savings and loan associations also use the forward commitment in their mortgage lending activities as do commercial banks in their business term-lending operations.

For the lenders there are a number of advantages to the forward commitment. It enables them to match their investment outlays to a fairly steady and predictable inflow of funds. Moreover, if they are loaned up, the forward commitment enables them to accommodate borrowers who usually do not have an immediate need for long-term funds. As Jones points out, the forward commitment also provides lenders with the opportunity to vary the incidence of their investments in response to expectations of future interest rates independently of their current supply of funds.[15] Obviously, this is not always ad-

---

[15] Jones, *Investment Policies of Life Insurance Companies*, p. 324. Jones discovered, however, that insurance companies took advantage of this opportunity to a limited extent.

vantageous. When cash flows were less than predicted in 1966 and in 1969–1970 as a result of an unanticipated increase in policy loans and mortgage loan repayments, life insurance companies, the major lenders in the private market, found that they had overcommitted.

The forward commitment is also advantageous to borrowers. Most importantly, it allows them to formulate their investment plans with greater certainty. Because the schedule of takedowns of a loan is designed to coincide with a borrower's need for funds, the forward commitment made in a private issue offers a convenience value; public issues usually are completely paid for at the time of sale. Because of this, lenders regard the forward commitment as a competitive device to enhance the attractiveness of private placements vis-à-vis public offerings.[16]

The forward commitment was once a feature in private agreements only. The device was introduced into public contracts at least as early as 1966. During that year no less than eight publicly offered industrial issues, totaling $490 million, contained deferred payment provisions. It is likely, however, that deferred payments were included in these agreements because institutional lenders had already committed all of their available funds. The evidence for this is the fact that 86.5% of the $490 million was paid to borrowers at the time of issue and the remainder, a few months later. In the private market the initial takedown of an issue usually occurs after the time of commitment and is a smaller fraction of the issue. Moreover, subsequent takedowns extend over a longer period.

The commitment agreement specifies the terms and provisions of the issue, the delivery dates or range of dates, and the terminal date of the commitment. The borrower is also required to notify the lender a certain minimum time before he takes down funds. If the borrower is unable to close the loan before an agreed-upon date, the lender can cancel the loan. Usually, however, he extends the commitment, sometimes at a penalty cost to the borrower in the form of a higher interest rate or a higher commitment fee.

The commitment fee, which varies between 0.5% and 1% of the face value of the loan, is paid by the borrower to the lender when the commitment involves a lag of several months before the loan is taken down. There is little agreement among observers over the economic rationale underlying this fee.

The agreement to honor a commitment is, in a sense, unilateral. Lenders regard the commitment as binding, whether it is written or unwritten; borrowers sometimes take a more flexible view.[17] The interest rate on the loan is set at the time of commitment and reflects prevailing rather than anticipated

---

16 *Ibid.*, p. 326.
17 Brimmer, *Life Insurance Companies in the Capital Market,* p. 104.

future market conditions.[18] Thus, borrowers can cancel their commitments and borrow at a lower interest rate in the event that interest rates fell between the time of commitment and takedowns. Unlike the call feature, however, borrowers do not appear to view the forward commitment as a means of reducing their interest costs in the event interest rates fall. In contrast, lenders seldom attempt to refinance the loan at a higher rate if interest rates rise between the time of commitment and takedowns.

Data on commitment cancellations (Table 1–4) do not provide convincing evidence that this risk justifies the commitment fee, however. The percentage of outstanding commitments canceled was higher during periods of relatively low interest rates in the early 1960s than in 1959 and 1966–1967, two periods of relatively high rates, but the differences were quite small.[19] Moreover, a downward revision in a borrower's actual need for funds could well be expected during a downturn in economic activity. Lenders themselves are probably more lenient in permitting borrowers' initial estimates to exceed subsequent needs during periods of low interest rates, when their supply of funds is relatively plentiful. These factors could well explain the observed relationship between cancellations and interest rates.

Another explanation of the commitment fee offered by industry experts is that it is designed to insure that the borrower will honor his commitment to take down the loan as scheduled. There is no reason why the fee will guarantee this, however. Once it has been paid, the fee is a sunk cost which is irrelevant to the borrower's decision concerning a takedown of the loan. In some cases, where the commitment fee is refundable if the loan is taken down, then it does encourage the takedown of commitments.

A third explanation of the commitment fee is that it represents compensation to the lender for the differential effect of a change in interest rates between the time of commitment and the times of takedowns. In planning a capital project the borrower is most concerned with having funds available at an assured rate and at assured times. The fact that interest rates might fall between the time of commitment and the times of takedowns is less important because the spread between the expected return on his investment and the interest cost of the loan is probably quite wide. In contrast, institutional investors in the private market typically operate on relatively narrow margins between gross returns and costs. Moreover, their capital to asset ratios are usually a small fraction of the ratios characterizing companies borrowing in this market. A given change in asset return, then, has a much greater effect

---

[18] There are apparently a few lenders who set rates at the time of takedown. See Jones, *op. cit.*, p. 328.

[19] The high percentage of cancellations in the third quarter of 1959 probably reflected investment cutbacks resulting from the steel strike.

TABLE 1–4

Security Forward Commitments of Major Life Insurance Companies
Outstanding and Canceled

1959–1970

(Dollar amounts in millions)

Quarter	Amount[1] Out- standing	Amount Can- celed	Cancel- lations as % of Amount Out- standing	Interest[2] Rates
1959—1	$1,550	$ 42	2.71%	4.41%
2	1,449	41	2.83	4.59
3	1,240	159	12.82	4.75
4	1,124	26	2.31	4.86
1960—1	1,450	44	3.03	4.87
2	1,435	81	5.64	4.78
3	1,385	80	5.78	4.64
4	1,293	82	6.34	4.65
1961—1	1,351	46	3.40	4.59
2	1,479	89	6.02	4.59
3	1,292	68	5.26	4.72
4	1,152	64	5.56	4.71
1962—1	1,564	39	2.49	4.69
2	1,631	102	6.25	4.60
3	1,773	60	3.38	4.63
4	1,665	85	5.11	4.55
1963—1	1,753	126	7.19	4.48
2	1,760	118	6.70	4.47
3	1,677	112	6.68	4.50
4	1,614	104	6.44	4.54
1964—1	1,697	68	4.01	4.56
2	1,856	135	7.27	4.59
3	1,968	96	4.88	4.57
4	1,994	109	5.47	4.58
1965—1	1,975	106	5.37	4.56
2	2,414	198	8.20	4.58
3	2,603	131	5.03	4.66
4	2,948	192	6.51	4.77
1966—1	2,819	93	3.30	4.98
2	2,892	90	3.11	5.21
3	3,227	92	2.85	5.52
4	3,405	70	2.06	5.67
1967—1	3,159	85	2.69	5.43
2	3,460	68	1.97	5.58
3	4,056	97	2.39	5.92
4	4,703	108	2.30	6.34

TABLE 1–4 (Continued)

Quarter	Amount[1] Out-standing	Amount Can-celed	Cancel-lations as % of Amount Out-standing	Interest[2] Rates
1968—1	*	*	—	6.42%
2	$4,815	$118	2.45%	6.59
3	4,654	110	2.36	6.43
4	4,900	94	1.92	6.60
1969—1	4,183	192	4.59	6.98
2	4,116	121	2.94	7.18
3	4,056	115	2.84	7.43
4	4,113	122	2.97	7.87
1970—1	3,548	125	3.52	8.26
2	3,232	114	3.53	8.48
3	3,166	113	3.57	8.75
4	3,068	108	3.52	8.54

[1] Quarterly average of month-end amounts.

[2] Quarterly average of monthly average interest rates on outstanding corporate bonds.

* Break in series, no data reported.

SOURCE: Life Insurance Association of America. Moody's Investor Service. (Reported in the Federal Reserve Bulletin.) (See footnote 2, p. 52.)

on the return on lenders' capital than on the return on borrowers' capital. Thus, the opportunity losses to the borrower and lender in the event that interest rates change are asymetrical. The commitment fee serves as compensation to the lender who suffers much greater opportunity losses between the time of commitment and takedowns if rates rise than the borrower suffers if rates fall.[20]

The commitment fee may, of course, reflect the structure of the private market. Lenders in the private market can enforce this practice because they are in a superior bargaining position relative to borrowers who usually have limited access to alternative sources of funds. If this is true, the size of the commitment fee should be a decreasing function of the size of the loan which serves as a measure of the borrower's access to alternative sources of funds. Unfor-

[20] Evidence of this explanation of the commitment fee is found in the direct relation between the length of the commitment period and the size of the fee, as reported by Jones (p. 331). Although the expected opportunity loss to the lender might not change, the variance of the opportunity loss certainly increases with an increase in the length of the commitment period. Thus, assuming that variance is an appropriate measure of risk, lenders charge a larger fee on longer commitments in order to compensate for the increased risk of an opportunity loss.

tunately, there are no data to determine this. However, Jones reports that lenders believe that fees are higher on small, low quality, issues.[21]

The forward commitment is very significant to the investment process of institutional lenders; anticipated takedowns account for a large proportion of available funds. Using commitment data compiled by the Life Insurance Association of America, Jones found that for successive months between January 1957 and December 1959 takedowns expected during the ensuing six months from commitments outstanding at the beginning of the month averaged 70% of the funds available for investment during that six months.[22] Similar data, reported on a quarterly basis by the LIAA since 1959, indicate that 6-month anticipated takedowns continued to represent around 70% of 6-month anticipated cash flows through the first half of the 1960s and then rose to an annual average of 88% and 81% respectively during the high interest rate periods of 1966 and 1969–1970.

Takedowns resulting from a forward commitment can extend from a few months to several years into the future. About two-thirds of total commitments are usually taken down within six months of the time of approval and about 80% within 12 months, according to Jones.[23] Data on the quarterly distribution of takedowns by the Fortune 500 companies during 1953–1969 reveal a similar pattern.[24] Of the $19.9 billion takedowns of private placements by this group during this period, 70.3% occurred in the quarter in which the SEC was first notified of the financing, 7.4% in the first quarter after first notice, 6.7% in the second quarter, 6.6% in the third quarter, and 9.0% in all subsequent quarters. This understates the time lag between commitments and takedowns, however, because lenders notify the SEC of a financing when the first takedown occurs. This can be from a few months to over a year after the commitment.[25]

---

[21] *Ibid.*, p. 331.

[22] *Ibid.*, p. 354.

[23] *Ibid.*, p. 356.

[24] The Fortune 500 company sample, referred to throughout the book, consists of the 500 largest industrial and the 50 largest commercial companies ranked annually on the basis of sales by *Fortune* magazine. For each of the years, 1955–1970, the sample exactly coincided with Fortune's list of 550 companies for that year. Fortune's 1955 list was used for 1953 and 1954 as well. The debt issues sold by this group were compiled from the files of the Securities and Exchange Commission beginning in 1953, the first year individual company financing records were available.

[25] Of the life insurance companies responding to a survey in mid-1967, nine indicated an average time lag between commitment and the first takedown of two to four months while eight indicated an average time lag of five to seven months. However, this probably understates the average time lag for all securities sold privately, weighted by their size. The respondents to the survey were chiefly small companies which accounted for a small volume of lending in the private market. Large life companies, which did not respond, usually initiate financings in which smaller companies subsequently participate and therefore experience longer time lags

In recent years the takedown schedule requested by borrowers has had an important influence on the cost of a private placement. In 1969–1970, for example, when life insurance companies had a limited supply of uncommitted funds, borrowers who wanted the immediate use of funds had to pay higher returns—usually in the form of warrants to purchase common stock. In contrast, during 1971 life insurance companies have been willing to make concessions to encourage the immediate takedown of commitments because of an unexpected increase in cash flows.

Other Provisions of the Private Placement Agreement

A variety of protective devices quite typically appear in privately negotiated loans, some of them analogous to the indenture features of public issues. There is usually a funded debt limitation; a limit on dividend payments; a provision that the borrower be "out of the banks" a few months of the year; a limitation on mortgages on property; a limitation on lease obligations by the debtor; some regulation of mergers or consolidations; a checkrein on expansion and/or diversifications; and a restriction on the buying in of the company's own common stock. Maintenance of a certain level of working capital is usually required. If the borrower engages in foreign business, the agreement may contain some limitation on the commitment of its funds to areas where they may become frozen and unavailable for debt repayments.

The protective provisions of the private placement agreement are generally considered to be more restrictive than those of a public offering agreement. But studies suggest that they exert only a modest restraint on the flexibility of borrowers.[26] This is because of the care which is taken in negotiating the initial provisions of the contract and the ease with which these provisions can be renegotiated. For example, the Commercial and Industrial Loan Department of the Prudential Life Insurance Company, which specializes in loans to small companies, has in recent years averaged about one provision change per loan per year. At the same time other lenders have demanded some compensation in the form of either a higher interest rate or shorter maturity for renegotiating the loan contract, especially during periods of higher interest rates such as 1966–1967 and 1969–1970.

---

between commitments and takedowns. The average monthly lag between the commitment date and first takedown date for a major life insurance company is shown in Figure 5–8.

[26] See, for example, Atamian, "Modifying Direct Placement Agreements."

CHAPTER 2

Borrowers in the Private Placement Market

IN THIS CHAPTER we examine the borrowers in the private placement market and their motives for participating in this market.

There are a number of advantages to the borrower in selling his debt in the private placement market. The legal, accounting, and other expenses of preparing a registration statement are eliminated, and compensation to the investment banker is also reduced because of the elimination of underwriting risks in the distribution process.

A second important advantage of a private placement is that it can be consummated in a fraction of the time required to distribute an issue through the public market. The sale can be completed a few days to a few weeks from the time the borrower decides to sell an issue. In the case of smaller issues requiring the negotiation of terms and provisions, it may take somewhat longer. In contrast, a public offering requires up to 90 days and, in some instances as much as six months, to prepare and to obtain SEC approval of the registration statement. It is also customary to wait an additional 20 days before the issue can be sold.

The SEC has attempted to accelerate the registration process for high-grade, seasoned companies that have sold bonds previously by introducing the S-7 or "short" registration form for use by companies that have achieved a high level of financial and earnings stability. In such cases the registration process itself may take as little as seven to ten days.

Timing is especially important to the borrower who is refunding an outstanding issue to reduce interest costs. The success of his decision depends in large part on his ability to obtain the current market rate of interest on the new issue. Although the market rate may be the same or even lower 90 days hence, the possibility that it might rise significantly limits the attractiveness of a public offering. The advantage in obtaining funds quickly is also important to other borrowers. Although the borrower and/or his agent frequently do not attempt to anticipate short-run interest changes in timing the sale of an issue, they do form judgments concerning the current state of the market and attempt to arrange their financing when the current market looks good, that is, when investors are buying and/or the supply of new issues coming to the market is limited. It is always more hazardous from the borrower's point of view to have to predict the state of the market two or three months hence. Rather than risk a chance of encountering a poor reception in the public market, some borrowers prefer to sell their issues privately even at a rate above the then going interest rate in the public market.

A third important advantage of the private placement method of sale lies in the flexibility of negotiation over the terms and provisions of the issue. The borrower has the chance to explain to the lender any unique features of his situation not easily dealt with in the confines of a prospectus. The borrower can also provide lenders with earnings projections, a practice not permitted in the prospectus of a public offering. This may be particularly important to the small and growing company whose earnings history is a poor indication of its future prospects. Because the borrower is dealing with a few knowledgeable investors—or maybe only one—he is able to bargain for terms and provisions which he considers important for the future success of his operations and to concede on other provisions of less importance. Moreover, the inclusion of covenants in debt issues which are not standard or are unfamiliar to the public market presents little problem in the private placement market; the lenders in that market have acquired considerable experience in investing in issues with unfamiliar loan contract features.

Another advantage that stems from the closeness of the bargaining relationship is that the terms and provisions of an issue can easily be renegotiated during its life. Although the ability to change the provisions of an issue is seldom used by large companies that are borrowing for general purposes, it is especially important to the small, rapidly growing companies that have a continual need for funds. It is valuable as well to heavy and continuous borrowers.

On the other side of the ledger, a disadvantage of the private placement method of sale is that the borrower is less able to repurchase the issue from existing owners to meet sinking fund requirements. If the market rate of interest rises after the issue has been sold and the market price of a public issue has concomitantly declined, this could result in important savings to the borrower.

A second disadvantage charged to private placements is that interest rates tend to be higher in the private market than in the public market on comparable issues. The difference presumably compensates lenders for the high degree of nonmarketability of private issues. Data on interest rate spreads by quality category (Table 2–1) indicate, however, that this is true only for higher

TABLE 2–1
Yields on Private Placements Minus Yields on
Public Offerings, by Quality Category
11-Year Average
1951–1961

| Class | Average Residuals | |
	Industrials	Public Utilities
1	.33%	.16%
2	.15	.20
3	.15	.12
4	—.03	.19
5	—.06	.05
6	—	.08

SOURCE: Cohan, *Yields on Corporate Debt Directly Placed*, p. 130.

quality issues; and even for these the differences are not large. Of course, these spreads are a 10-year average; and for higher quality issues, the quarterly yield spreads have varied between 10 and 150 basis points (depending on the yield series used) as discussed more fully in Chapter 5. Differences in the average yields of public offerings and private placements tended to be an increasing function of issue quality and were even negative in the case of low quality industrial issues.

The differences in cost are even smaller when distribution expenses are considered. The reduction in distribution expenses on a private placement is equivalent to almost a 1% difference in interest cost for small issues and amounts to almost a 0.10% difference for large issues (Table 4–10).

The negative relation between issue quality and the spread in yields between public offerings and private placements probably results from the disparity between real and apparent financial strength among small companies with lower credit ratings. Lenders in the public market rely on traditional ratios, such as "times interest earned" and "debt/equity," to evaluate the quality of borrowers and issues. This is especially disadvantageous to small companies whose ratios frequently understate their real financial strength; that is, their ability to repay their debt. Institutional lenders in the private market, on the other hand, rely on a more thorough analysis of the underlying financial variables to assess the probability of repayment and, in turn, the quality of an issue.

The positive relation between quality and yield spreads also might reflect the fact that investors in the public market generally are more averse to risk than investors in the private market and thus demand relatively higher yields on lower quality issues.

To determine the spread in yields between the public and private markets as a function of quality, Cohan first defined homogeneous quality classes chiefly on the basis of accepted financial ratios.[1] A positive relation between the quality of issues and yield spreads might have been anticipated since Cohan largely ignored the terms and provisions of an issue in his definition of comparable quality. It seems likely that lower quality issues sold in the public market are less standardized than higher quality issues sold in this market. As a result, the lower quality borrower, far more than the high quality borrower, pays a higher nominal rate on a public offering relative to a "comparable" private placement.

Finally, the positive relation between quality and yield spreads might have stemmed from a difference in the pricing process between the public and private markets. In the public market, issues are sold chiefly on the basis of interest rates. The same holds true for issues of high quality, large borrowers in the private market. For other issues in the private market, the interest rate on the loan is still an important factor in determining its acceptability to lenders, but negotiations tend to focus on nonprice variables in the contract. Lenders frequently substitute more restrictive provisions for higher interest rates on such loans. This strategy not only reduces the risk of the issue itself, but also serves as a device for rationing funds during periods when there is a limited supply available in this market. Thus, Cohan's result can also be attributed to the negative relation between the credit standing of the borrower and the emphasis on the nonprice dimensions of issues sold privately.

These yield comparisons are of limited value, however, because they consider only the quality of issues. Except for high quality issues sold by large companies, private placements and public offerings are not readily comparable. Most of the issues sold privately contain provisions or reflect situations which investors in the public market would not accept or would discount quite heavily. Hence, it is likely that if the borrower attempted to offer exactly the same issue in the public market, he would have to provide an interest rate concession which would increase the cost (including underwriting expenses) above the rate paid in the private market. It is also possible that the borrower could not sell the issue in the public market at any acceptable rate. Or the necessary changes might be so restrictive that they would cancel the anticipated benefits of the loan.

The advantages of a private placement clearly vary among companies on

---

[1] Cohan, *Yields on Corporate Debt Directly Placed*, pp. 26–37.

TABLE 2–2
Public Utility Financing by Industry Category
1948–1970
(Dollar amounts in millions)

Year	TOTAL				ELEC., GAS, WATER			
	Pub.	Priv.	Tot.	% Priv.	Pub.	Priv.	Tot.	% Priv.
1948	$ 2,694	$ 745	$ 3,439	21.6%	$ 1,244	$ 562	$ 1,806	31.1%
1949	1,976	959	2,935	32.6	1,042	572	1,614	35.4
1950	2,196	880	3,076	28.6	1,294	633	1,927	32.8
1951	1,906	825	2,731	30.2	1,119	611	1,730	35.3
1952	2,426	1,069	3,495	30.6	1,209	642	1,851	34.6
1953	2,316	977	3,293	29.6	1,265	674	1,940	34.7
1954	3,036	1,208	4,244	28.4	2,065	797	2,863	27.8
1955	2,496	975	3,471	28.1	1,080	555	1,635	33.9
1956	2,301	902	3,203	28.2	1,219	597	1,816	32.8
1957	4,041	1,209	5,250	23.0	2,477	656	3,134	20.9
1958	3,790	1,192	4,982	23.9	2,353	525	2,877	18.2
1959	2,406	1,399	3,805	36 7	1,643	625	2,268	27.5
1960	3,082	880	3,962	22.2	1,896	387	2,283	16.9
1961	2,452	1,267	3,719	34.0	1,669	671	2,340	28.6
1962	3,264	818	4,082	20.0	1,855	416	2,272	18.3
1963	2,863	1,286	4,149	30.9	1,646	604	2,249	26.8
1964	2,405	1,348	3,753	35.9	1,686	454	2,140	21.2
1965	2,638	1,466	4,094	35.8	1,773	559	2,332	23.9
1966	5,102	1,685	6,787	24.8	2,643	474	3,116	15.2
1967	6,421	1,531	7,952	19.3	3,703	514	4,217	12.2
1968	5,922	1,966	7,888	24.9	3,905	502	4,407	11.4
1969	7,473	1,800	9,273	19.4	4,798	612	5,410	11.3
1970	13,695	1,570	15,265	10.3	7,418	598	8,016	7.5
Total	$86,891	$27,957	$114,848	24.3%	$51,002	$13,240	$64,242	20.6%

NOTE: Components may not add to totals due to rounding.
SOURCE: Securities and Exchange Commission.

the basis of their size and access to alternative sources of funds, the purpose to which the proceeds will be put, the nature of their business, and the importance of the interest rate as a cost item, as well as a number of other factors. The particular motive for using the private market may also vary from one sale to the next for issues of the same company.

There is a clear industry pattern to the use of the private market. Real estate and financial companies sold 63% of their debt in the private market between 1948 and 1970; industrial and miscellaneous companies sold 55%. But public utilities sold only 24% of their debt privately. We proceed to examine these three categories of borrowers and their motivations for using the private placement market.

Public Utilities

In the years 1948–1970, electric, gas, and water companies (EGW), communication companies, and railroads relied heavily on the public market to distribute their debt, respectively financing only 20.9%, 12.5%, and

TABLE 2–2 (Continued)

	COMMUNICATION				OTHER TRANSPORTATION				RAILROAD			
Year	Pub.	Priv.	Tot.	% Priv.	Pub.	Priv.	Tot.	% Priv.	Pub.	Priv.	Tot.	% Priv.
1948	$ 831	$ 52	$ 882	5.8%	$ 1	$ 126	$ 127	99.2%	$ 618	$ 5	$ 623	.8%
1949	475	49	525	9.3	1	336	337	99.7	458	2	460	.4
1950	285	54	340	15.8	75	181	256	70.7	542	12	554	2.1
1951	458	55	513	10.7	3	155	157	98.7	326	4	330	1.2
1952	627	70	697	10.0	118	305	424	71.9	472	52	524	9.9
1953	730	63	793	7.9	25	234	260	90.0	296	6	302	1.9
1954	526	84	610	13.7	5	288	293	98.2	440	39	479	8.1
1955	884	103	987	10.4	5	302	307	98.3	527	15	542	2.8
1956	642	84	726	11.5	71	209	280	74.6	369	12	381	3.1
1957	1,186	136	1,322	10.2	34	417	450	92.6	344	0	344	0
1958	1,145	161	1,305	12.3	54	505	558	90.5	238	1	238	.4
1959	520	93	613	15.1	92	659	751	87.7	151	22	174	12.6
1960	883	92	976	9.4	109	383	492	77.8	194	18	211	8.5
1961	536	169	705	23.9	119	375	494	75.9	128	52	180	28.8
1962	1,114	146	1,260	11.5	79	247	326	75.7	216	9	226	3.9
1963	761	184	945	19.5	75	449	524	85.6	381	49	431	11.3
1964	349	320	668	47.9	84	527	611	86.2	286	47	333	14.1
1965	471	338	808	41.8	125	547	673	81.2	259	22	281	7.8
1966	1,491	323	1,814	17.8	637	880	1,517	58.0	331	8	338	2.3
1967	1,542	243	1,786	13.6	899	771	1,670	46.2	277	4	280	1.4
1968	1,470	253	1,723	14.7	349	1,164	1,513	76.9	198	47	245	19.2
1969	1,832	133	1,965	6.8	646	960	1,606	59.8	197	95	292	32.5
1970	4,898	161	5,059	3.2	810	707	1,517	46.6	569	104	673	15.4
Total	$23,656	$3,366	$27,022	12.5%	$4,416	$10,727	$15,143	70.8%	$7,817	$625	$8,441	7.4%

7.2% privately. In contrast, "other" transportation companies—chiefly airlines—sold 70.8% of their debt privately (Table 2–2).

In describing motives for borrowing publicly and privately, EGW and communication companies and railroads may be considered as a single group not only because of similar divisions in their borrowing in the public and private markets but also because of the coincidence of factors influencing their distribution choices.

There appear to be two reasons—one legal and the other economic—why this group placed so small a percentage of their debt privately. On the one hand, a large number of companies are required by their state commissions to sell their debt through public sealed bidding. In addition, the SEC along with the Interstate Commerce Commission, which regulates railroads, and the Federal Power Commission, which regulates electric utility issues, have strongly resisted the attempts of these groups to provide any call protection in their issues. The Commissions were motivated by the belief that liberal call provisions are not penalized in the new issue market. It is generally conceded that investors in the public market have been less insistent on restrictive call features. The spread in yields between callable and 5-year deferred callable public utilities issues (Figure 1–1) indicates, however, that even investors in the public market are aware of the value of a restrictive call feature. Many public utilities, which might otherwise have wished to use the private market, were prevented from doing so because of the buyers' insistence on deferred call features. In response to this, in 1969 the SEC first permitted public utilities falling under its jurisdiction to provide five years of call protection.

The economic reasons why EGW, communication companies, and railroads have not relied on the private market is that the particular advantages of the private market, such as reduced distribution expenses, flexibility in negotiations, and the ease of renegotiation, do not outweigh the interest cost saving that has been obtained through public sales. Being subject to regulation and protected both from economic competition and from a widely fluctuating demand for their products, the utilities have been able to provide a fairly standard set of provisions on new issues and to maintain high credit ratings which the investors in the public market particularly value. Moreover, their steady growth has obviated the need to renegotiate loan provisions during the life of an issue.

Thus, for the very reasons that a private placement offers little advantage, issues of public utilities are especially appealing to the typical buyer of publicly offered securities. The public utilities have not been able to justify the increased interest cost of borrowing in the private market by the rather modest advantages it conferred.

There is one major exception to the above observations and this is the private market's advantage of timing when a company is undertaking a refunding to secure a lower interest cost. The utility, in that case, may prefer to pay a slightly higher interest cost in the private market than to wait and risk the chance of missing a "good" market completely.

Two public utility industries have at times placed great reliance on the private market: the gas pipeline industry in the first postwar decade; the airlines from 1955 through 1970.

The gas pipeline companies grew rapidly after World War II, constructing pipelines for carrying natural gas from the southwest fields to the middle west and northeast markets. These companies had an assured source of supply and demand, along with contracts insuring profitable operation over long periods of time, and they sought to finance their investment chiefly by debt. Because these companies were unseasoned, however, buyers of public offerings would not accept the companies' high debt ratios. As a result, this group relied chiefly on the private placement market for financing during the first postwar decade (Table 2–3). Once the gas pipelines acquired investment stature, they relied more heavily on the public market to finance their needs.

The airline industry's emergence as a major borrower in the corporate bond market coincided with the advent of the jet age in the late 1950s (Table 2–4). The heavy reliance on the private market by airlines initially reflected

TABLE 2–3
Straight-Debt Borrowing by Gas Pipeline Companies
1945–1962
(In millions of dollars)

Year	Public	Private	Total	% Privately Placed
1945	$ 9	$ 10	$ 19	53%
1946	20	63	83	76
1947	50	155	205	76
1948	64	214	278	77
1949	50	228	278	82
1950	115	176	291	61
1951	123	293	416	70
1952	40	178	218	82
1953	170	232	402	58
1954	202	57	259	22
1955	75	409	484	85
1956	110	205	315	65
1957	315	77	392	20
1958	320	157	477	33
1959	303	379	682	56
1960	266	74	340	22
1961	360	210	570	37
1962	325	127	452	28

SOURCE: Freitas, "Private Placements and their Role in the Growth of Selected Industries," p. 55.

their low credit standing and the resulting poor reception their issues would have experienced in the public market. The other advantages of private issues, namely, the ability to tailor the issue to the borrower's particular needs and the ability to renegotiate the terms and provisions, were also important considerations in the airlines' preference for the private market. Moreover, the forward commitment mechanism was particularly useful in the financial planning of airlines because of the long delays between orders and deliveries of airplanes.

In recent years airlines have begun to lease rather than buy their airplanes under equipment trust arrangements. This change was necessitated by the huge financing requirements of the second generation of jet aircraft. Under the equipment trust arrangement, banks, finance companies, or individuals typically supply around 25% of the cost of an airplane. In return, they receive a full equity participation which entitles them to all of the depreciation and the residual value of the equipment. They also receive a 7% investment tax credit if the planes were ordered before mid-1968, the date when the tax credit was repealed. The trustee in the arrangement, who leases the equipment to the airline, borrows the remaining 75% on a straight-debt basis.

TABLE 2–4

Borrowing by Airlines,

1951–1970

(In millions of dollars)

| Year | Public | | Private[1] |
	Straight-Debt	Convertible	
1951	0	0	$ 10
1952	0	0	0
1953	0	0	0
1954	0	0	25
1955	0	$ 4	270
1956	0	5	172
1957	0	0	0
1958	0	13	44
1959	0	47	70
1960	0	25	331
1961	0	127	243
1962	0	0	21
1963	$ 15	120	183
1964	0	67	95
1965	0	156	376
1966	0	494	602
1967	0	660	674
1968	0	102	876
1969	70	325	463
1970	249	84	232

[1] Includes both straight-debt issues and issues with warrants.

SOURCE: "Corporate Financing Directories," *Investment Dealers' Digest.*

Until 1969 airlines' sales in the public market were confined almost exclusively to convertible bond issues. In part, this reflected the airlines' need to maintain debt/equity ratios which were acceptable to the investment community. However, since airlines found it difficult to provide standard contracts, convertibles also represented the only feasible method of borrowing in the public market.

Airlines initially sold equipment trust certificates in the private market, but beginning in 1969 they began to sell them in the public market as well. In part this shift to the public market resulted from a deterioration of airlines' earnings. The majority of airlines were no longer able to meet the legal minimum earnings requirement for New York State life insurance companies of one-and-one-half times interest and lease payments.[2] In addition, the shift reflected a limited availability of funds from life insurance companies, the major

[2] Lenzner, "Private Placements—The Hinges are Turning."

buyers of the long-term obligations of airlines in the private market. When selling straight-debt issues in the public market, airlines usually have had to guarantee the notes, a practice not required for the sale of equipment trust certificates in the private market.

The decision of airlines to sell straight-debt rather than convertible issues in the public market reflected the declining earnings pattern in this industry during the late 1960s and the poor earnings forecast for the early 1970s. In addition, during much of 1970 the investment community was relatively unreceptive to convertible issues; and this substantially increased their costs in comparison with straight-debt issues.

Real Estate and Financial Companies

Real estate companies, finance companies, commercial banks, and other financial institutions have used the private placement market to distribute a major fraction of their debt during the postwar period. During 1948–1970 this group sold 63% of its debt privately. As shown in Table 2–5 covering the period 1951–1970, commercial banks relied least on the private market, selling only 27% of their debt privately. Finance companies, consisting of the 50 largest companies (ranked according to their accounts receivables) through 1967, and all finance companies in 1968–1970, sold 44% of their debts issues in the private market. "Other" companies, consisting chiefly of real estate companies but also including smaller finance companies through 1967 and other financial institutions, borrowed almost exclusively in the private market —selling over 85% of their debt privately.

Finance companies have relied heavily on the debt market during the postwar period, in part a result of their rapid growth. The financial assets of these companies increased from $3.8 billion in 1945 to $60.3 billion in 1970. These companies traditionally have financed around 90% of their loans through borrowing.

Because of their high debt/equity ratios, small differences in the cost of funds can have a significant effect on the earnings per share of their common stock. Thus, a finance company is especially sensitive to the costs of alternative sources of funds and attempts to maintain a debt structure which minimizes these costs.

To accomplish this, a finance company has a wide range of alternatives: short-term debt in the form of commercial paper and/or bank loans; long-term debt in the form of senior, senior-subordinated, and junior-subordinated obligations; capital in the form of preferred and common stock and convertible debentures. In choosing among these alternatives, the finance company must consider not only current differences in interest costs of these alternatives but future differences as well. For example, even though the interest cost on com-

TABLE 2-5
Real Estate and Financial Companies Financing by Industry Category
1951–1970
(Dollar amounts in millions)

Year	Finance Companies[1]				Commercial Banks[2]				Other Companies[3]				Total			
	Pub.	Priv.	Total	% Priv.	Pub.	Priv.	Total	% Priv.	Pub.	Priv.	Total	% Priv.	Pub.	Priv.	Total	% Priv.
1951	$ 40	$ 53	$ 93	57.0%					$ 23	$ 168	$ 191	88.0%	$ 63	$ 221	$ 284	77.8%
1952	43	102	145	70.3					16	205	221	92.8	59	307	366	83.9
1953	455	342	797	42.9					38	541	579	93.4	493	883	1,375	64.2
1954	170	108	278	38.8					14	410	424	96.7	184	518	702	73.8
1955	593	271	864	31.4					26	477	503	94.8	619	748	1,368	54.7
1956	339	394	733	53.8					15	617	632	97.6	354	1,011	1,364	74.1
1957	618	139	757	18.4					54	570	624	91.3	672	709	1,381	51.3
1958	264	83	347	23.9					23	411	434	94.7	287	494	781	63.3
1959	314	382	695	55.0					63	590	653	90.4	377	972	1,349	72.1
1960	854	497	1,351	36.8					105	566	671	84.4	959	1,063	2,023	52.5
1961	312	381	693	55.0					126	750	876	85.6	438	1,131	1,569	72.1
1962	143	374	517	72.3					125	790	915	86.3	268	1,164	1,431	81.3
1963	571	593	1,164	50.9	$ 155	$ 79	$ 234	33.8%	29	1,384	1,413	97.9	755	2,056	2,810	73.2
1964	359	804	1,163	69.1	228	254	482	52.7	165	1,581	1,746	90.5	752	2,639	3,391	77.8
1965	642	685	1,327	51.6	628	139	767	18.1	136	1,533	1,669	91.9	1,406	2,357	3,762	62.7
1966	203	316	519	60.9	58	38	96	39.5	2	1,131	1,133	99.8	263	1,485	1,748	85.0
1967	575	293	868	33.8	230	67	297	22.5	110	974	1,084	89.9	915	1,334	2,249	59.3
1968	386	254	640	39.7	314	15	331	4.5	175	1,016	1,189	85.5	874	1,284	2,160	59.4
1969	683	204	887	23.0	87	44	130	33.8	705	1,017	1,722	59.0	1,474	1,264	2,739	46.1
1970	837	192	1,030	18.6	27	14	41	34.1	2,015	773	2,788	27.7	2,879	979	3,859	25.4
Total	$8,401	$6,466	$14,867	43.5%	$1,727	$650	$2,377	27.3%	$3,965	$15,504	$19,469	79.6%	$14,091	$22,619	$36,710	61.6%

[1] The 50 largest finance companies, ranked by *The American Banker*, through 1967; all finance companies 1968–1970.

[2] Includes bank holding companies.

[3] Real estate and other finance companies. This category is composed chiefly of real estate issues. It also includes issues of small finance companies through 1967 and issues of other financial institutions.

NOTE: Components may not add due to rounding.

SOURCE: Large finance companies and commercial banks, "Corporate Financing Directories," *Investment Dealers' Digest*, 1951–1967; SEC, 1968–1970. Real estate and finance companies total, SEC, 1951–1970.

mercial paper might be below the interest rates on long-term obligations, a finance company could achieve a lower net interest cost in the long run by selling long-term debt if it expects a substantial increase in short-term and long-term interest rates.

A finance company must also consider the relation between its debt structure and that accepted as normal by institutional investors. To facilitate lenders' and investors' evaluation of a finance company's credit worthiness, i.e., riskiness, an ideal or standard structure has evolved in the investment community. The standard is expressed in terms of the percentage of total debt each type of debt should represent.[3] A finance company is penalized in the form of higher interest costs on its debt for substantial departures from this norm in either direction—risk or conservativeness. If, for example, a company failed to maintain an adequate percentage of subordinated debt, the cost of its senior debt would rise. At the same time, it would not be economic to maintain a highly conservative debt structure by increasing the percentage of subordinated debt: the cost of its junior debt would likely rise while the cost of its senior debt would probably not fall by an amount insufficient to offset the marginal differences in cost between the two kinds of debt.

A finance company's choice between a public offering and a private placement to sell long-term debt depends on a number of additional considerations. Cost difference is important. On average the difference in net interest costs (after distribution expenses) between public and private issues is less for finance company issues than for issues of companies in other borrower categories. This probably results from a difference in the assessment of the risk in owning finance company obligations between the buyers of private and public issues. Buyers of privately placed issues—chiefly the large insurance companies and private pension funds—are experienced investors who are willing to accept the high debt/equity ratios of finance companies. They recognize that the high ratios are a consequence of the nature of finance companies' business. The buyers of publicly offered issues—largely state and local retire-

---

[3] Chapman and Jones, *Finance Companies: How and Where They Obtain Their Funds.* For example, the debt structure of large sales finance companies conforms to the distribution shown in the accompanying table. In general, the small finance companies maintain higher percentages of subordinated debt to total debt than do the large companies. See also Jacobs, "Sources and Costs of Funds of Large Sales Finance Companies."

Percentage of Long-Term Capital Funds	
Senior Debt	80%
Subordinated Debt	7
Junior-Subordinated Debt	3
Net Worth	10
	100%

ment systems, the smaller life insurance companies and smaller private pension funds, and individuals—are less experienced and hence more suspicious of these high ratios. As a consequence they demand higher returns than those on other comparable publicly offered corporate obligations to make them acceptable portfolio investments. These differences in risk assessment have narrowed the interest rate spread between publicly offered and privately placed issues in recent years to the point where only the larger finance companies which issue debt in amounts of $10 million or more find it advantageous to sell debt publicly on a cost basis alone. Virtually all other finance companies sell their debt issues exclusively in the private placement market.

Among those finance companies which sell their obligations in both markets, the cost difference is only one consideration in their choice of whether to sell a public or a private issue. The choice also represents a response to the structure of the supply of and demand for the debt issues of finance companies. Because of their rapid growth during the postwar period along with their heavy reliance on borrowed funds, finance companies have issued large amounts of debt both absolutely and in relation to their assets. As a result the issues of finance companies have lost any scarcity value they might have possessed during the early postwar years. To the extent that they can distribute their debt to the large number of investors, finance companies can reduce the overall cost of their long-term borrowing by avoiding a satiation of any one segment of demand. Thus, a finance company uses the private placement market to reach one group of investors and the public offering market to reach the other. It might issue its debt privately even though it cost more at any given moment of time in order to keep the buyers in the public market receptive to future issues.

Almost all the subordinated debt of these companies is sold in the private market. Senior-subordinated and junior-subordinated issues are usually sold in smaller amounts than senior issues. On smaller size issues, the distribution expenses of a public sale are usually sufficiently higher than those associated with a private placement to offset any interest cost savings the public sale might provide. Subordinated issues also provide returns which are attractive to the large institutional investors who buy primarily on the basis of yield.

Timing is an important factor in the choice of markets. If the bond market is unsettled and future interest rate movements are uncertain, a finance company will prefer to place its debt privately because it can be sold in a matter of hours or days. There have been as little as 5 and 10 basis points of difference between the two markets after distribution expenses, so relatively small movements in rates can quickly erase any interest cost saving from a public sale.

Flexibility in both determining and renegotiating the terms and provisions of the agreement during the life of the issue appear to be less important to the finance companies than to other categories of borrowers. Finance company loan agreements are fairly standard and appear to require only infrequent revisions.

The call provision in its debt obligations is an important factor in determining the future profitable operations of a finance company. Although a substantial portion of a finance company's liabilities are long-term maturities, its assets in the form of accounts receivables have relatively short-term maturities. Both the outstanding volume and the return on accounts receivables can change subtantially in fairly short periods of time. To obtain corresponding flexibility on the liability side of the balance sheet in terms of both the volume of debt outstanding and its cost, finance companies issue large amounts of commercial paper.

At the same time, to meet the standards of an acceptable debt structure set by the investment community, finance companies must also finance a substantial portion of their receivables with long-term debt and thus continually face the potential problem of having to finance low-return short-term assets with debt which may have been acquired during previous periods of high interest rates.

The more restrictive call provisions associated with privately placed issues increase a finance company's exposure to the risk that it will be burdened with high fixed charges at a time when both the volume of accounts receivables and consumer loan rates are falling. To avoid this possibility, some finance company issues provide for the redemption of the issue after a period of five years in the event that the volume of receivables declines below their level at the time of sale of the issue.

It appears, however, that finance companies have not attempted to bargain seriously for more liberal call features and have not been responsive to the difference in the call provisions on issues sold publicly and privately. One reason is that the difference in call protection on publicly offered and privately placed issues has not been substantial. For example, the average length of the deferred call period has been about eight years on public issues and about ten years on private issues. The penalty premiums for calling an issue, however, have been slightly smaller on publicly offered issues. Furthermore, interest rates in the capital market have followed a general upward trend since the call provision began to take on meaning in the mid-1950s. The inability to refund high-cost debt has not acquired any significance in the debt management experience of finance companies.

Commercial banks became important borrowers in the corporate bond market beginning in 1963. The progressive deterioration of banks' capital/asset ratios during the postwar period accelerated during the early 1960s. Bank assets grew rapidly during this latter period as a result of bank efforts to com-

pete more aggressively for time deposits. Because of the rising costs of acquiring these deposits, however, the growth in bank earnings—and, in turn, capital
—failed to match the growth in assets. Banks quickly found themselves with
inadequate capital positions. The authorities relaxed regulations in 1963 to
permit banks to treat debt as equivalent to equity in a bank's capital structure.
Debt thus served as a low-cost alternative to common stock.

An additional impetus to the sale of debt by larger banks in financial
centers was the 1961 introduction and subsequent growth of certificates of
deposits (CDs). These deposits with typical maturities of three to nine months
were actively traded in the secondary market and competed with Treasury
bills, commercial paper, and other money market instruments for the short-
term funds of investors. To change its supply of CDs outstanding, a bank
simply varied the (posted) rates it was willing to pay in relation to those paid
by comparable banks. Thus, within the interest rate ceiling specified by the
Federal Reserve's Regulation Q, a bank could increase its deposits and assets
as fast as it desired, provided, of course, it had the capital necessary to support
such expansion.[4] Many banks which did not sold long-term debt.

Commercial banks sold approximately two-thirds of their debt issues in
the public market between 1963 and 1970 (Table 2–5). This figure belies the
importance of the private market in the distribution of bank issues, however.
When banks first began to issue debt, even some of the largest ones sold their
debt privately. In 1963, for example, $155 million of bank debt was sold
publicly by two borrowers and $95 million was sold privately by three bor-
rowers.

Because of the lack of precedent for their sale, the difficulties in establishing standards, and the potentially unfavorable reaction of a bank's customers
to a low rating, issues of banks were not rated by Moody's and Standard and
Poor's rating services. The absence of a rating prevents some investors in the
public market, such as state and local retirement systems, from buying them.
In addition, the lack of market seasoning and investor experience with bank
obligations created problems in the public market. Bank issues were quickly
accepted by investors in both markets, however. During the first half of 1965
there were seven issues sold publicly totaling $609 million. During this same
period, 30 issues totaling $104 million were sold privately. Of these privately
placed issues, the largest was $12 million; the smallest was $0.2 million; six
issues were less than $1 million.[5] Indicative of the seasoning of bank issues

---

[4] For example, on the basis of current capital/asset ratios of around 8%, the sale of a
$10 million debenture would support the sale of $120 million CDs.

[5] For a discussion of bank debt financing, see Jessup, "Bank Debt Capital: Urchin of
Adversity to Child of Prosperity."

which occurred during this period, the United California Bank of Los Angeles sold a $35 million issue privately in 1963 and a $35 million issue publicly in 1965.

The market for bank debt has quickly developed into one resembling the market for the issues of industrial and miscellaneous companies (discussed in the next section). Further seasoning of bank issues should permit smaller banks to sell their debt publicly if they desire. The typical advantages of private placements, such as the flexibility of negotiation and the ease of renegotiation, do not appear to be important to commercial banks. Thus, the distribution choices of banks in the future probably will depend on interest and distribution cost differences between the public and the private markets.

It seems reasonable to expect banks to play an important role in the corporate bond market in the future. The volume of bank financing fell during 1966–1970 but this decline was probably temporary. The growth rate of banks, especially the larger ones, declined during this period as a result of a more restrictive monetary policy and this temporarily reduced the banks' need for additional capital. A portion of bank debt financing during 1964 and 1965 was undertaken in anticipation of future growth which failed to materialize. It is unlikely that the net return on bank assets will be sufficient to enable net worth alone to increase in step with the future capital requirements of banks.[6] Banks might safely support debt issues equal to their net worth, according to one industry expert.[7] On June 30, 1970, the $2.1 billion outstanding debt issues of all commercial banks represented only 5% of net worth.

Real estate companies have relied quite heavily on the private placement market to distribute their debt. The most popular loan arrangement—and the one accounting for a major portion of the real estate loans placed privately—is known as a sale-and-lease-back arrangement. A company first establishes a real estate subsidiary. The subsidiary then purchases new property or existing property from the parent company and leases it back to the parent either directly or indirectly. The subsidiary finances the purchase of the property through the sale of a long-term obligation. Oil companies regularly establish such subsidiaries when they want to expand service station properties. The subsidiary issues its debt to finance the construction and ownership of the properties and then leases the stations to independent operators. To minimize the interest costs on the loan, the parent company guarantees the lease payments of the independent operators. The same type of arrangement is also used by food chains to finance stores and fixtures. This arrangement enables a company

---

[6] Cates, "Are Debentures Still a Luxury?"

[7] *Ibid.*

to maintain ownership of property and obtain the depreciation on the property as a noncash expense—without deteriorating its debt equity ratio.

Commercial banks have also entered into sale-and-lease-back arrangements involving bank property. To the banks, the advantages are twofold. First, it frees up capital which can be used to support the acquisition of new or higher yielding assets. The Federal Reserve uses a formula in the examination of banks which allocates a bank's capital by category of assets. The capital allocation is presumably designed to cover any loss in the capital value of the assets should a liquidation of assets be required. The capital allocation varies according to the maturity and marketability of the assets in the category. The capital allocated to fixed property is 100% of book value while the capital allocated to loans averages about 20% of book value. The capital freed from the sale of property, then, can be used to support a volume of loans equal to five times the book value of the fixed property. The second advantage of a sale-and-lease-back of property is that a bank usually acquires additional capital because the selling price of the property to the subsidiary is based on current market values—usually above the book value of the property.

A second type of real estate financing arrangement closely related to the sale-and-lease-back arrangement is known as "off-balance sheet financing." This differs from the sale-and-lease-back in only one respect. The lessee has the option of buying back the leased property for $1.00 at the termination of the lease. The Internal Revenue Service has ruled that such an option confers ultimate ownership of the property to the lessee and hence gives it the right to include the depreciation on the property in its own income statement. Of course, in the event that the real estate subsidiary is wholly owned, this merely transfers the depreciation from the subsidiary's income statement to the parent company's income statement, but the significant advantage of the IRS ruling is that it enables the real estate company (lessor) to be independent of the lessee.

A number of investment houses have established real estate subsidiaries to finance these special projects. The real estate subsidiary—a new one for each project—buys land specified by a lessee, such as a food chain, sells it to an investor, and then leases it back on a long-term basis. The subsidiary constructs the specified buildings and then leases them to the food chain. The subsidiary's investment in the property is financed through a note, usually secured by assignment of the lease, which is placed privately with a corporate pension fund or other institutional lender. The major benefits accrue to the parent company, the investment house, in the form of depreciation on the property—a noncash expense which is deducted from its income. Investment bankers have also served as brokers in these financing arrangements, selling the tax-shelter aspects to investor groups who are typically clients of the firms.

Privately placed securities are also issued in connection with the financing of urban renewal projects. A number of loan arrangements might be involved in such a financing including common and preferred stock, several layers of senior and subordinated debt, and mortgages.

There are few significant differences between a real estate note placed privately and a mortgage; in most instances the loan can be made using either form of financing. A common distinction between a real estate note placed privately and a mortgage is that on a note the primary source of security is an assignment of the lease and the secondary source, the mortgage on the property. On a mortgage the primary and secondary sources of security are reversed. The difference often depends simply on whether the loan originated in the mortgage department or in the investment department of the institutional lender. Agents themselves prefer to place such loans with the investment department because the latter is usually willing to acquire the loan at a lower interest rate than the mortgage department. This is because the investment department regards the loan as a corporate bond and evaluates it on the basis of the credit of the lessee; the mortgage department looks at it as a mortgage and evaluates it on the basis of the quality of the property. Interest rates on corporate bonds were generally lower than interest rates on mortgages in almost every year covered by our study.

Certain types of real estate loans are more suited for one form of financing or the other. Shopping center financing, for example, lends itself to mortgage financing. There are a large number of leases, representing different credit risks and covering various lengths of time. If an assignment of the lease is the primary source of security, it would prove to be quite cumbersome because of the multitude of terms which would have to be written into it. In addition, the owner rather than the lessee usually pays the taxes and insurance on the property. On the other hand, a note is preferable to a mortgage in arrangements where there is a single lessee, the maturity of the leases are uniform, and the lessee pays the insurance and taxes on the property.

Virtually all real estate notes are sold privately. Since the arrangements surrounding the issue of such notes are quite complicated, this is not surprising. There are issues, however, which appear to be suitable candidates for sale in the public market—e.g., the indirect obligations of large industrial and commercial companies issued in connection with sale-and-lease-back and off-balance sheet financing. Such issues, however, have not yet been accepted by most investors in publicly offered obligations, because they do not completely understand the motives underlying these forms of financing and regard the indirect nature of the lessee's obligation with some suspicion. Privately placed indirect borrowings typically require a higher interest rate—equivalent to the difference in return on two securities with a one letter difference in rating—but this is much less than the interest rate which investors in the public market would require.

Insurance companies and corporate pension funds which are familiar with sale-and-lease-back financing place a smaller value on the probability of default than do investors in the public market. Thus, the differences in the assessment of the risk in owning these issues among investors have acted to narrow the spread between the public and private markets and to encourage the sale of real estate obligations in the private placement market.

The borrowers themselves also favor the private placement method of sale. Because of the unfavorable publicity which has attended sale-and-lease-back financing, they prefer to avoid the wide distribution of ownership that would result from a public sale.

Industrial and Miscellaneous Companies

As a group, industrial companies probably have the greatest freedom to vary their distribution choices in response to changes in economic variables. Substantial differences in borrowing behavior do occur, however, among industrial companies based chiefly on size. During the period 1953–1970, for example (Table 5–6), large industrial and miscellaneous companies, the Fortune 500 companies, sold 37.4% of their debt privately. In contrast, all other companies in this category sold 74.7% of their debt privately.

Small companies tend to sell small issues, and for small issues the distribution expense of a private placement is substantially less than for a public offering. In addition, small companies do not have the financial security either in the form of an assured growth in earnings or in the form of a low-risk balance sheet to offer a standardized set of terms and provisions on their issues. As a result small companies borrow chiefly in the private market.

Large companies tend to sell large issues, and the differences in distribution expenses for such issues in the public and private markets are quite small. Moreover, large companies typically have the financial security to meet a standardized set of provisions. As a result, they have relied much more on the public market than small companies to finance their needs.

The ability of large industrial companies to vary their financing between the public and private markets is evidenced in the number of Fortune 500 companies that sold debt issues in both markets. Of the 498 companies comprising the Fortune 500 lists between 1953 and 1970 that sold two or more debt issues, 277 or 56% sold issues in both markets. Of these 277, 139 sold convertible bond issues only in the public market while the other 138 companies sold at least one straight-debt issue in the public market.[8] Of the 138 companies that sold straight-debt issues publicly, 95 or 69% first sold a private placement. This pattern is not unexpected in view of the fact that as companies grow, they become more secure financially and thus are in a better position to qualify for a public offering. At the same time, 80 of the 138 companies sold at least one private placement after they had sold a straight-debt issue. Finally, 37 of the 138 companies pursued a multiple distribution strategy, varying their choice of distribution channels several times during the period of study.

Insight into the motives influencing the distribution decisions of companies borrowing in both markets has been provided by their replies to a questionnaire. This questionnaire was sent to a number of such companies, and it asked them to rank by relative importance (critical, important, not important, and not considered) the factors which influenced their decision for each of their issues sold during the 1960s.

The most influential factor for issues sold both publicly and privately was the cost of borrowing. It was a relatively more important factor in the decision to borrow publicly rather than privately (Table 2–6). On the one hand, companies selling private issues estimated that they could have sold the same issues publicly at a 15.5 basis point lower cost. Yet, companies selling public issues estimated that it would have cost them 16.6 basis points more to sell the same issues privately. This insignificant difference might have been the coincidental result of the spreads prevailing at the particular times at which the respondents' issues were sold. In combination with the importance of yield differentials on their distribution choices, however, a more reasonable explanation of the similarity of estimated spreads would appear to be the following. Because interest rates are higher in the private market, a private sale must be justified by other advantages accruing to it. Other factors are less important in a public sale because the interest cost is lower; this serves as sufficient justification. In the case of private borrowing, the spread in rates appears to operate chiefly as a constraint on the choice of markets. After borrowers satisfied themselves that the spread was sufficiently narrow, they

---

[8] Approximately 85% of all convertible bond issues have been sold in the public market (Table 5–2) because such issues carry a strong appeal to individual investors who can participate only in the public market. In addition, such issues must be registered anyway at the time of conversion. Less financially secure companies may choose to sell a convertible rather than a straight-debt issue in the public market because this market is much less insistent on a standard set of terms and provisions for such issues. Without further research, it is not possible to determine the fraction of the 139 companies that borrowed in the public market because they had decided to issue a convertible bond and the fraction that sold a convertible bond because it was the only form of financing which was not prohibitively expensive. This problem is discussed at greater length in Chapter 5.

TABLE 2–6

Average Weight of Factors Influencing Distribution Decisions
of Companies Replying to Questionnaire

FACTORS	*Average Weight*[1]
Companies Selling Public Issues (26 Issues)	
1. Nominal interest rate was lower on a public issue	6.87
2. Investment banker recommended	6.47
3. Company desired to reach a wide range of investors	5.37
4. Standardized provisions could be offered	4.27
5. The call feature was less restrictive	3.50
6. Funds were not available in the private market	3.13
7. Public issue could be repurchased in the secondary market to meet sinking fund requirements	3.00
8. There was no need to consummate the sale quickly	2.93
Companies Selling Private Placements (23 Issues)	
1. The nominal interest rate was not substantially higher	6.50
2. The distribution costs were lower	6.00
3. No SEC registration was required	5.67
4. The issue could be sold more quickly	5.20
5. Investment banker recommended	5.15
6. The terms and provisions provided greater flexibility	4.83
7. The funds were available through forward commitments at more convenient times	3.50

[1] Based on a scale of 0 to 10 where the four possible responses were assigned the following weights: Critical = 10.00
Important = 6.67
Not important = 3.33
Not considered = 0

justified their decisions on the basis of other considerations such as the absence of SEC registration and the speed of sale. As might be expected, given the size of the companies surveyed, other factors such as the desirability of flexible terms and provisions were unimportant.

The continuance of cost considerations in the public offering decision is evident not only in the relative importance attached to the interest factor but also in the surprisingly high average weights attached to the recommendation of investment bankers and the desire to reach a wider range of investors. Field interviews indicate that this latter argument is used frequently by investment bankers to justify a public offering. This suggests that in their replies the companies simply repeated their investment bankers' arguments. It is difficult to identify the advantages of a wide distribution, however. In public offerings, the major buyers through most of the period examined were also institutional investors, and even the largest public issues seldom have more than 1,000 purchasers.

TABLE 2-7

Industrial Corporate Bond Sales by Industry

Summary 1950–1964

(Dollar amounts in millions)

SIC #	Industry	Public	Private	Total	% Public	Average[1] Size of Co. in Ind.	Rank % Public	Rank Average Size
33	Primary Metal Industries	$ 2,516	$2,301	$ 4,817	52.2%	155	4	3
29	Petroleum Refining & Related Industries	2,774	450	3,224	86.0	86	1	1
37	Transportation Equipment	1,681	1,280	2,961	56.8	136	3	2
28	Chemical & Allied Products	1,214	915	2,129	57.0	178	2	6
35	Electrical Machinery	681	1,036	1,717	39.1	196	7	7
36	Food & Kindred Products	784	864	1,648	47.6	163	5	4
20	Machinery Except Electrical	629	709	1,338	47.0	164	6	5
	Total	$10,279	$7,555	$17,834				
	Total Sales, 312 Sample Cos.	$11,254	$8,383	$19,637				

[1] Arithmetic average of 1964 Fortune 500 rankings of companies included in an industry category.

SOURCE: "Corporate Financing Directories," *Investment Dealers' Digest.*

Only a few borrowers considered lack of available funds in the private market to be the most influential variable in their decision to borrow publicly. A substantial number of market observers, however, consider this to be one of the more important factors explaining the sharp rise in public offerings in recent years. Its unimportance in the above survey might in part be explained by the fact that the majority of financings reported occurred during the early 1960s when funds were plentiful in the private market.

There is additional evidence of the influence of company size on the distribution decision. The 312 largest companies in *Fortune* magazine's list of the 500 largest manufacturing companies at the end of 1963 were grouped according to their SIC industry classification number, and their borrowing history over the 15-year period, 1950–1964, was summarized (Table 2–7).

The oil industry, which had the largest average size of company, sold a much smaller percentage of their debt (14%) in the private market than did any other industry. At the opposite extreme, the electrical machinery industry, which had the smallest average size of firm, sold by far the highest percentage of their debt (60%) in the private market. The five other industries sold between 43% and 53% of their debt in the private market. Moreover, with the exception of the chemical industry, the rank of the industry based on the average size of the firm differed by no more than one with its rank based on the percentage of debt placed privately. On the basis of these data, it appears clear that the size of the firms in an industry has a definite, predictable influence on the industry's use of the private placement method to obtain external funds.

CHAPTER 3

Lenders in the Private Placement Market

IN THIS CHAPTER we examine the portfolio policies and the role of the three major lenders in the private market—life insurance companies, private pension funds, and state and local government retirement funds.

Certain characteristics common to the liability and cost structures of all three institutions have made privately placed corporate bonds an attractive investment at various times during the postwar period. All three, for example, have experienced a substantial net inflow of funds. This inflow has been virtually immune to cyclical and shorter-run reverses with the exception of life insurance companies that were subjected to substantial cash outflows in the form of loans to policyholders during 1966 and 1969–1970. The flow of funds has served to reduce the importance of liquidity and marketability in their portfolio choices. Furthermore, the commitments of these institutions in the form of future payments to policyholders (or beneficiaries) or to pensioners are either fixed in amount or relatively stable and predictable over time. Accustomed to holding fixed-income securities to maturity anyway, these investors usually have found that the relatively greater return on private placements more than compensates for the limited marketability of these issues.

Within this common framework, however, there are certain differences among these institutions in their legal liabilities, in legal restrictions on their choice of assets, and in the structure of portfolio administration. These differences have significantly varied the portfolio policies of these institutions as well as the role they play in the private placement market. Private pension funds, for one, have placed a much greater emphasis on acquiring variable income securities, i.e., common stock, than either life insurance companies or state and local retirement funds. Only in recent years have these latter groups accelerated their purchases of common stock.

During the early postwar years, life insurance companies supplied the major portion of funds to the corporate bond market (Table 3–1). Although life insurance companies continued to supply substantial amounts of funds to this market during subsequent years, their position of dominance was progressively eroded through the mid-1960s. Private pension funds began increasing their acquisitions in the 1950s; state and local retirement funds started doing the same in the 1960s. Other institutional lenders, such as mutual savings banks, and individuals have been chiefly a residual source of funds to the corporate bond market, varying acquisitions in response to changes in the returns on corporate bonds and other financial assets; these investors have not been active in the private market.

Only life insurance companies have consistently supplied substantial funds to the private market throughout the postwar period. In comparison, private pension funds have had a varied pattern of activity in the private market. The more aggressive funds have pursued portfolio objectives in the private market similar to those of the large life insurance companies, but on balance private pension funds have tended to acquire higher quality issues. After progressively increasing their activity in the private market through the first half of the 1960s, private pension funds abruptly reduced their purchases in recent years. In response to the increased importance placed on portfolio performance, these funds have come to regard the incremental returns on private placements as inadequate compensation for the loss of flexibility in managing their debt and equity portfolios.

State and local government retirement funds did not become an important supplier of funds to the private market until the early 1960s and then, because of limited investment management facilities and legal restrictions, they bought only higher quality rated issues which featured standard contracts. Sales of this kind of issue in the private market declined during recent periods of high interest rates, such as 1966 and 1969–1970; and it seems probable that the role of state and local retirement funds in the private market has also diminished. Larger state and local funds recently have begun to improve the sophistication of their portfolio administration and could potentially widen their selection, but this development probably will have a greater impact on their activity in the stock market than in the private placement market.

Life Insurance Companies

Life insurance companies have been the most active and consistent participants in the private market during the postwar period. Because of their highly specialized investment staffs, the insurance companies have also been virtually the sole supplier of funds to smaller, less financially secure companies which require flexible terms and special provisions.

TABLE 3-1
Net Acquisitions of Corporate Bonds[1]
by Lender Category
1946-1970
(Dollar amounts in billions)

Year	Life Insurance Companies		Private Pension Funds		State and Local Retirement Funds		Other Institutional[2] Investors		Individuals and Other Investors		Total Corporate Bond Sales
	Amount	Percent	Amount	Percent	Amount	Percent	Amount	Percent	Amount	Percent	
1946	$1.8	180%	$0.3	30%	*	—	$ 0.2	20%	$–1.3	–130%	$ 1.0
1947	3.0	100	0.3	10	*	—	0.5	17	–0.7	–23	3.0
1948	4.2	88	0.3	6	$0.1	2%	0.3	6	–0.2	–4	4.8
1949	2.6	79	0.3	9	0.1	3	0.4	12	–0.1	–3	3.3
1950	1.8	78	1.0	43	0.2	9	0.2	9	–0.9	–39	2.3
1951	2.7	69	0.7	18	0.1	3	0.5	13	–0.1	–3	3.9
1952	3.1	62	1.1	22	0.2	4	0.4	8	0.1	2	5.0
1953	2.8	61	1.1	24	0.5	11	0.3	7	*	—	4.6
1954	2.0	53	1.3	34	0.6	16	0.1	3	–0.2	–5	3.8
1955	1.8	45	0.9	23	0.5	13	–0.5	–13	1.4	35	4.0
1956	2.1	43	1.6	33	0.6	12	–0.4	–8	1.0	20	4.9
1957	2.6	35	1.9	25	0.8	11	0.9	12	1.3	17	7.5
1958	2.5	37	1.5	22	0.8	12	0.9	13	1.1	16	6.8
1959	2.2	49	1.2	27	0.9	20	–0.1	–2	0.4	9	4.5
1960	1.8	32	1.6	29	1.2	21	0.7	13	0.4	9	5.6
1961	2.5	45	1.2	21	1.7	30	–0.4	–7	0.6	11	5.6
1962	2.5	42	1.2	20	1.9	32	0.7	12	–0.5	–8	5.9
1963	2.8	42	1.5	23	1.9	29	0.7	11	–0.2	–3	6.6
1964	2.3	32	1.6	23	1.9	27	1.3	18	–0.1	–1	7.1
1965	2.8	33	1.5	17	2.1	24	1.1	13	1.1	13	8.6
1966	2.4	20	1.9	16	2.5	21	2.1	18	3.2	27	11.8
1967	3.8	22	0.9	5	3.4	20	5.5	32	3.6	21	17.2
1968	3.9	26	0.7	5	2.5	17	2.4	16	5.7	38	15.1
1969	1.5	10	0.6	4	3.0	20	3.3	22	6.3	43	14.8
1970	1.5	6	1.6	7	3.9	16	3.1	13	13.7	58	23.7

[1] Includes foreign bonds.
[2] Includes state and local governments, commercial banks, mutual savings banks, and other insurance companies.
* Less than ± $0.05 billion.
NOTE: Components may not add to totals due to rounding.
SOURCE: Board of Governors, Federal Reserve System, *Flow-of-Funds Accounts: 1945–1968* and *Flow-of-Funds Accounts, First Quarter, 1971*.

The financial assets of life insurance companies have grown at a 6.3% average annual rate during the postwar period. Reflecting this growth, life companies' net acquisition of credit market instruments increased progressively from $3.5 billion in 1946 to $8.8 billion in 1970 (Table 3–2). In the early postwar years, life insurance companies liquidated substantial amounts of U.S. Government securities, accumulated during the war, and invested the proceeds in corporate bonds and mortgages. Between the early 1950s and 1968, corporate bonds accounted for around 40% of life insurance companies' net purchases of credit market instruments; bonds competed chiefly with mortgages as the insurance companies' major investment. In 1969 and 1970, however, net acquisitions of corporate bonds fell to only 18% of net credit market purchases.

This decline was chiefly the result of an increase in "other" loans—chiefly of loans to policyholders. Other loans accounted for 37% of net credit market purchases during 1969–1970, up sharply from the previous high of 19% in 1966 and an average of around 5% for the 20 years prior to that.

Policy loans increased to 9.4% of investment funds in 1966 and to a high of 15.2% in 1969 (Table 3–3).[1] Between 1957 and 1965 these loans accounted for only 3.5% to 6.9% of investment funds. Data on policy loans are reported by the Life Insurance Association of America (LIAA) in their sample of major life insurance companies.[2]

Even without the increase in loans to policyholders, life insurance companies' net purchases of corporate bonds would have fallen in 1969–70. These bonds accounted for only 28% of their purchases of credit market instruments net of the increase in other loans. Life insurance companies had accelerated their purchases of common stocks as part of a vigorous effort to compete with commercial banks for private pension fund accounts. Before 1959 life insurance companies were not permitted to invest their pension fund reserves separately from their other reserves.[3] As a result, their pension funds accounts

---

[1] The sharp increase in policy loans during recent high interest rate periods resulted from the fact that the maximum rates which life insurance companies were allowed to charge on such loans—currently 5% in New York and slightly higher elsewhere—were far below the rates which borrowers would have had to pay commercial banks or finance companies. Because of their own limited supply of funds during these periods, banks themselves encouraged borrowers to take advantage of this opportunity.

[2] The life insurance companies included in the LIAA's sample represented between 60% and 64% of the industry's assets between 1957 and 1966, about 70% in 1967, and around 80% in 1968–1970.

[3] In 1959 Connecticut and New Jersey authorized separate accounts for the management of pension funds and New York followed in 1962. All but one state had authorized separate accounts by 1970. See *Institutional Investor Study, Report of the Securities and Exchange Commission*, Vol. II, pp. 642–643. For a discussion of the growth of separate accounts, see Bishop, *The Response of Life Insurance Investments to Changes in Monetary Policy, 1965–1970*, pp. 53–55.

TABLE 3-2
Net Acquisitions of Credit Market Instruments by
Life Insurance Companies
1946–1970
(Dollar amounts in millions)

Year	Corporate Bonds Amt.	Pct.	Corporate Stock Amt.	Pct.	Mortgages Amt.	Pct.	U.S. Govt. Securities Amt.	Pct.	State and Local Govt. Sec. Amt.	Pct.	Other[1] Loans Amt.	Pct.	Total Credit Market Instruments
1946	$1.8	51%	$0.3	9%	$0.5	14%	$ 1.0	29%	$-0.1	-3%	$-0.1	-3%	$3.5
1947	3.0	97	0.2	6	1.6	52	-1.6	-52	*	—	*	—	3.1
1948	4.2	117	*	—	2.1	58	-3.2	-89	0.3	8	0.1	3	3.6
1949	2.6	70	0.2	5	2.1	57	-1.5	-41	0.2	5	0.2	5	3.7
1950	1.8	47	0.3	8	3.2	84	-1.8	-47	0.1	3	0.2	5	3.8
1951	2.7	73	0.1	3	3.2	85	-2.4	-65	*	—	0.2	5	3.7
1952	3.1	69	0.2	4	1.9	42	-0.8	-18	*	—	0.1	2	4.5
1953	2.8	57	0.1	2	2.0	41	-0.4	-8	0.2	4	0.2	4	4.9
1954	2.0	41	0.3	6	2.7	55	-0.8	-16	0.6	12	0.2	4	4.9
1955	1.8	35	0.1	2	3.5	67	-0.5	-10	0.2	4	0.3	6	5.2
1956	2.1	41	*	—	3.6	71	-1.0	-20	0.2	4	0.2	4	5.1
1957	2.6	52	*	—	2.2	44	-0.5	-10	0.1	2	0.5	10	5.0
1958	2.5	49	0.1	2	1.8	35	0.1	2	0.3	6	0.2	4	5.1
1959	2.2	42	0.2	4	2.1	40	-0.3	-6	0.5	10	0.5	10	5.2
1960	1.8	33	0.4	7	2.6	48	-0.5	-9	0.4	7	0.8	15	5.4
1961	2.5	44	0.5	9	2.5	44	-0.4	-7	0.3	5	0.4	7	5.7
1962	2.5	38	0.4	6	2.7	42	0.1	2	0.1	2	0.7	11	6.5
1963	2.8	42	0.2	3	3.6	54	-0.4	-6	-0.2	-3	0.5	7	6.7
1964	2.3	31	0.5	7	4.6	62	-0.3	-4	-0.1	-1	0.4	5	7.4
1965	2.8	34	0.7	8	4.9	60	-0.4	-5	-0.3	-4	0.6	7	8.2
1966	2.4	30	0.3	4	4.6	57	-0.3	-4	-0.4	-5	1.5	19	8.1
1967	3.8	45	1.1	13	2.9	35	-0.3	-4	-0.1	-1	1.0	12	8.4
1968	3.9	43	1.4	16	2.5	28	-0.1	-1	0.2	2	1.2	13	9.0
1969	1.5	18	1.7	20	2.0	24	-0.4	-5	*	—	3.4	41	8.3
1970	1.5	17	2.0	23	2.3	27	*	—	0.1	1	2.9	33	8.8

[1] Mostly loans to policyholders.
* Less than ± $0.05 billion.
NOTE: Components may not add to total due to rounding.
SOURCE: Board of Governors, Federal Reserve System, *Flow-of-Funds Accounts*.

TABLE 3–3

Net Increase in Policy Loans as a Percentage of Life Insurance Companies'
Investment Funds before Policy Loans
1957–1970

Year	Policy Loans as % of Investment Funds
1957	4.4%
1958	3.6
1959	4.4
1960	6.9
1961	4.9
1962	4.4
1963	3.5
1964	3.6
1965	3.5
1966	9.4
1967	6.4
1968	7.3
1969	15.2
1970	12.2

SOURCE: Life Insurance Association of America, "Sample of Major Life Insurance Companies."

were subject to the investment restrictions on their reserves, which, for example, limited common stock holdings to 5% of assets. Commercial banks, which faced no such restrictions on their investments, progressively increased their share of the private pension fund industry's assets—all of that gained at the expense of life insurance companies. The accelerated decline in bond prices that began in late 1965 and the continued growth in stock prices through most of the 1960s prodded the insurance companies into becoming more competitive in managing separate pension fund accounts. The insurance companies had been slow to take advantage of the investment freedom that the regulation changes offered them, but by 1970 the cash flow generated from these separate accounts had increased to $1.8 billion, equivalent to more than 25% of the net increase in ledger assets during that year.[4]

Life insurance companies' purchases of corporate bonds have become progressively concentrated in the private placement market. This development is chronicled in Table 3–4 which shows the purchases of public and private issues by 28 major life insurance companies, representing about 80% of the industry's assets between 1946 and 1966, the last year for which data are available. These companies increased the percentage of corporate bonds acquired in the private market from around 55% in the early postwar years to

---

[4] LIAA's sample of major life insurance companies.

TABLE 3-4
Acquisitions of Publicly Offered and Privately Placed Corporate Bonds by 28 Life Insurance Companies 1946-1966
(Dollar amounts in millions)

Year End	Public Utilities				Industrial & Misc. Companies[1]				Total Corporate				
	Public Offerings	Private Placements	Total	% Private	Public Offerings	Private Placements	Total	% Private	Public Offerings	Private Placements	Total	% Private	% Indus. & Misc. Co.
1946	$ 967	$331	$1,298	25.5%	$317	$1,556	$1,872	83.1%	$1,284	$1,887	$3,171	59.5%	59.0%
1947	1,427	512	1,939	26.4	262	1,747	2,009	87.0	1,689	2,259	3,948	57.2	50.9
1948	1,280	614	1,894	32.4	107	2,400	2,507	95.7	1,388	3,014	4,402	68.5	57.0
1949	669	616	1,285	47.9	262	1,801	2,063	87.3	931	2,417	3,347	72.2	61.6
1950	882	696	1,578	44.1	66	1,642	1,707	96.2	948	2,338	3,285	71.2	52.0
1951	343	784	1,127	69.6	180	2,688	2,867	93.7	523	3,472	3,994	86.9	71.8
1952	328	773	1,101	70.2	225	3,233	3,458	93.5	554	4,006	4,559	87.9	75.8
1953	323	746	1,069	69.8	174	2,768	2,943	94.1	497	3,515	4,011	87.6	73.4
1954	591	927	1,518	61.1	229	2,760	2,989	92.3	820	3,686	4,506	81.8	66.3
1955	422	560	982	57.0	188	2,944	3,132	94.0	609	3,503	4,113	85.2	76.1
1956	246	646	892	72.4	125	2,756	2,881	95.7	370	3,401	3,771	90.2	76.4
1957	199	501	700	71.6	118	3,182	3,300	96.4	317	3,683	4,000	92.1	82.5
1958	241	459	700	65.6	275	2,562	2,837	90.3	516	3,023	3,538	85.4	80.2
1959	98	778	876	88.8	55	2,993	3,048	98.2	153	3,771	3,923	96.1	77.7
1960	107	365	472	77.3	100	2,615	2,715	96.3	207	2,981	3,188	93.5	85.2
1961	109	448	557	80.4	113	3,287	3,400	96.7	222	3,734	3,957	94.4	85.9
1962	163	304	467	65.1	91	3,813	3,904	97.7	253	4,117	4,370	94.2	89.3
1963	179	358	537	66.7	107	4,638	4,746	97.7	286	4,996	5,282	94.6	89.9
1964	105	545	650	83.8	36	4,531	4,567	99.2	141	5,076	5,217	97.3	87.5
1965	121	272	393	69.2	118	5,473	5,590	97.8	239	5,744	5,983	96.0	93.4
1966	305	359	664	54.1	127	4,637	4,765	97.3	432	4,996	5,429	92.0	87.8

[1] Includes real estate and financial companies.

NOTE: Valuation basis is cost, not par. Components may not add to totals due to rounding. Beginning in 1956, maturities of one year or less are excluded. In 1956, maturities of one year or less was $802 million for the industrial and miscellaneous category, but was believed to be substantially less than this in the years before 1956.

SOURCE: Life Insurance Association of America, 1967 Record of Life Insurance Investments.

around 90% in the early 1960s. Moreover, the proportion of issues acquired in the private market was relatively immune to increases and decreases in the proportion of all corporate debt sold privately (Figure 3–1). This reflects the ability of the highly specialized staffs of life insurance companies to acquire high yielding, lower quality issues quite independently of the overall demand for funds in the public and private markets. As a result of the increased activity in the private market, the 28 major life insurance companies had acquired 82% of their corporate bond holdings from private placements in 1966; in 1948 that proportion was only 54% (Table 3–5).

These life insurance lenders have consistently purchased 90% or more of their industrial, real estate, and financial corporation bonds from the private market every year since 1952. By the early 1960s this percentage was consistently above 97% (Table 3–4).

In contrast, the 28 life insurance companies have purchased a substantially smaller percentage of public utility issues in the private market, though even this percentage has increased from less than 30% in the years immediately following the war to between 70% and 80% in the 1960s. Inhibited by regulatory public restrictions, utilities have sold only 24.3% of their issues in the private market between 1948 and 1970.[5] As a fraction of total public utility issues owned by insurance companies, private placements increased from 32% in 1948 to 47% at the end of 1966, considerably less than the percentage of industrial and miscellaneous corporate bonds acquired through private placements.

During the 1950s life insurance company acquisitions of private placements accounted for a very high percentage of all issues sold privately (Figure 3–2). While life insurance company purchases of privately placed issues continued to increase during the 1960s, the percentage of privately placed issues acquired by the 28 companies fell sharply beginning in 1960 to only 66% in 1966 (Figure 3–2). The entry of state and local retirement funds as lenders in the private market appears to be largely responsible for this decline, although private pension funds were also active in the private market during this period. State and local funds confined their purchases to the issues of companies with higher credit ratings which were attracted to the private market by the relatively favorable terms on which funds were available. This condition appears to have stemmed from the fact that the demand for funds on the part of corporations was quite modest at a time when the supply of funds available in the private market was augmented by the entry of state and local funds into this market.

Although the entry of state and local retirement funds as lenders in the

---

[5] See Table 2–2.

TABLE 3–5
Ownership of Publicly Offered and Privately Placed Corporate Bonds by 28 Life Insurance Companies
1948–1966
(Dollar amounts in millions)

Year End	Public Utilities				Industrial & Misc. Companies[1]				Total Corporate				
	Public Offerings	Private Placements	Total	% Private	Public Offerings	Private Placements	Total	% Private	Public Offerings	Private Placements	Total	% Private	% Indus. & Misc Co.
1948	$7,117	$3,269	$10,386	31.5%	$ 915	$ 5,978	$ 6,893	86.7%	$ 8,033	$ 9,248	$17,280	53.5%	39.9%
1949	7,528	3,712	11,240	33.0	1,125	7,211	8,336	86.5	8,653	10,923	19,576	55.8	42.6
1950	7,866	4,132	11,998	34.4	1,098	8,062	9,160	88.0	8,965	12,193	21,158	57.6	43.3
1951	7,900	4,699	12,599	37.3	1,154	9,823	10,978	89.5	9,055	14,521	23,577	61.6	46.6
1952	7,993	5,233	13,226	39.6	1,297	11,728	13,025	90.0	9,290	16,960	26,250	64.6	49.6
1953	8,331	5,763	14,094	40.9	1,407	13,333	14,740	90.5	9,738	19,097	28,835	66.2	51.1
1954	8,512	6,147	14,659	41.9	1,469	14,521	15,991	90.8	9,982	20,668	30,649	67.4	52.2
1955	8,639	6,463	15,102	42.8	1,479	15,632	17,112	91.4	10,119	22,096	32,214	68.6	53.1
1956	8,607	6,839	15,446	44.3	1,370	17,021	18,391	92.6	9,976	23,861	33,837	70.5	54.3
1957	8,706	7,048	15,754	44.7	1,411	18,540	19,951	92.9	10,117	25,588	35,705	71.7	55.9
1958	8,845	7,241	16,086	45.0	1,583	19,701	21,285	92.6	10,428	26,942	37,370	72.1	57.0
1959	8,838	7,529	16,367	46.0	1,542	21,207	22,750	93.2	10,380	28,737	39,117	73.5	58.2
1960	8,831	7,537	16,368	46.0	1,549	22,491	24,040	93.6	10,380	30,028	40,408	74.3	59.5
1961	8,695	7,684	16,379	46.9	1,577	24,061	25,638	93.8	10,271	31,745	42,016	75.6	60.6
1962	8,720	7,647	16,367	46.7	1,576	25,739	27,315	94.2	10,296	33,385	43,681	76.4	62.5
1963	8,586	7,637	16,223	47.1	1,558	27,862	29,420	94.7	10,144	35,499	45,643	77.8	64.4
1964	8,400	7,398	15,798	46.8	1,420	29,649	31,069	95.4	9,820	37,047	46,866	79.0	66.3
1965	8,150	7,242	15,392	47.1	1,376	31,998	33,374	95.9	9,526	39,179	48,705	80.4	68.5
1966	7,777	7,036	14,813	47.5	1,413	33,855	35,268	96.0	9,189	40,892	50,081	81.7	70.4

[1] Includes real estate and financial companies.
NOTE: Valuation basis is cost, not book value. Components may not add to totals due to rounding.
SOURCE: Life Insurance Association of America, 1967 Record of Life Insurance Investments.

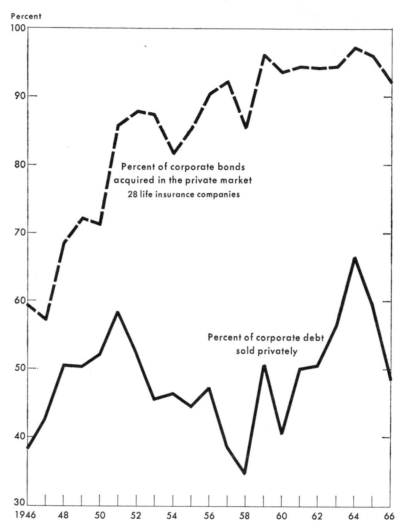

FIGURE 3–1
Percentage of Corporate Debt Sold Privately
Percentage of Corporate Bonds Acquired in the Private Market by 28 Life
Insurance Companies
1946–1966

private market represented a secular change in the composition of supply, the erosion of life insurance companies' share of the private placement market during the 1960s was more cyclical in character. Companies selling issues to state and local funds largely confined their borrowing to the public market during the latter years of the 1960s and in 1970. It seems reasonable to assume that state and local funds shifted their acquisitions to the public market in

FIGURE 3–2

Private Placements and the Acquisition of Private Placements by 28 Life
Insurance Companies
1946–1966

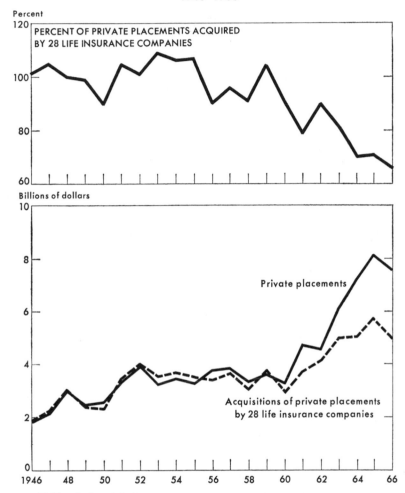

SOURCE: Tables 3–4 and 5–1.
NOTE: The acquisitions of the 28-company sample have been inflated by various reporting
procedures. Before 1956 purchases of commercial paper and other short-term issues were included in this series. The series also includes secondary market acquisitions. Moreover, as noted
in the 1969 report of the LIAA, the figures "are substantially inflated by the inclusion of exchanges and noncash items" (p. 26). In contrast, the SEC records only the net cash increases
in refundings and exchanges and excludes secondary market transactions.

response. In addition, private pension funds sharply reduced their acquisitions
of private placements in the late 1960s. It is not possible to determine exactly
the extent to which the life insurance companies' share of the private market
has increased in recent years because the LIAA series on the acquisition of

private placements by the 28 life insurance companies has not been compiled since 1966. The LIAA has compiled the acquisitions from outstanding securities commitments in their sample of major life insurance companies (Table 3–6).

TABLE 3–6

Acquisitions from Outstanding Forward Commitments
by Life Insurance Companies
1957–1970
(Dollar amounts in millions)

Year	Acquisitions[1]	% of Private Placements
1957	$2,913	75.9%
1958	2,950	88.9
1959	2,874	79.1
1960	2,768	84.5
1961	3,139	66.5
1962	3,502	76.5
1963	4,121	66.9
1964	4,180	57.7
1965	4,771	58.5
1966	4,385	58.1
1967	4,989	71.6
1968	N.A.	—
1969	4,695	83.6
1970	4,952	101.5

[1] Includes state and local bonds and other noncorporate securities.

SOURCES: Acquisitions, Life Insurance Association of America, "Sample of Major Life Insurance Companies." Private placements, Table 5–1 (Securities and Exchange Commission).

The percentage of private placements accounted for by life insurance companies' acquisitions progressively declined from around 80% in the late 1950s to less than 60% in 1964–1966. This percentage then rose sharply to reach 100% in 1970.[6]

The life insurance companies' almost exclusive role as lenders to financially less secure companies, requiring the special advantage of a private placement, was in no way affected by the activity of state and local pension funds in the private market during the early 1960s. Data on new commitments, reported in the LIAA's sample of major life insurance companies, show that throughout the 1960s the largest proportion (usually 40% to 50%) of new authorizations was made each year to companies rated Number 4 in quality—corresponding to Moody's Baa rating (Table 3–7). This reflects the life in-

[6] Part of the increase in 1967–1970 resulted from an increase in the LIAA sample size as reported in footnote 2. In addition, securities other than corporate bonds represented a small fraction of life insurance company acquisitions.

TABLE 3-7

Authorizations of Life Insurance Companies for Private Placements, Classified by Quality and Types of Issues
1960–1970

(% of total authorizations invested in each category)

Year	Issues Classified by Quality [1]					Other Issues							Total	
	1	2	3	4	Total	Foreign	Canadian [2]	Convertible	With Warrants [3]	Mineral Production [3]	All Other	Total	Percent	Amount (in millions)
1960	0.7	4.8	26.1	42.8	74.5	7.1		1.5			16.8	25.5	100.0	$ 2,271
1961	1.1	5.9	25.0	46.6	78.7	3.7		0.6			17.0	21.3	100.0	2,702
1962	0.2	6.0	18.2	52.4	76.8	12.0		0.6			10.6	23.2	100.0	3,360
1963	0.5	6.5	19.8	50.3	77.2	6.7		0.6			15.6	22.8	100.0	3,408
1964	1.5	6.4	16.3	53.1	77.3	7.7		0.5			14.5	22.7	100.0	3,995
1965	0.6	5.8	18.0	47.4	71.8	7.8		0.5			19.9	28.2	100.0	5,127
1966	0.9	9.1	21.8	44.7	76.5	1.0	4.8	1.0	2.8	1.9	12.1	23.5	100.0	4,061
1967	1.2	7.5	22.5	46.2	77.3	0.7	3.9	2.0	4.2	1.5	10.4	22.7	100.0	4,647
1968	0.9	2.7	12.7	42.1	58.4	0.6	14.2	3.8	8.3	1.3	12.8	41.6	100.0	3,586
1969	0.4	4.6	13.2	35.8	54.0	1.2	8.0	7.9	20.3	0.2	8.4	46.0	100.0	2,654
1970	0.7	3.2	16.7	41.7	62.3	—	2.6	3.1	13.0	0.5	12.4	37.0	100.0	2,002
Total	0.8	5.9	19.0	46.3	72.1	4.6	3.0*	1.8	4.1*	0.5*	13.8	27.9	100.0	$37,804

[1] Numerical ratings are designed to correspond respectively, with Moody's Aaa, Aa, A, and Baa ratings.

[2] Included in Foreign: 1960–1965.

[3] Included in All Other: 1960–1965.

* 1966–1970 totals as % of total (1960–1970) authorizations.

NOTE: Components may not add to totals due to rounding.

SOURCE: Life Insurance Association of America, "Average Yields on Directly Placed Corporate Bond Authorizations," various reports.

surance companies' preference for higher risk-higher return loans. The interest in lower quality issues, as well as the changing character of the private placement market, is also revealed in the growth in issues with equity features. Convertible bonds and issues with warrants accounted for only 4% of authorizations in 1966 but for 28% in 1969 and 22% in 1970.

Within the life insurance industry, the large companies have been the most active participants in the corporate bond market as well as in the private placement market during the postwar period. In a survey conducted in 1958, the 15 largest life insurance companies accounted for 75% of the assets of the sample group; they owned 89% of all industrial and miscellaneous issues of the group and 83% of all corporate bonds (Table 3–8). In comparison the 15 largest companies held only 76% of the public utility issues owned by the sample companies, again because of the limited sale of public utility issues in the private market. The concentration of privately placed issues in the portfolios of the largest life insurance companies is evidenced in Table 3–9 which summarizes data compiled by Brimmer for the year 1958. This table indicates that not only did a fewer number of smaller life insurance companies (those in size groups 3 and 4) participate in the private market, but that those which did acquired a smaller percentage of their issues in this market.

One reason for the limited participation of smaller life insurance companies in the private market is that they cannot afford to maintain a staff specializing in administering a portfolio of such issues. Moreover, the fact that smaller companies have limited resources and in most instances can acquire only small portions of an individual issue has also acted to restrict their entry into the private placement market. The distribution process in the private market tends to limit the number of investors in an issue.[7] The agent usually offers the issue first to investors who are capable of buying the entire issue or at least a substantial portion of it. The borrower also prefers this procedure because it increases the speed and flexibility with which potential renegotiations of the terms and provisions of the issue can be conducted. And the large life insurance companies prefer to minimize the number of other buyers for essentially the same reason. A few companies traditionally buy entire issues whenever their resources permit since this eliminates the possibility of concessions to other members of the buying group over the terms and provisions of the issue. All three participants—the borrower, his agent, and the large investor—act to restrict the small institutional investor's participation in the private market.

Without personnel capable of administering a private placement portfolio, the smaller life insurance companies are reluctant to acquire issues with

---

[7] Discussed in Chapter 4.

TABLE 3–8

Distribution of Total Assets and Corporate Bonds by Size Group
of Largest Life Insurance Companies
1957

(Dollar amounts in millions)

Asset Range of 15 Companies in Each Group	Assets of Group		Corporate Bonds Held					
			Industrial & Misc. Cos.		Public Utilities[1]		Total	
	Amount	% of Total	Amount	% of Total	Amount	% of Total	Amount	% of Total
1 ($1,329–$15,536)	$72,891	74.7%	$18,891	88.8%	$14,108	75.7%	$32,999	82.7%
2 ($514–$1,273)	10,898	11.2	1,291	6.1	2,123	11.4	3,414	8.5
3 ($236–$497)	5,213	5.3	508	2.3	836	4.5	1,344	3.4
4 ($143–$234)	2,704	2.8	190	0.9	482	2.6	672	1.7
5 ($100–$141)	1,774	1.8	129	0.6	365	2.0	494	1.2
6–10 ($25–$99)	4,107	4.2	262	1.3	726	3.8	988	2.5
Total	$97,587	100.0%	$21,271	100.0%	$18,640	100.0%	$39,911	100.0%

[1] Includes railroad issues.

SOURCE: Brimmer, *Life Insurance Companies in the Capital Market*, p. 209.

TABLE 3–9

Percentage of Corporate Bonds Acquired in the Private Placement Market
by Size Group of Life Insurance Companies

1958

% of Bonds Acquired in the Private Placement Market	Size Group[1]				
	1 ($376–$14,732)	2 ($121–$357)	3 ($53–$111)	4 ($25–$52)	Total
Industrial & Miscellaneous					
0%	0	11	13	17	41
1%–50%	5	9	10	7	31
51%–100%	23	8	5	3	39
Total Companies	28	28	28	27	111
Public Utilities[2]					
0%	3	14	11	20	48
1%–50%	10	8	15	5	38
51%–100%	15	6	2	2	25
Total Companies	28	28	28	27	111

[1] Range of asset sizes of companies in category.
[2] Excludes railroad issues.
SOURCE: Brimmer, *Life Insurance Companies in the Capital Market,* p. 204.

unusual features where the degree of risk is difficult to assess. Nevertheless, there is no apparent reason why the risk-return portfolio configurations desired by these companies should be so conservative as to preclude acquisition of the issues of finanically less secure companies, if such issues were made available to them. Certainly, the number of issues sold in the private market is sufficiently large and the character of these issues sufficiently diverse so that smaller investors could satisfy their selection criteria despite their limited investment management facilities.[8]

Private Pension Funds

The role of private noninsured[9] pension funds as lenders in the corporate bond market increased progressively throughout the postwar period until the

---

[8] In 1967, for example, the *Investment Dealers' Digest* listed over 1,200 privately placed issues in its semiannual reviews.

[9] Private insured pension funds, which are managed by life insurance companies, until recently were commingled with the other life insurance company assets and thus invested in the same way. In recent years, life insurance companies have been allowed to segregate their pension fund reserves from other reserves and to invest with fewer restrictions, particularly with respect to common stock acquisitions. At the end of 1970, however, segregated reserves amounted to only $4.9 billion of the $41.2 billion insured pension funds. Consequently, in the following discussion we consider only noninsured funds. In the flow-of-funds accounts, insured pension funds are included as part of the life insurance industry.

early 1960s. It has abruptly declined since then. Data on their activity in the private market are available but fragmentary. The individual funds appear to have displayed considerably more heterogeneity in their participation in this market than either life insurance companies or state and local retirement funds.

The book value of private pension fund assets grew at a 15.7% average annual rate between the end of 1945 and 1970. As a consequence, private pension funds' net acquisition of credit market instruments increased from $0.7 billion in 1946 to $6.6 billion in 1970 (Table 3–10). Corporate bonds

TABLE 3–10

Net Acquisitions of Credit Market Instruments
Private Noninsured Pension Funds
1946–1970

(Dollar amounts in billions)

Year	Corporate Bonds		Corporate Stock		Mortgages		U.S. Government Securities		Total Credit Market Instruments
	Amount	Percent	Amount	Percent	Amount	Percent	Amount	Percent	
1946	$0.3	43%	$0.1	14%	*	—	$0.3	43%	$0.7
1947	0.3	43	0.1	14	*	—	0.3	43	0.7
1948	0.3	43	0.1	14	*	—	0.3	43	0.7
1949	0.3	43	0.1	14	*	—	0.3	43	0.7
1950	1.0	63	0.5	31	*	—	0.1	6	1.6
1951	0.7	70	0.3	30	*	—	0.1	10	1.0
1952	1.1	65	0.5	29	*	—	0.2	12	1.7
1953	1.1	55	0.5	25	*	—	0.3	15	2.0
1954	1.3	62	0.7	33	*	—	0.1	5	2.1
1955	0.9	45	0.7	35	$0.1	5%	0.3	15	2.0
1956	1.6	64	0.9	36	0.1	4	—0.2	—8	2.5
1957	1.9	66	1.1	38	0.1	3	—0.2	—7	2.9
1958	1.5	48	1.4	45	0.2	6	*	—	3.1
1959	1.2	34	1.7	49	0.2	6	0.2	6	3.5
1960	1.6	42	1.9	50	0.3	8	—0.1	—3	3.8
1961	1.2	32	2.3	61	0.3	8	0.1	3	3.8
1962	1.2	30	2.2	55	0.3	8	0.2	5	4.0
1963	1.5	35	2.2	51	0.3	7	0.4	9	4.3
1964	1.6	36	2.2	49	0.5	11	0.1	2	4.5
1965	1.5	29	3.1	60	0.6	12	*	—	5.2
1966	1.9	35	3.7	67	0.5	9	—0.5	—9	5.5
1967	0.9	18	4.6	90	0.1	2	—0.6	—12	5.1
1968	0.7	12	4.7	81	*	—	0.4	7	5.8
1969	0.6	10	5.4	87	0.1	2	0.1	2	6.2
1970	1.6	24	4.6	70	*	—	0.4	6	6.6

* Less than ± $0.05 billion.
NOTE: Components may not add to total due to rounding.
SOURCE: Board of Governors, Federal Reserve System, *Flow-of-Funds Accounts.*

were the principal investment of these funds during the early postwar period. Through 1958 net acquisitions of corporates accounted for approximately 55% of this group's net purchases of credit market instruments.

After 1958 private pension funds' corporate bond purchases tended to level off. As the growth of cash inflows continued, such purchases declined to less than 27% of the acquisitions of credit market instruments during 1959–1970. The role of private pension funds in the corporate market also declined. The percentage of net corporate bonds purchased by this group fell from a level of around 30% during the middle 1950s to an average of 5% during 1967–1970 (Table 3–1). In place of corporate bonds, private pension funds acquired increasing amounts of common stock. The shift reflected a growing awareness, undoubtedly promoted by the more aggressive fund managers, of the importance of higher portfolio returns in reducing an employer's contributions to a fund. For example, a one percentage point increase in the portfolio's return from 4% to 5% reduces an employer's contributions by 20%.[10]

Private pension funds have covered the entire risk-return spectrum in their portfolio choices in the private market. On balance, however, they appear to have occupied a middle position between the spirited investment style of the life insurance companies and the supercaution of the state and local retirement funds.

At the end of 1970 the book value of private pension fund assets totaled $95.9 billion. Corporate pension funds represented about 90% of this amount while the funds of nonprofit organizations and multi-employer plans, the other 10%. The major portions of private pension funds are managed by commercial banks, although investment advisory services and life insurance companies have become aggressive competitors in recent years. The *Institutional Investor Study* of the Securities and Exchange Commission tallied the management of 371 pension accounts which had $47.2 billion assets in June 1969: 253 with assets of $24.2 billion were managed by banks; 35 with assets of $1.3 billion were managed by investment advisors; 56 with assets of $3.5 billion were insured (that is, managed by life insurance companies); 27 with assets of $14.2 billion were self-managed.[11]

Within the banking industry itself, a handful of New York City banks appear to manage the largest fraction of all bank-managed pension fund money. Although the number of plans and volume of funds managed by individual banks are closely guarded secrets, one market observer estimates that the five largest bank pension departments manage over 50% of such reserves. The Institutional Investor Study survey tends to confirm this. Of the 253 bank-managed accounts, four banks managed 47% by number and 54% of the assets of these accounts.[12]

Considerable differences in investment policies exist among the com-

---

[10] Andrews, "Noninsured Corporate and State and Local Government Retirement Funds in the Financial Structure," pp. 428–429.

[11] *Institutional Investor Study, Report of the Securities and Exchange Commission,* Vol. 3, p. 1006.

[12] *Ibid.,* p. 1007.

mercial banks which manage private pension funds. Differences are also evident among the pension funds managed by the same bank, depending on the investment management discretion permitted by the corporation client. In the private placement market the more performance-oriented bank pension departments have adopted investment policies similar to those of life insurance companies. One bank fund manager notes: "In our acquisitions of private placements [during the early 1960s] we competed with life insurance companies strictly on the basis of interest return. Naturally, we favored lower quality issues which frequently contained special terms and features." In general, however, bank-managed funds appear to have pursued more conservative lending policies in the private market than life insurance companies.

The profile of private issues acquired by one major bank pension department between 1954 and 1967 is shown in Table 3–11. During this period, A-rated issues accounted for 65% of all private issues acquired by the department; Aa-rated issues accounted for another 24%. Since public utility issues generally receive higher ratings than industrial and miscellaneous issues, the proportion of utility bonds was high—averaging 40%. It is quite evident that the banks' investment strategy changed around 1963. Acquisitions of Baa and Ba rated issues began increasing. Purchases of industrial and miscellaneous issues also increased sharply, beginning in 1965. This pattern was probably typical of many banks' response to the growing emphasis placed on performance and the increased competition from state and local retirement funds for higher quality issues.

No aggregate data on the activity of private pension funds in the private placement market are available. One industry expert has estimated that in 1965 privately placed issues represented well over 50% of corporate pension funds' purchases of corporate bonds. This percentage appears to have dropped sharply in subsequent years, however. As part of increasing interest in performance, corporate pension funds shifted their acquisition of credit market instruments from bonds to stocks during the 1960s. In addition, they began to place a higher value on maintaining flexibility of their debt portfolios. Even though the incremental returns on private placements increased over those on publicly offered issues, after 1965 private pension funds found the premium insufficient to compensate for their limited marketability. They have acquired an increasing percentage of their corporate bonds in the public market since 1965.

The extent of this shift into publicly offered issues is evident in the acquisition patterns of public and private issues reported by two major bank pension fund departments. In 1964, for example, net acquisitions of private placements by these banks accounted for over 98% of net corporate bond purchases. By 1967 this percentage had fallen to less than 70%, and the decline since then

TABLE 3-11

Private Placements Acquired by a Major Bank Pension Fund Department by Quality and Industry Category

1954–1967

(% of issues in each category)

Year	Quality Category					Industry Category				Total Number of Issues
	Aaa[1]	Aa	A	Baa & Ba	Total	Public Utilities	Industrial & Misc. Companies	Real Estate & Financial	Total	
1954	10.0%	80.0%	10.0%	—	100.0%	50.0%	40.0%	10.0%	100.0%	10
1955	8.3	—	91.7	—	100.0	50.0	8.3	11.7	100.0	12
1956	—	31.6	68.4	—	100.0	26.4	36.8	36.8	100.0	19
1957	4.8	23.8	71.4	—	100.0	57.1	23.8	19.1	100.0	21
1958	—	16.0	84.0	—	100.0	32.0	8.0	60.0	100.0	25
1959	—	23.3	73.3	3.4%	100.0	43.3	13.3	43.3	100.0	30
1960	8.7	21.7	69.6	—	100.0	52.2	8.7	39.1	100.0	23
1961	—	33.3	66.7	—	100.0	56.4	10.3	33.3	100.0	39
1962	2.9	31.4	65.7	—	100.0	37.1	20.0	42.9	100.0	35
1963	—	15.4	80.8	3.8	100.0	30.8	11.5	57.7	100.0	26
1964	8.1	18.9	56.8	16.2	100.0	29.8	21.6	48.6	100.0	37
1965	5.9	26.5	47.1	20.5	100.0	29.4	58.8	11.8	100.0	34
1966	11.5	19.2	42.3	27.0	100.0	38.5	42.3	19.2	100.0	26
1967	—	8.3	66.7	25.0	100.0	41.7	41.7	16.6	100.0	12
	4.0%	24.4%	64.5%	7.2%	100.0%	40.1%	23.8%	36.1%	100.0%	349

[1] Ratings estimated by department.

has been even more dramatic. The few purchases that these funds have made in the private market since 1967 were almost completely limited to issues with equity options.

Reflecting their increased emphasis on portfolio flexibility, private pension funds sharply increased their acquisitions of corporate bonds in 1970—largely at the expense of corporate stock purchases (Table 3–10). In view of the fact that stock prices were depressed during the year and corporate bond rates were at postwar highs, it seems reasonable to infer that the relative price appreciation potential of corporate bonds was the motivating factor in this shift.

State and Local Retirement Funds

During the postwar period, state and local retirement funds progessively increased their acquisitions of corporate bonds to the point where they surpassed life insurance companies as the major institutional lender in the corporate bond market. In 1970 state and local funds supplied $3.9 billion net funds to the corporate bond market, over two times the $1.5 billion supplied by life insurance companies (Table 3–1).

The role of state and local retirement funds in the private market has been quite modest, however, in comparison with life insurance companies and private pension funds. They not only have acquired a smaller percentage of corporate bonds in this market than the other groups, but also have limited their acquisitions to higher quality issues with standard contracts.

The increasing role of state and local retirement funds in the corporate bond market stemmed in part from the growth in their reserves. The book value of state and local funds' assets increased at a 13% average annual rate during the postwar period; and their net acquisition of credit market instruments grew from $0.3 billion in 1946 to $6.2 billion in 1970 (Table 3–12). In addition to the increase in cash inflows, dramatic shifts in the composition of state and local retirement fund portfolios in favor of corporate bonds also occurred during the postwar period up to 1967. Between 1946 and 1956, for example, corporate bonds accounted for 32% of state and local funds' net purchases of securities; between 1957 and 1960, for 51%; and between 1961 and 1967, for 75%. During 1968–1970 state and local retirement funds accelerated their acquisitions of corporate stock. In reflection of this, acquisitions of corporate bonds fell to 61% of net credit market purchases. But to explain completely the growing role of state and local retirement funds in the corporate bond market as well as their limited role in the private placement market it is helpful to first review the character of portfolio administration in such funds.

In general, the investment policies of state and local funds have been much more conservative than those of life insurance companies and corporate

TABLE 3-12
Net Acquisitions of Credit Market Instruments
State and Local Retirement Funds
1946–1970
(Dollar amounts in billions)

Year	Corporate Bonds		Corporate Stock		State and Local Obligations		U.S. Government Securities		Mortgages		Total Credit Market Institutions
	Amount	Percent	Amount	Percent	Amount	Percent	Amount	Percent	Amount	Percent	
1946	*	*	*	—	$ 0.1	33%	$ 0.2	67%	*	—	$0.3
1947	*	*	*	—	0.1	33	0.2	67	*	—	0.3
1948	$0.1	25%	*	—	0.1	25	0.2	50	*	—	0.4
1949	0.1	20	*	—	0.2	40	0.2	40	*	—	0.5
1950	0.2	29	*	—	0.2	29	0.2	29	*	—	0.7
1951	0.1	14	*	—	0.2	29	0.4	57	*	—	0.7
1952	0.2	22	*	—	0.2	22	0.5	56	*	—	0.9
1953	0.5	42	*	—	0.2	17	0.5	42	*	—	1.2
1954	0.6	40	*	—	0.3	20	0.5	33	$0.1	7%	1.5
1955	0.5	38	*	—	0.3	23	0.3	23	0.1	8	1.3
1956	0.6	42	*	—	0.4	29	0.3	21	0.1	7	1.4
1957	0.8	50	$0.1	6%	0.4	25	0.1	6	0.1	6	1.6
1958	0.8	53	0.1	7	0.4	27	*	—	0.2	13	1.5
1959	0.9	45	0.1	5	0.3	15	0.5	25	0.3	15	2.0
1960	1.2	55	0.1	5	0.2	9	0.3	14	0.5	23	2.2
1961	1.7	71	0.2	8	-0.1	-4	0.2	8	0.4	17	2.4
1962	1.9	79	0.2	8	-0.5	-21	0.4	17	0.3	13	2.4
1963	1.9	79	0.2	8	-0.5	-21	0.4	17	0.4	17	2.4
1964	1.9	68	0.3	11	-0.4	-14	0.6	21	0.5	18	2.8
1965	2.1	64	0.4	12	-0.3	-9	0.4	12	0.7	21	3.3
1966	2.5	66	0.5	13	-0.1	-3	0.2	5	0.8	21	3.8
1967	3.4	97	0.7	20	-0.1	-3	-1.0	-29	0.5	14	3.5
1968	2.5	56	1.3	29	*	—	0.4	9	0.4	9	4.5
1969	3.0	64	1.7	36	-0.2	-4	-0.2	-4	0.3	6	4.7
1970	3.9	63	2.1	34	-0.3	-5	-0.3	-5	0.9	15	6.2

* Less than ±$0.05 billion.

NOTE: Components may not add to totals due to rounding.

SOURCE: Board of Governors, Federal Reserve System, *Flow-of-Funds Accounts.*

pension funds at comparable points in time. The investment policies of public funds are controlled by governmental bodies that have tended to favor safety of principal at the expense of additional income. In addition, through most of the 1950s many governing bodies treated their pension funds as a vehicle for serving other purposes. Many funds, for example, were allowed to invest only in U.S. Government securities and in the tax-exempt issues sold by their districts. This restriction was designed to improve the market for issues sold by these districts and thus lower their interest costs; but since pension funds are themselves tax-exempt, this restriction was not in the best interests of the employees covered by such funds.

A second factor encouraging the conservative investment policies of state and local funds has been the paucity of competent personnel to manage their investment portfolios. This is universally true in the case of smaller funds, and until a few years ago it was also true of the majority of large funds. Smaller funds typically are managed by a board of trustees which infrequently includes persons with expertise in investments. The management of medium-sized funds usually is a part-time responsibility of a member of the treasurer's or controller's office. Only the largest funds employ full-time investment officers but even in these instances the supporting staff is frequently limited in competence and experience.[13]

In recent years a number of the larger and more progressive funds have engaged outside investment advisory groups to aid them in their portfolio administration.[14] Of 105 public pension funds with $38.0 billion assets surveyed by the *Institutional Investor Study* of the SEC in 1969: 72 were self-managed; 14 were bank-managed; 18 were investment-advisor-managed; one was managed by a life insurance company.[15] Even where public pension funds used banks and investment advisors, the influence of the outside manager on the fund's portfolio choices appears to be limited. Of 20 outside managed funds surveyed in the *Institutional Investor Sudy,* for example, only one manager had sole investment authority. Six had day-to-day authority within guidelines set by the board of trustees of the fund. All the rest had to consult with the acting officer of the board before trades.[16]

Restrictions on the investments of state and local funds were progressively relaxed beginning in the 1950s, which led to a surge of investments in corpo-

---

[13] To illustrate this, the investment staff managing the $1.8 billion New Jersey State Investment Fund was paid a total of $235,000 in 1967. See Hardy, "New Jersey's State Pension Fund: 866 Bonds, 75 Stocks and 1 Generation Behind," p. 26.

[14] "Oregon Blazes the Pension Trail," pp. 26 ff.

[15] *Institutional Investor Study, Report of the Securities and Exchange Commission,* Vol. 3, p. 1151.

[16] *Ibid.,* p. 1157.

rate bonds. Corporate bonds were superior to mortgages, the only competing investment, since they could be administered with much less effort and experience than a comparably sized mortgage portfolio. Moreover, the fact that corporate issues were more standardized than mortgages and were marketable and quality identifiable undoubtedly facilitated their acceptance by state and local legislatures. Only in recent years have public funds begun to invest a more significant fraction of their net inflows in common stocks. It appears that a handful of funds, many of which retain advisors, have been responsible for the major portion of these purchases.

To determine the role and activity of these state and local funds in the public and private corporate markets more precisely, a questionnaire was sent to the major state and local retirement funds (Exhibit 3–1). Partial or complete replies were received from 51 funds with assets of $28.2 billion in 1967.[17] This represented 71% of the assets of all state and local pension funds at the end of fiscal year 1967.[18] Their aggregate size indicates that the activity of these funds in the corporate bond market provides a fairly accurate measure of this industry's participation in the market.

In 1960 the large majority (73%) of the 45 funds reporting these data were already active in the public market. This number increased through the 1960s; by 1967 all but two funds were participants in the public market. The large funds tended to enter the corporate market before the smaller funds did (Table 3–13). In 1960, for example, all 8 of the funds with $1 billion or more in assets were acquiring issues in the public market compared with only 6 of the 12 funds with assets of less than $100 million.

Some funds accelerated the shift to corporate bonds by liquidating municipal bonds.[19] Seven of the funds followed the opposite pattern, reducing the proportion of their portfolios invested in corporate bonds after 1960. In each case, the fund already had a substantial portfolio of corporate bonds and began

---

[17] All eight of the public funds with $1 billion or more in assets, as reported in *State and Local Pension Funds,* Investment Bankers Association of America, replied to the questionnaire. The assets of these funds totaled $18.9 billion. Two of these, the New York City Retirement System and the Ohio Teachers Retirement System (with assets of $6.1 billion), did not report their activity in the private placement market.

[18] Virtually all of the funds reported on a fiscal year basis. Thus, a fund's purchases of corporate bonds during 1967, for example, represented purchases between July 1, 1966, and June 30, 1967.

[19] For example, the New York City Retirement System held $1,985 million or 66% of its assets in the obligations of New York City in June 1961. During the next four years, it liquidated $527 million of these issues; and with the growth in reserves, New York City obligations fell to only 35% of the New York Retirement System's assets in June 1965. Corporate bond purchases of $1,263 million during this four-year period amounted to 115% of the net increase in assets.

EXHIBIT 3–1
State and Local Government Retirement Fund
Questionnaire

1. What was the size of your fund (including all subsidiary funds managed) at the end of 1966?_____ At the end of 1967?_____

2. What percentage of your portfolio was invested in corporate bonds at the end of 1960?_____ At the end of 1963?_____ At the end of 1967?_____

3. a) What percentage of your corporate bonds portfolio consists of securities which were privately placed?_____ When did you begin to buy private placements?_____

   b) Please indicate the amounts invested in publicly offered and privately placed corporate bonds for the following years.

Year	Public Offerings	Private Placements	Total
1960			
1961			
1962			
1963			
1964			
1965			
1966			
1967			

   c) Of your corporate bond portfolio, what is the categorical breakdown? (In amount or percent)

      utilities_____
      industrials_____
      real estate_____
      finance_____

	Public	Private (equivalent)
Aaa	_____	_____
Aa	_____	_____
A	_____	_____
Baa	_____	_____
no rating	_____	_____

4. a) What restrictions, legal or otherwise, apply to the quality or industry from which you may obtain private placements or public offerings?

   b) Has the composition of your corporate bond portfolio changed substantially since 1960? If so, what were the major changes?

shifting into common stock. This pattern was a forerunner of the industry-wide shift into corporate stock which first became significant in 1968.

The entry of state and local retirement funds as lenders in the private market tended to occur after their entry into the public market. In 1960, for

TABLE 3–13

Number of Reporting State and Local Government Retirement Funds
Investing in Publicly Offered and Privately Placed
Corporate Bonds by Size Category
1960, 1963, 1967

Size Category[1] (in millions)	Number of Funds in Category	1960		1963		1967	
		Public	Private	Public	Private	Public	Private
Over $1,000	8	8	4	8	8	8	8
$500–$1,000	4	3	0	4	1	4	3
$250–$499	11	8	2	10	6	11	9
$100–$249	10	8	0	8	4	10	6
Less than $100	12	6	0	9	2	10	4
Total	45	33	6	39	21	43	30

[1] As reported at the end of 1967.
Source: Survey of State and Local Government Retirement Funds' Purchases of Corporate Bonds.

example, only 6 of the 45 reporting funds invested in private placements. By 1967 this number had increased to 30—but this was still less than the number of funds participating in the public market. Again, the largest funds tended to lead the industry in entering this market. By 1963, for example, all 8 of the billion dollar funds were active in the private market compared with only 6 of the 22 funds with assets of less than $250 million. The leadership of the large funds in this movement is not surprising since they have more professional management than smaller funds. Smaller funds also have been excluded from investing in the private market by the minimum purchase lot requirement which is inherent in the distribution structure.

The percentage of corporate bonds acquired in the private market by the reporting funds increased from 22% in 1960 to 37% in 1965, then declined to 33% in 1967 (Table 3–14). At the end of 1967 these funds had 26% of their corporate bond portfolios invested in privately placed issues. The later entry of the 28 small funds (with assets of less than $1 billion) into the corporate market is reflected in the increasing fraction of their total purchases of the 34 reporting funds from 15% in 1960 to 37% in 1967.

Both large and small funds acquired roughly 30% of their corporate bond issues in the private market during the 8-year period. The large funds slowly and somewhat unevenly increased their acquisitions of private issues from 26% of corporate bond purchases in 1960 to 38% in 1967. The small funds acted differently. They did not acquire any issues in the private market in 1960. But once they entered this market, they rapidly increased their activity to the point where private issues represented almost half (46%) of their corporate bond purchases in 1965. The proportion then fell sharply to

TABLE 3–14

Reporting State and Local Government Retirement Funds' Purchases of
Publicly Offered and Privately Placed Corporate Bonds
by Size of Fund
1960–1967

(Dollar amounts in millions)

Year	Large Funds[1] (Assets greater than $1 billion)				Small Funds[2] (Assets less than $1 billion)				Totals[3]				% of Total Purchases by Small Funds
	Public	Private	Total	% Private	Public	Private	Total	% Private	Public	Private	Total	% Private	
1960	$248	$ 85	$334	25.5%	$ 60	0	$ 60	0.0%	$ 309	$ 85	$ 394	21.6%	15.2%
1961	383	164	547	29.9	170	$ 18	188	9.5	553	182	735	24.7	25.6
1962	522	136	657	20.6	183	38	220	17.1	705	173	878	19.7	25.2
1963	523	158	680	23.2	146	102	247	41.0	669	259	928	27.9	26.7
1964	500	162	662	24.5	148	109	256	42.3	648	270	918	29.5	27.9
1965	456	224	680	32.9	190	161	351	45.9	646	385	1,031	37.3	34.1
1966	537	272	808	33.6	297	178	476	37.6	834	450	1,284	35.1	37.1
1967	621	377	997	37.8	442	144	586	24.6	1,062	521	1,583	32.9	37.0

[1] Includes 6 funds with $10.6 billion in assets.
[2] Includes 28 funds with $6.7 billion in assets.
[3] At the end of 1967, these 34 funds owned $9.1 billion corporate bonds or 43% of the industry's holdings.
NOTE: Components may not add to totals due to rounding.
SOURCE: Survey of State and Local Government Retirement Funds' Purchases

25% in 1967. An examination of the activity of individual funds indicates that this decline between 1965 and 1967 was the result of substantial purchases of publicly offered issues by a few funds, permitted for the first time to buy corporate bonds in 1965. Because of the character of the private issues acquired by state and local funds, however, such a relative decline might well have happened anyway with the rapid increase in corporate borrowing in 1965.

Because of high minimum quality restrictions imposed by governing bodies and inadequate staffing, a large majority of state and local funds are unable to purchase the issues of financially less secure companies. With respect to minimum quality restrictions, 8 of 46 reporting funds could purchase only Aa or higher rated issues; 24, A or higher rated issues. Only 2 could purchase Baa or higher rated issues. The acquisitions of 6 of the other 12 reporting funds were governed by the regulations applicable to life insurance companies or to savings banks in their states; 2, by the "prudent man" rule; and 2, by other criteria such as the borrower's earnings history.[20] Only 2 of the 46 funds had no quality restrictions on their portfolio choices. Reflecting these restrictions, only 1% of the $3.3 billion corporate bonds owned by 20 reporting funds at the end of 1967 carried ratings lower than A, although 8% were not rated (Table 3–15). These quality restrictions also are reflected in the com-

TABLE 3–15

Quality Composition of State and Local Retirement Funds'
Corporate Bond Portfolios[1]

1967

(Dollar amounts in millions)

Moody's Equivalent Credit Rating	Public Offerings		Private Placements		Market Origin of Issues Not Identified		Total	
	Amount	Percent	Amount	Percent	Amount	Percent	Amount	Percent
Aaa	$ 577	29.5%	$148	23.7%	$197	25.8%	$ 922	27.6%
Aa	536	27.5	199	31.8	261	34.2	996	29.8
A	608	31.2	221	35.4	287	37.6	1,116	33.4
Baa	25	1.3	0	0	8	1.0	33	1.0
Nonrated	204	10.5	57	9.1	11	1.4	272	8.2
	$1,950	100.0%	$625	100.0%	$764	100.0%	$3,339	100.0%

[1] Includes 20 funds with $8.2 billion in assets.

[20] A unique restriction was placed on the investments of the New Mexico Public Employees Retirement Administration. The fund was allowed to invest in A or higher rated corporate bonds only if such issues provided at least a 4% return and the return was at least 1% higher than the return on Government issues of the same maturity.

position of state and local fund holdings by borrower category. At the end of 1967, 39 reporting funds with corporate bond holdings of $11.5 billion had 70% of their portfolios invested in public utility issues, 26% invested in industrial issues, and 5% in real estate and financial issues.

Even in the absence of quality restrictions on their portfolio choices, the state and local funds do not have the personnel or facilities to purchase any but the most conventionally constructed privately placed issues containing standard terms and provisions. During the first half of the 1960s such issues did account for an unusually large proportion of private placements, and their sale in the private market contributed importantly to the rapid increase in the percentage of debt sold privately during this period. The percentage of corporate debt sold privately increased from 41% in 1960 to a postwar high of 67% in 1964 (Table 5-1). In large part this development can be attributed to the entry of state and local funds into the private market. The demand for long-term funds on the part of corporations was relatively modest during this period. By augmenting the supply of funds available in the private market, the state and local funds contributed to a reduction in yield differentials between the public and private markets. As a result, several major industrial corporations which could borrow in either market, and thus were quite sensitive to changes in yield differentials, found it profitable to borrow in the private market for the first (and only) time.[21] State and local funds were the major purchasers of these issues; their yields were too low to attract life insurance companies and corporate pension funds.

With the rapid increase in corporate borrowing beginning in 1965, the percentage of debt sold privately by this group of large companies fell sharply, though their absolute volume of sales in the private market remained at the level reached in 1964.[22] Without this, the percentage of corporate bonds acquired in the private market by reporting state and local funds might have declined by more than the four percentage points it actually did.

Although the more progressive state and local funds recently have begun to seek outside investment consultation, these arrangements are more likely to produce an increase in common stock acquisitions rather than of lower quality private placements. In the absence of fundamental changes in the internal structure of portfolio administration by state and local funds, their activity in the private market probably will fluctuate in response to changes in the division of financing between the public and private markets on the part of companies which can provide standard contracts and thus can borrow in either market.

---

[21] Some of these issues are identified on p. 106.

[22] This is shown in Table 5-6, which reports the borrowing of Fortune 500 companies, a proxy for large, financially secure companies that can borrow in either market.

Summary

Of the three major institutions lending in the private market during the postwar period, only life insurance companies have been a consistent major supplier of funds to financially less secure borrowers that require nonstandard contracts on their issues and thus benefit from the unique advantages of this market. For a time in the 1950s and early 1960s corporate pension funds also supplied funds to this group of borrowers, but their activity in the private market has diminished rapidly in recent years. In response to the growing emphasis placed on portfolio performance, corporate pension funds accelerated their acquisitions of common stocks and have placed greater importance on marketability in their purchases of bonds. Life insurance companies have chosen to remain active in the private market and to seek higher portfolio returns through the more frequent use of equity options. State and local government retirement funds, a late entry as lenders in the private market, have confined their purchases to high quality issues with standard contracts because of regulatory restrictions and limited investment management facilities. In the future, the percentage of their funds invested in private placements will depend chiefly on the distribution decisions of high quality borrowers, capable of borrowing in either the public or the private market.

CHAPTER 4

The Distribution of Private Placements
in the New Issues and Secondary Markets

THE DISTINCTIVE FEATURE of the distribution of new issues in the private placement market is that issues are sold directly by borrowers to lenders. Most new public issues, by contrast, are sold first to investment banking syndicates, which in turn resell the issues to the investing public. In the private market, an investment banker may serve as an intermediary between the borrower and lender(s)—acting as agents or finders rather than as underwriters. In many private placements, however, the investment banker plays no role; borrower and lenders negotiate directly with each another.

There is virtually no secondary market for most private placements. This is the result, in part, of legal restrictions on resale. However, issues such as these are, with nonstandard terms and provisions, would have limited marketability even in the absence of legal restrictions. Those few private issues which feature standard contracts and which are distributed to a comparatively large number of buyers are fairly actively traded; even for these issues, however, the volume of secondary market transactions is modest compared with the trading in publicly offered issues.

In this chapter we examine the distribution of private placements in the new issue and the secondary markets. First, we focus on the role of intermediaries in the distribution of new issues. Second, we briefly examine the distribution of new issues when no intermediary is involved. Then we examine the distribution costs of securities sold in the public and private markets. Finally we consider the secondary market for private placements.

The Role of Intermediaries in the Distribution of New Issues

Intermediaries distribute the major portion of new issues in the private market. A very few firms operate exclusively as agents in the sale of private issues; most of these intermediaries, however, are investment bankers who also distribute new issues in the public corporate market.

Characteristics of New Issues Distributed by Investment Bankers

The average size of private issues sold by investment bankers and other agents is somewhat larger than those private placements sold without the use of an agent. According to one survey by the Securities and Exchange Commission, 57% of the volume of privately placed issues were distributed by an agent or finder[1] (Table 4–1).[2] Another survey found that investment bankers

TABLE 4–1
Corporate Bonds Placed Privately
Classified by Method of Offering and by Size of Issue
1951, 1953, 1955
(Dollar amounts in millions)

| Method of Offering | Size of Issue | | | | | | Total |
	Under $0.5	$0.5– $0.9	$1.0– $4.9	$5.0– $9.9	$10.0– $19.9	$20.0 & Over	
Directly by Issuer							
Number	264	218	443	86	58	68	1,137
Amount	$ 72.9	$136.0	$ 803.9	$ 386.6	$ 547.9	$1,989.4	$3,936.7
Through Agent or Finder							
Number	166	176	426	110	72	82	1,032
Amount	$ 47.1	$109.6	$ 811.0	$ 630.3	$ 764.3	$2,900.0	$5,262.3
Total							
Number	430	394	869	196	130	150	2,169
Amount	$120.0	$245.6	$1,614.9	$1,016.9	$1,312.2	$4,889.4	$9,199.0
% Through Agent or Finder							
Number	38.6	44.7	49.0	56.1	55.4	54.7	47.6
Amount	39.3	44.6	50.2	62.0	58.2	59.3	57.2

SOURCE: Securities and Exchange Commission, *Cost of Flotation of Corporate Securities: 1951–1955*, p. 62.

accounted for approximately 61% of the volume of new issues sales in 1959.[3] Our survey of the same data from the *Investment Dealers' Digest* for 1967

---

[1] Securities and Exchange Commission, *Cost of Flotation of Corporate Securities, 1951–1955*, p. 62.

[2] A very small, but unidentified, portion of these issues was distributed by firms specializing in the distribution of private placements. These are considered later (see pp. 89–90).

[3] Walter, *The Investment Process*, p. 333.

revealed that the volume of new issues sold through intermediaries had declined only slightly to 60% (Tables 4–2 and 4–3). And the Investment

TABLE 4–2

Distribution of Private Placements by Method, Size of Issue,
and Category of Borrower 1959

(Dollar amounts in millions)

Size of Issue	Public Utilities		Financial Companies		Industrial & Misc. Companies		Total	
	Inter-mediary	Non-inter-mediary	Inter-mediary	Non-inter-mediary	Inter-mediary	Non-inter-mediary	Inter-mediary	Non-inter-mediary
$0.1								
Number	—	5	—	—	3	7	3	12
Amount	—	$ 1	—	—	*	$ 1	*	$ 1
$0.1–$0.5								
Number	6	17	4	9	11	75	21	101
Amount	$ 2	$ 5	$ 1	$ 3	$ 3	$ 23	$ 6	$ 30
$0.5–$1.0								
Number	6	14	4	10	12	70	22	94
Amount	$ 5	$ 11	$ 3	$ 8	$ 9	$ 53	$ 17	$ 72
$1.0–$5.0								
Number	49	19	22	18	85	148	156	185
Amount	$187	$ 57	$ 66	$ 54	$ 255	$ 444	$ 508	$ 555
$5.0–$10.0								
Number	10	4	8	3	35	29	53	36
Amount	$ 75	$ 30	$ 60	$ 23	$ 270	$ 218	$ 405	$ 270
$10.0–$25.0								
Number	6	—	6	1	36	16	48	17
Amount	$105	—	$105	$ 18	$ 630	$ 280	$ 840	$ 298
$25.0 & over								
Number	6	—	7	—	11	14	24	14
Amount	$300	—	$350	—	$ 550	$ 700	$1,200	$ 700
Total								
Number	83	59	51	41	193	359	327	459
Amount	$674	$104	$585	$106	$1,717	$1,719	$2,976	$1,929

* Less than $0.5 million.

NOTE: These amounts were estimated as follows: the midpoint of each size category was multiplied by the number of issues in the category. For issues in the $25 million or over category, it was assumed that the average size of issues was $50 million. Components may not add to total due to rounding.

SOURCE: Walter, *The Investment Process*, p. 333.

Bankers Association of America has estimated that for the 1950–1963 period as a whole, 60% of the volume of all private placements were sold with the aid of intermediaries.[4]

In contrast with these volume figures, intermediaries were involved in

---

[4] Investment Bankers Association of America, "Today's Challenge to Investment Bankers: Report of the Securities Study Committee," p. 1.

TABLE 4-3

Private Placements Sold Directly and Through Intermediaries by Size of Issue and Category of Borrower

1967

(Dollar amounts in millions)

Size of Issue	Public Utilities				Financial Companies[1]				Industrial & Misc. Companies				Total					
	Inter-mediary		Direct		Inter-mediary		Direct		Inter-mediary		Direct		Inter-mediary		Direct			
	No.	Amt.	No.	Amt.	No.	Amt.	No.	Amt.	No.	Amt.	No.	Amt.	No.	Amt.	No.	Amt.	No.	Amt.
Less than $0.1	—	—	2	$ 0.2	2	$ 0.2	—	—	3	$ 0.3	13	$ 1.3	5	$ 0.5	15	$ 1.5	20	$ 2.0
$0.1–$0.5	4	$ 1.8	27	8.6	12	4.6	8	$ 2.5	24	9.1	150	52.8	40	15.5	185	63.9	225	79.4
$0.5–$1.0	7	6.3	19	14.7	10	8.9	12	10.7	42	38.5	115	94.2	59	53.7	146	119.6	205	173.3
$1.0–$5.0	52	141.6	34	86.9	34	89.8	59	145.1	109	283.3	203	594.5	195	514.7	296	826.5	491	1,341.2
$5.0–$10.0	32	247.3	8	58.7	16	130.2	9	74.5	33	238.8	48	373.1	81	616.3	65	506.3	146	1,122.6
$10.0–$25.0	25	395.4	5	75.2	2	26.0	7	117.6	50	824.9	29	488.5	77	1,246.3	41	681.3	118	1,927.6
$25.0 & over	11	706.2	6	329.1	7	441.0	—	—	23	1,005.6	14	570.0	41	2,152.8	20	899.1	61	3,051.9
Total	131	$1,498.6	101	$573.4	83	$700.7	95	$350.4	284	$2,400.5	572	$2,174.4	498	$4,599.8	768	$3,098.2	1,266	$7,698.0

[1] Includes real estate and leasing companies.

SOURCE: *Investment Dealers' Digest.*

distributing a substantially *smaller* percentage of the *number* of issues sold in the private market. In the SEC survey, for example, investment bankers and other agents distributed only 48% of the number of issues sold privately; in the 1959 survey, 41%; and in our 1967 survey, 40%. In all three studies the data indicated that issues involving agents were significantly larger. In the SEC survey these averaged $5.1 million; issues sold directly averaged $3.5 million. In Walter's 1959 survey these issues averaged $9.4 million; those sold directly, only $4.2 million. Our 1967 survey showed that issues sold through agents averaged $9.2 million; issues sold directly averaged $4.0 million.

The chief reason for this consistent pattern is that investment bankers cannot distribute very small issues economically, but they are well equipped to distribute larger ones. The minimum cost to the investment banker in handling a private placement is between $10,000 and $20,000. He customarily charges a fee of 3% or less of the proceeds of an issue. So the minimum size of an issue sold with the aid of an investment banker tends to be around $500,000.

Another factor that contributes to this pattern is the fact that small issues are usually sold by smaller, less financially secure companies and require direct negotiation of terms. These issues are acquired by the larger life insurance companies which are skilled in the negotiating process and which have their own particular preferences regarding the structure of the contract. Under these circumstances the usefulness of an agent is quite limited.

Larger issues typically are sold by larger, financially secure companies, with relatively standardized terms and provisions. Such issues are bought chiefly by state and local retirement systems and smaller life insurance companies—investors which tend to acquire smaller positions in individual issues. Thus, the aid of an intermediary is almost essential to reach successfully the large and diverse groups necessary to absorb the issues. The investment banker is knowledgeable about which institutions have funds to invest and what type of issues each one prefers. As a result, the investment banker presumably can sell an issue at a lower net interest cost than the company could if it attempted to solicit lenders directly. The fact that the terms of these larger issues are relatively standardized implies that only a modest amount of expertise is required to sell them. Thus, at relatively little cost these issues get wide exposure via the investment house's salesmen who are in frequent contact with institutional investors.

Investment bankers also appear to play an especially important role in distributing the issues of corporations borrowing for the first time in the private placement market. Once a borrower has established outlets for his issues, he can by-pass the investment banker and negotiate directly with the lender. A common provision of the loan agreement in smaller private placements, for example, gives existing owners of outstanding issues the right of first refusal of subsequent issues sold by the borrower.

Finance companies and public utilities rely more heavily on the use of intermediaries to distribute their privately issued debt than do other borrowers (Tables 4–2 and 4–3). In Walter's 1959 survey, for example, investment bankers distributed about 82% of the dollar volume of finance company and public utility issues; they sold only 51% of the volume of industrial and miscellaneous issues.

The debt issues of public utilities usually carry high credit ratings and standard terms. Intermediaries offer a substantial service in reaching the wide range of investors who purchase such issues.

Finance companies rely on intermediaries to distribute their issues for somewhat different reasons. Finance company issues typically contain complicated provisions, are tailored to the borrower's needs, and are sold to sophisticated institutional investors. Such considerations, by themselves, would tend to reduce the usefulness of intermediaries. But these considerations are less important in the distribution decision than another feature of finance companies' borrowing: the high frequency with which such issues are sold. In a study of the borrowing practices of finance companies, Chapman and Jones found, for example, that 50 large finance companies sold 481 issues during the period 1946–1956, or an average of about one issue per year for each company.[5] The five largest sales finance companies alone sold 126 issues or an average of 2.5 issues per year. Although the study covered the first postwar decade only, the continued growth of finance companies since then suggests that similar findings undoubtedly would extend to more recent years. The frequency of these sales forces the finance companies to reach all segments of the market in order to avoid saturating any one of them. In fact, because of finance companies' continuing and large need for funds, institutional lenders probably discourage formation of more permanent ties with them. And the finance companies themselves are less concerned with establishing continuing sources of funds than with obtaining the lowest interest cost on each sale of debt.

In circumstances such as these, where the relation between the borrower and lenders is somewhat impersonal, investment bankers are also helpful in deciding on the terms and provisions of an issue. Because of their continual contact with participants in the market, investment bankers are in the best position to know the current spreads between junior and senior issues and the availability of funds for each. They can thus tailor an issue to those investors

---

[5] Chapman and Jones, *Finance Companies: How and Where They Obtain Their Funds,* p. 35.

who have excess funds. They can also develop the most competitive package because they are aware of other issues being offered in the market.

The institutional investors that purchase public utilities issues also buy the issues of large industrial and miscellaneous companies with high credit ratings. As a result, these issues also tend to be distributed with the aid of investment bankers. Intermediaries are used less frequently to distribute "other" industrial issues, however. Because these issues are usually of lower quality, they appeal to the larger life insurance companies which take much larger fractional positions in individual issues than other lenders do. The lower quality issues have provisions tailored to the particular needs of the borrower; renegotiations occur frequently. The relation between borrowers and lenders resembles that between commercial banks and their loan customers. Continuing financing relations between borrowers and lenders in this sector of the market are common if only because it enables lenders to maintain greater control over their previous investments in the company. The value of an investment banking house in distributing new issues in such circumstances is quite limited.

Investment Bankers Participating in Private Placements

Although the number of investment banking houses which act as agents for borrowers in the private market is quite large, the major portion of the issues are handled by a relatively small number of houses. According to Walter's summary of the *Investment Dealers' Digest* report of private placements, 211 houses originated private placements during the three and a half years ending in 1959.[6] However, only eight houses averaged as much as one placement per month during the 3-year period.[7] The larger investment bankers tended to specialize in issues of particular industries: First Boston, Kidder Peabody, Goldman Sachs, and Salomon Brothers specialized in the sale of finance company issues; Eastman Dillon, Union Securities specialized in real estates issues.[8]

Specialization in the distribution of issues of a particular group of borrowers probably occurred by accident in many instances, but it can also be traced to conscious policy decisions on the part of certain houses. For example, Kidder Peabody and First Boston's specialization in public utility issues probably arose from their ability to take advantage of well-organized distribution facilities. Specialization is also a prerequisite for the distribution of finance and real estate company issues because of their complicated provisions and the expertise needed to sell them.

---

[6] Walter, *op. cit.*, pp. 334–335.

[7] *Ibid.*, p. 335.

[8] *Ibid.*

There are several ways in which a potential borrower and an investment banker may be introduced prior to the sale of a private placement. If the investment house has developed a reputation for placing issues of a particular industry, other firms in the industry may contact the house directly to handle their financing. Word-of-mouth referrals through common business acquaintances are also an important source of new business. If the investment banker has done a satisfactory job in placing the issues of one company, it is likely that this company will recommend the banker to other companies. The investment banker's own salesmen also generate referrals. However, this source appears to be less important than others, because the salesmen's contacts are chiefly restricted to institutional buyers and usually do not include potential borrowers.

Some of the more aggressive investment banking houses actively seek out candidates for new business through a systematic study of the future financing needs and the present financing arrangements of corporations. If a company is growing fast, it may need external financing; it may be encumbered with debt which is either too costly or too restrictive and the investment banker may suggest a new financing or a refunding of outstanding issues. This prospecting, however, does not appear to be nearly as successful in producing new business as referrals.

Investment bankers also try to solicit the customers of their competitors. For example, after a company has sold an issue, an investment banker might argue that his firm could have distributed the same issue at a lower cost. Such claims are of doubtful effectiveness unless, of course, the borrower's present underwriter or agent did a discernibly poor job in selling an issue. The infrequency of changes in borrower-investment house connections suggests that this method of soliciting business is not very productive.[9]

The Distribution of New Issues by Investment Bankers

The distribution of new issues in the private placement market is significantly different from a public offering. The intermediary can show a new issue to only a limited number of potential buyers, for one. A publicly offered issue, in contrast, may be shown to an unlimited number of buyers. Second, the intermediary has considerable flexibility in selecting the appropriate sector of the private market and then packaging an issue to appeal to investors in

---

[9] Evidence of this can be found in the "Corporate Financing Directory, 1950–1960," *Investment Dealers' Digest*. This shows that corporations very infrequently changed investment bankers. In recent years, however, account switching by major corporations appears to have accelerated. See Thackray, "Investment Banking Breaks Formation," and Hayes, "Investment Banking: Power Structure in Flux."

this sector. Finally, the investment banker serves as an agent or a finder in the private market rather than as an underwriter.

The sale of an issue qualifies as a private placement if the offeree does not need the "protection afforded by registration"; that is, if the investor can obtain the same or more information than is contained in the registration statement and is professionally competent.[10] If it does qualify, then it presumably can be shown to an unlimited number of prospective buyers. Investment banker distributors, however, tend to regard the exemption from registration (under Section 4(1) of the Securities Act of 1933) as serving to limit the number of prospective investors to whom an issue may be shown. This limit has been defined neither in the law nor by the Supreme Court nor by the SEC, but both the regulatory authorities and the investment community have interpreted the law as placing some restraint on the number of offerees.

In general, investment bankers agree that the number of investors to whom an issue can be shown is an increasing function of the size of the issue, although they are not specific about the precise nature of the relationship. One agent said that a large issue—say $100 million in size—which appealed to smaller insurance companies and the state and local retirement systems active in this market, could be shown to as many as 200 investors. Another said that as long as the issue did not have any "frosting," that is, speculative features such as warrants, convertibility, or an unusually high call price, it could be shown to an unlimited number of investors.[11] If it did have any speculative features, then the maximum number of offerees was much less—around 25.[12]

Since he must target his market so carefully, an investment banker has considerable discretion in packaging an issue for the private market. To sell such an issue, an agent must first identify the segment of the market with available funds, the segment most likely to be attracted to a specific issue, and then he must design the terms and provisions of the issue to enhance a successful sale in that segment of the market. He should know the investment preferences of individual institutions on yield, quality, and call protection.

"Showing an issue" consists of providing a potential investor with the name of the borrowing company. An agent may discuss an issue with an in-

---

[10] SEC vs. Ralston Purina Co., 346 U.S. 126 (1953).

[11] The usual first call price is one year's interest or, equivalently, the coupon rate of the issue. Any call price significantly above this would be regarded as an issue containing an incentive feature.

[12] This latter limit can be traced to the Commission's ruling in the Crowell-Collier case of 1957. This case involved the sale of a $3 million convertible bond in 1955 and a $1 million debenture in 1956 and will be discussed on p. 104 in connection with resales of privately placed issues in the secondary market.

vestor, identifying the industry of the borrower and the tentative interest rate to see if the investor has an interest. This does *not* constitute an offering for the purposes of reporting to the SEC. The investment banker's method of showing an issue depends in large part on the sector of the market in which the issue is distributed. If, for example, the issue contains a standard set of provisions which need little explanation, as in the case of most public utility issues and high quality industrial issues, it may be placed on an active list to be shown by the salesmen of the house to institutional investors.

On the other hand, if the issue possesses any unusual features, the same person or group in an investment banking house acts as both negotiator and seller of an issue. This group has acquired an intimate knowledge of both the borrower and the issue itself and is thus in the best position to explain the reasons for the unusual features. The intermediary may arrange direct meetings between the borrower and those institutions likely to be interested in the issue.

If he is selling a borrower's first issue, the agent usually contacts a larger, well-known buyer in the hope of obtaining either a complete or a partial commitment for the issue. It is quite easy to sell the remainder of an issue to smaller investors after a portion of it has been sold to a larger investor. In the trade, the large company that is the first investor in an issue is known as a "bell cow." The "bell cow" in a private placement is most commonly one of the large life insurance companies. The commitment of the large buyer signifies not only that the issue is priced right but also that the interests of the smaller lenders will be satisfied both in the initial negotiations and in future renegotiations of the terms and provisions of the issue. At least one investment house decides on the institutions to whom an issue will be shown by compiling a master list of the various amounts which each investor might buy from estimates by the firm's salesmen. Then the institutions are solicited in order of their rank on the master list.

Sometimes an issue cannot be placed on the basis of the tentative provisions and rate. In this event the intermediary has usually obtained some feedback on acceptable terms and provisions from investors who turned it down. Thus, any changes required to place the issue are usually quite specific. The changes might not be approved by the borrower, of course, in which case he might switch intermediaries; this is very unusual.

The extent of negotiations between the intermediary and potential buyers over the terms and provisions of an issue varies a great deal depending on the industry of the borrower, the agent, and the market conditions. For larger issues in the industrial and miscellaneous category, the tentative provisions—particularly the interest rate—are rarely changed. Recommended changes might be looked upon unfavorably by the borrower and could be used by other investment bankers to place the agent at a competitive disadvantage in handling future issues of the borrower. Under these circumstances, some agents prefer to underprice the issue rather than risk the possibility of an incomplete sale. For example, the agent might set the yield on the issue at 8% initially even though he believes that there is a fairly good, but certainly smaller, chance that he could place it at 7¾%. Other agents argue that it is their responsibility as a representative of the borrower to attempt to complete the sale at the lowest possible rate even if the likelihood of doing so is relatively low. Finance companies usually prefer their agents to pursue this strategy; that is, to attempt first to sell the issue at a yield slightly below competitive rates when the chances of a complete sale are quite small. In such instances, increases from the initial yield frequently occur, but they are fully expected by the borrower. Market conditions can also influence an agent's pricing strategy. If market conditions are unstable, an agent might choose to under-price the issue slightly in order to avoid the possibility of missing the market and having to place the issue at a still higher rate.

Other Intermediaries in the Private Placement Market

Investment bankers account for virtually all the sales of new private issues through intermediaries. The small remaining fraction is distributed by firms which deal exclusively as agents in the private market. These companies owe their existence to their ability to specialize in ways which are not economic for the larger investment banking houses. This, in turn, has enabled them to distribute at a profit issues which the larger houses consider too small to handle.

The firm of Robert Fulton Maine is one of the better known of these specialized intermediaries. It has concentrated on the distribution of finance company issues and over the years has become associated with a group of such companies whose financing needs they handle on a continuing basis. By becoming familiar with the financial structure of the companies in this industry, they have reduced the costs both of investigating companies and of preparing loan agreements. They have also acquired specialized knowledge of the buyers of these issues and thus reduced the costs incurred in distributing new issues. Finally, by specializing they have earned a reputation among potential borrowers and investors as experts in this area of financing. This has further eased their task of finding and selling new issues.

In the larger investment houses industry expertise is usually acquired and utilized in the underwriting department—not in the sales department. An institutional salesman who has to be responsible for handling all the investment needs of his account cannot acquire the specialized knowledge which is important in selling issues of the small finance companies in which a firm such as Robert Fulton Maine specializes. Thus, on small issues which have a relatively complicated set of loan provisions, the agent specialist is capable of distributing the issues more efficiently than the larger houses.

What limits these agents from distributing larger issues appears to be more a function of the size of the issuer than the size of the issue. When the borrower is small, its only source of long-term debt funds is the private market. As it grows, it can attract funds from the public market as well. In addition, it can often sell common stock at higher price/earnings ratios than it could at an earlier stage in its growth. For both types of financing an investment banker is usually required. Thus, as a company increases in size, it simply outgrows the ability of an agent specialist to handle all its financing needs.

In addition, when an investment house handles a variety of services for a borrower, it can cost and price any individual service on a marginal basis. The private distribution of securities, which may have been unprofitable on a full cost basis, could become profitable on a marginal cost basis.

The Direct Distribution of New Issues

Most private placements (by number) are sold directly by the borrower to the lender without the aid of an intermediary. A substantial fraction of this business represents the sale of new issues to lenders who are already owners of a company's outstanding issues.[13] Life insurance companies prefer to lend to current or previous borrowers because it obviates the need to investigate the company and it provides the lender with greater control over the company's financial operations. In the case of repeat loans where only a few lenders are involved, an intermediary has no important role; he is not needed to distribute the issue; and the terms and provisions can be worked out through direct negotiations. A repeat borrower might find an intermediary advantageous if he was able to obtain funds on better terms from other lenders than he was getting from his present lender(s).

A borrower can make *initial* contact with a lender—without the help of an intermediary—through a variety of channels. By far the most important of these is word-of-mouth referrals. Referrals originate with accountants and lawyers; with current borrowers. Investment bankers refer loans to insurance companies when these loans fall below the $500,000-$1 million range and cease to be profitable to them. A major source of referrals is the company's local banker. If the company needs funds for a longer period of time than the maximum maturity of a term loan, a bank may organize a financing package; it supplies the company with short-term and intermediate-term funds; and an institutional investor supplies the borrower's long-term needs through a private placement. In the early 1960s, when they had an ample supply of funds, banks

---

13 Walter, *op. cit.,* p. 333.

preferred to extend the maturity of their loans rather than arrange a short-term and long-term financing package with institutional lenders. As a result, referrals declined as a percentage of private placements. In recent years of credit stringency, however, banks have not only reduced the maturity of their term loans but also rejected a larger fraction of borrowers' requests for funds. Their referrals, in turn, have increased at a time when the institutions themselves were experiencing a reduction in funds available for investments.

There is little evidence that insurance companies systematically search for new business as commercial banks do. (Banks, of course, have a dual motive: obtaining deposits as well as making new loans.) A notable exception to the rule, however, is the Commercial and Industrial Loan Department of Prudential Insurance Company which concentrates on making loans of $2 million and under to companies with assets ranging between $250,000 and $25 million. The department was formed in 1956; and by the end of 1970 it had made loans to 1,035 companies totaling $1.2 billion. More than 200 loans were made during 1970. In recent years about 60% of the C&I department's loans were made to existing borrowers; and virtually all of these were made directly without the aid of a referral. Of the 40% of the loans which were made to new borrowers, about 80% came from referrals by local bankers, accountants, and lawyers in response to the department's solicitation efforts. To seek out, negotiate, and administer new loans the department maintains a staff of around 70, all but 8 of whom are located at regional offices of the Prudential around the country. The job of the field representative is to search for new customers, to do a thorough credit analysis of the prospective borrower, to negotiate the terms and provisions of prospective loans, and to oversee these loans once negotiations have been completed. In recent years, modifications of existing loans have averaged almost one per year.

Although other large life insurance companies undoubtedly search for small loans, none apparently has extended this beyond the region immediately surrounding their home office. Of course, Prudential's advantage in this respect stems from the presence of a regional office system which the company previously had established for the purpose of mortgage lending.

Size of Issues and Distribution Costs
in the Public and Private Markets

The private placement market is a small issue market. Over one-third of all the debt issues sold privately from 1951 to 1955 were less than $1 million in size (Table 4–4).[14] In the same period, less than 2% of publicly offered is-

---

[14] The source of these data is the *Cost of Flotation of Corporate Securities 1951–1955* published by the Securities and Exchange Commission in June 1957. The data used cover

TABLE 4–4

Size of Corporate Debt Issues Offered Publicly and Privately

1951–1955

Size of Issue (in millions)	Offered Publicly		Offered Privately	
	Number of Issues	% of Total	Number of Issues	% of Total
Less than $0.3	0	—	202	9.3%
$0.3–$0.4	0	—	228	10.5
$0.5–$0.9	5	1.9%	394	18.2
$1.0–$1.9	15	5.7	463	21.3
$2.0–$4.9	29	10.9	406	18.7
$5.0–$9.9	44	16.6	196	9.0
$10.0–$19.9	72	27.2	130	6.0
$20.0–$49.9	79	29.8	94	4.4
$50.0 & over	21	7.9	56	2.6
	265	100.0%	2,169	100.0%

SOURCE: Securities and Exchange Commission, *Cost of Flotation of Corporate Securities, 1951–1955*, pp. 20, 37, 62.

sues were under $1 million. At the opposite end of the size spectrum, only 13.0% of the privately placed issues were $10 million or more compared with 64.9% of all public offerings. For most of the postwar period, the average size of privately placed issues has varied between one-fourth and one-third of the average size of publicly offered issues (Table 4–5). The average size of issues sold in both markets declined during the early years, but a subsequent increase in the size of publicly offered issues during 1952–1954 was not matched by a comparable increase in the size of privately placed issues. The failure of the average size of privately placed issues to grow is not surprising. Although the frequency of large issues sold in this market no doubt increased as the size of companies grew, the frequency of sales by small borrowers likewise increased as economic activity expanded.

Differences in the average size of public and private issues sold by the Fortune 500 companies, a relatively homogeneous size group, exhibited less of a disparity than the issues sold by all corporate borrowers (Table 4–6). For the 1953–1970 period, the average size of private placements of the Fortune group was 42% of the average size of their public offerings. The average size of both private placements and public offerings tended to rise irregularly during this period. No noticeable cyclical pattern in the ratio of

approximately 50% by number and 60% by volume of all registered public offerings, excluding investment company issues, during the years 1951, 1953, and 1955; and approximately 75% by number and 80% by volume of all private offerings except by U.S. railroads, banks, and similar institutions during these years. Conclusions similar to those reached here from earlier data appear in Conklin, "Direct Placements."

TABLE 4–5
Average Annual Size of Corporate Bond Issues
1945–1963
(In millions of dollars)

Year	Public Offerings	Private Placements
1945	$22.51	$6.85
1946	21.00	8.82
1947	19.49	6.35
1948	15.22	6.51
1949	15.38	5.65
1950	12.79	4.19
1951	9.15	5.88
1952	13.03	5.83
1953	14.96	6.16
1954	20.20	5.73
1955	15.13	4.98
1956	14.46	5.96
1957	17.91	5.24
1958	21.62	4.71
1959	12.38	4.61
1960	15.02	4.32
1961	15.73	4.55
1962	16.73	4.77
1963	20.11	5.48

SOURCE: Friend et al., *Investment Banking and the New Issues Market*, p. 344.

private placements to public offerings is evident. At the same time this ratio was quite high in 1964, a year of modest financing when several major corporations sold issues in the private market (see page 106 and Table 5–6); and the ratios were quite low in 1958 and 1970, two years of relatively heavy corporate financing. In these years only the smaller members of the Fortune group found it advantageous to borrow in the private market.

Since there are limits to the amount a company can borrow as dictated by investors' assessments of and willingness to assume risk, it seems likely that issue size should be directly related to borrower size. In the case of issues sold in the public market (Table 4–7), the data indeed suggest that the issue size category containing the largest number of issues increases progressively with the size of borrower category. At the same time, small companies sell larger issues relative to their asset size than do large companies, reflecting the economies to small companies of selling larger size issues.

One of the major advantages of the private placement method of sale lies in the reduced costs of distribution. The magnitude of these savings over issues sold publicly can be large as was revealed in the SEC study of the cost of flotation during 1951, 1953, and 1955 (Table 4–8). No study of the costs of distributing private issues has been undertaken since the 1957 SEC study.

TABLE 4–6
Average Annual Size of Corporate Bond Issues
Fortune 500 Companies
1953–1970
(Dollar amounts in millions)

Year	Public Offerings	Private Placements[1]	Private Placements as % of Public Offerings
1953	$69.7	$11.2	.16%
1954	54.4	17.7	.33
1955	30.9	16.7	.54
1956	29.6	19.0	.64
1957	30.6	17.6	.58
1958	56.4	17.7	.31
1959	27.2	12.0	.44
1960	24.9	14.6	.59
1961	44.0	20.0	.46
1962	28.6	19.3	.68
1963	50.1	20.4	.41
1964	30.9	28.7	.93
1965	44.1	28.2	.64
1966	53.7	34.0	.63
1967	58.9	25.2	.43
1968	59.8	26.6	.45
1969	42.7	20.7	.49
1970	72.7	16.9	.23
Average	$50.6	$21.2	.42%

[1] Recorded on the date of the first takedown.

While there may have been some changes in these costs since this period, depending on the intensity of competition among underwriters and agents, it seems unlikely that these have been sufficient to modify the major relationships which are evident in the data.[15]

[15] The underwriters' cost of distributing issues publicly has been compiled subsequently. For the issue size categories shown in Table 4–7, the underwriting spreads as a percentage of gross proceeds for 1961 and 1963 (along with 1951–1955) where:

Size (in millions)	1951–1955	1961	1963
$0.50	—	6.5%	—
$0.50–$0.99	7.5%	6.9	4.7%
$1.00–$1.99	5.8	6.2	7.9
$2.00–$4.99	2.4	4.5	3.9
$5.00–$9.99	1.0	1.4	1.6
$10.00–$19.99	0.9	1.2	0.9
$20.00–$49.99	0.8	1.1	0.8
$50.00 and over	0.9	0.9	0.8

SOURCES: 1951–1955: Table 2–7. 1961 and 1963: Friend et al., *op. cit.*, p. 408.

(*footnote continued on p. 98*)

TABLE 4-7

Cost of Flotation

Publicly Offered Corporate Bonds Classified by Size
of Company and Size of Issue

Number of Issues and Cost of Flotation as
Percentage of Proceeds

1951, 1953, and 1955

(Size of issue in millions)

Size of Company (Asset size in millions)	Under $0.5	$0.5– $0.99	$1.0– $1.99	$2.0– $4.99	$5.0– $9.99	$10.0– $19.99	$20.0– $49.99	$50.0 & Over	Total
					Number of Issues				
Less than $1	0	0	0	0	0	0	0	0	0
$1– $4.9	0	5	3	3	0	0	0	0	11
$5– $9.9	0	0	7	5	1	0	0	0	13
$10– $19.9	0	0	3	9	3	0	0	0	15
$20– $49.9	0	0	1	9	11	5	0	0	26
$50– $99.9	0	0	1	3	22	21	4	0	51
$100–$199.9	0	0	0	0	7	30	13	0	50
$200–$499.9	0	0	0	0	0	15	33	4	52
$500 & over	0	0	0	0	0	1	29	17	47
Total	0	5	15	29	44	72	79	21	265

(continued on page 96)

Table 4–7 (Continued)

Size of Company (Asset size in millions)	Under $0.5	$0.5– $0.99	$1.0– $1.99	$2.0– $4.99	$5.0– $9.99	$10.0– $19.99	$20.0– $49.99	$50.0 & Over	Total[1]
				Cost of Flotation as % of Proceeds					
Less than $1									
$1– $4.9	—	11.49%	10.73%	9.02%	—	—	—	—	10.24%
$5– $9.9	—	—	7.86	5.79	4.81%	—	—	—	6.27
$10– $19.9	—	—	8.05	3.48	3.04	—	—	—	4.02
$20– $49.9	—	—	5.87	2.45	2.22	2.06%	—	—	2.13
$50– $99.9	—	—	4.70	2.35	1.51	1.65	2.47%	—	1.50
$100–$199.9	—	—	—	—	1.57	1.49	1.52	—	1.48
$200–$499.9	—	—	—	—	—	1.33	1.27	1.31%	1.22
$500 & over	—	—	—	—	—	1.08	1.22	1.17	1.16
All issues									
Mean	—	11.49	8.17	3.78	1.83	1.52	1.33	1.19	—
Median	—	10.24	8.00	3.33	1.53	1.44	1.23	1.18	1.49

[1] Percentages in this column are medians for all issues in each company size interval.

SOURCE: Securities and Exchange Commission, *Cost of Flotation of Directly Placed Corporate Securities, 1951–1955.*

TABLE 4-8
Distribution Costs: Corporate Bond Market
by Size of Issue
1951, 1953, and 1955
(As % of proceeds)

Size of Issues (in millions)	Publicly Offered				Privately Placed				
					Through Agents		All Issues[1]		
	Number of Issues	Underwriter's Compensation	Distribution Expenses	Total Cost	Number of Issues	Agent's Fee	Number of Issues	Distribution Expenses	Total Cost with Agent's Fee[2]
Less than $0.3	—	—	—	—	64	1.86%	189	1.49%	3.35%
$0.3–$0.4	5	7.53%	3.96%	11.49%	82	1.60	208	1.06	2.66
$0.5–$0.9	15	5.80	2.37	8.17	158	1.31	345	0.83	2.14
$1.0–$1.9	29	2.37	1.41	3.78	183	0.97	392	0.59	1.56
$2.0–$4.9	44	1.01	0.82	1.83	161	0.69	330	0.43	1.12
$5.0–$9.9	72	0.88	0.64	1.52	90	0.49	154	0.34	0.83
$10.0–$19.9	79	0.85	0.48	1.33	59	0.31	108	0.32	0.63
$20.0–$49.9	21	0.88	0.32	1.19	64*	0.22	120	0.22	0.44
$50.0 & over									—
Total[3]	265	0.90%	0.59%	1.49%	861	0.83%	1,846	0.43%	1.26%

[1] Include issues placed through agents.
[2] Assumes distribution expenses are the same on issues placed through agents and issues placed directly.
[3] Median percentages.
* $20 million and over.
SOURCE: Securities and Exchange Commission, *Cost of Flotation of Directly Placed Corporate Securities, 1951–1955.*

The distribution cost declines quite rapidly as a function of the size of issues for both publicly offered and privately placed issues. The spread in cost between the two channels of distribution also narrows—falling from 8.1% in the $0.5–$0.9 million category to about 0.8% in the $20 million and over category. The spread narrows, of course, because the costs on public offerings have much further to fall. For the $0.5–$0.9 million size category, the smallest for which a comparison between the two markets is possible, the total cost of distributing an issue privately was only 1.9% if the borrower sold the issue directly to a lender and 3.4% if an agent was used. In comparison, the distribution cost of a publicly offered security was almost 11.5%.

The behavior of the underwriter's compensation reflects chiefly differences in the risks involved in underwriting small and large issues. As measured by the investment banker's compensation, the risk of underwriting declines as the size of the issue increases. The underwriter's compensation falls rapidly as a function of issue size to 1.1% in the $5.0–$9.9 million category, but then tends to level off at about 0.9% for all larger categories. But this turns out to be more a reflection of the increase in the size of the borrower selling the issue than an increase in the size of the issue itself. When the costs of flotation of debt issues offered to the public are cross-classified by size of issue and asset size of borrower (Table 4–9), the influence of the size of issuers can be seen explicitly if the size of issue is held constant. The underwriter's compensation on issues of $1.0–$1.99 million, for example, declines from 8.18% for borrowers with $1.0–$4.9 million in assets to 2.50% for borrowers with $50–$99.9 million in assets. On issues of $2.0–$4.99 million compensation decreases from 7.31% for issuers with $1–$4.9 million in assets to 1.36% for issuers with $50–99.9 million in assets.

The reasons for the sharp decline in the underwriter's compensation as a function of borrower size reflects, in part, the large costs of preparing the issues of small companies for sale. It also reflects the greater risks in pricing the issues of smaller companies. The number of potential buyers for the issues of small companies undoubtedly is more limited than the number of buyers for the issues of larger, well-known companies. Should the underwriter misjudge the best offering price of the issue of a small company, his subsequent price concessions to attract sufficient investor interest would be considerably greater than those necessary to clear the market for issues of well-known companies. Recognizing these risks, underwriters increase their compensation

----

(footnote 15 continued)

The changes in underwriting costs between 1951–1955 and 1963 presented a diverse pattern as a function of issue size. Although underwriting costs fell sharply for issues in the $0.50–$0.99 million category, they rose substantially for issues in the $1.00–$9.99 million categories. They are about the same for issues of $10.00 million or more.

on the issues of small companies.[16] It is also likely that investment bankers take advantage of their superior bargaining position with small borrowers who have limited access to funds and increase their compensation on such issues. As issuer size increases, the amount and percentage of compensation become more responsive to competitive conditions among underwriters.

If size of issuer is held constant, the underwriter's compensation declines little, if at all, with increasing size of an issue for small companies. Borrowers with assets in the $1–$4.9 million size category, for example, paid 7.55% in underwriter's compensation to sell issues of $0.5–$.99 million in size; 8.18% to sell issues $1.0–$1.99 million in size; and 7.31% for issues $2.0–$4.99 million in size. For intermediate-sized borrowers, costs declined somewhat more with an increase in issue size. Companies with assets between $5 and $9.9 million paid 5.50% in underwriter's compensation for issues between $1 and $1.99 million in size; but they paid only 3.88% for issues in the $5–$9.9 million size range. Firms with assets of $100 million or more, however, experience an increase in the cost of underwriter's compensation with increasing issue size.

The decline in underwriter's compensation as the size of the issue increases in part reflects economies of scale in the distribution process. One would expect, however, that as the size of an issue increased relative to the size of the issuer—at least for small borrowers—the risks of underwriting the issue and, in turn, the underwriter's compensation would increase. What also seems plausible is that a borrower size composition effect is present within the smaller issuer size categories; that is, the larger borrowers within a category sold the larger issues in a category. This would tend to limit any increase in the underwriter's compensation as a function of issue size for a given borrower size. As observed, compensation does increase as a function of issue size for larger borrowers. It seems likely that the higher compensation percentages reflected the increased risks to underwriters faced with the task of distributing larger issues; the higher borrower debt/equity ratios possibly associated with larger issues might also influence the coupon rate on the issue as well as the underwriting spreads.

The costs of registration (such as the Federal revenue stamp tax, state taxes, SEC fees, listing and trustee fees, printing and engraving, and legal, accounting, and engineering fees involved in preparing the prospectus) are mostly fixed, and so distribution expenses as a percentage of the proceeds of an issue should decline as issue size is increased. These distribution expenses are largely independent of the size of the borrowers for the different issue size

---

[16] For a discussion of the pricing decision of competitively bid, publicly offered corporate bonds, see Christenson, *Strategic Aspects of Bidding for Corporate Securities.*

TABLE 4-9

Cost of Flotation

Publicly Offered Corporate Bonds Classified by Size of Company and Size of Issue

Compensation and Distribution Expense as Percentage of Proceeds

1951, 1953, and 1955

(Size of issue in millions)

Size of Company (Asset size in millions)	Under $0.5	$0.5–$0.99	$1.0–$1.99	$2.0–$4.99	$5.0–$9.99	$10.0–$19.99	$20.0–$49.99	$50.0 & over	Total[1]
					Compensation as % of Proceeds				
Less than $1	—	—	—	—	—	—	—	—	—
$ 1–$ 4.9	—	7.55%	8.18%	7.31%	3.88%	—	—	—	6.50%
$ 5–$ 9.9	—	—	5.50	3.71	2.25	—	—	—	4.48
$ 10–$ 19.9	—	—	5.48	1.98	1.27	—	—	—	2.75
$ 20–$ 49.9	—	—	4.50	1.31	0.77	1.42%	—	—	1.02
$ 50–$ 99.9	—	—	2.50	1.36	0.67	1.00	1.95%	—	0.79
$100–$199.9	—	—	—	—	—	0.83	1.09	—	0.68
$200–$499.9	—	—	—	—	—	0.71	0.82	0.99%	0.68
$500 & over	—	—	—	—	—	0.50	0.70	0.85	0.67
All issues									
Mean	—	7.53	5.80	2.37	1.01	0.88	0.83	0.88	—
Median	—	6.50	3.50	2.25	0.79	0.68	0.70	0.85	0.80

Table 4-9 (Continued)

Size of Company (Asset size in millions)	Under $0.5	$0.5–$0.99	$1.0–$1.99	$2.0–$4.99	$5.0–$9.99	$10.0–$19.99	$20.0–$49.99	$50.0 & over	Total[1]
				Distribution Expenses as % of Proceeds					
Less than $1	—	—	—	—	—	—	—	—	—
$ 1–$ 4.9	—	3.96%	2.55%	1.71%	—	—	—	—	2.50%
$ 5–$ 9.9	—	—	2.36	2.08	0.94%	—	—	—	2.00
$ 10–$ 19.9	—	—	2.57	1.50	0.79	—	—	—	1.08
$ 20–$ 49.9	—	—	1.37	1.14	0.95	0.64%	—	—	0.96
$ 50–$ 99.9	—	—	2.20	0.99	0.74	0.65	0.52%	—	0.69
$100–$199.9	—	—	—	—	0.89	0.66	0.44	—	0.57
$200–$499.9	—	—	—	—	—	0.62	0.45	0.33%	0.46
$500 & over	—	—	—	—	—	0.58	0.52	0.31	0.40
All issues									
Mean	—	3.96	2.37	1.41	0.82	0.64	0.48	0.32	—
Median	—	3.14	2.20	1.24	0.85	0.61	0.44	0.34	0.59

[1] Percentages in this column are medians for all issues in each company size interval.

SOURCE: Securities and Exchange Commission, *Cost of Flotation of Directly Placed Corporate Securities, 1951–1955.*

categories (Table 4–8), although in some instances distribution costs tended to decline for issues of a given size as size of the borrower increased. In view of the fact that the costs of distributing an issue are a function of the size of an issue but largely independent of the size of the borrowers, this is what we would expect.

The effect of the cost of distribution on the interest cost of a loan depends on two factors: the coupon on the issue and its date of maturity. The effect of a variation of the coupon on the interest cost for a given discount from par is quite small, however, in comparison with the effect of the issue's maturity and is not discussed here.[17]

The effect of the distribution expenses on the net interest cost to the borrower for a 5% coupon issue sold at par and maturing in 20 years is presented in Table 4–10. The maturity of most private placements falls within this range. Suppose that a corporation floats an $800,000 issue of 20-year bonds with a 5% coupon paying interest semiannually and that the issue is sold at par. The cost of flotation (from Table 4–8) is 11.49%, so that the issuer receives 88.51% of the par value of the issue. This is equivalent to an

TABLE 4–10

Interest Rate Equivalents of Distribution Costs[1]

5% Bond Maturing in 20 Years[2]

Size of Issue (in millions)	Public Offerings			Private Placements		
	Under-writer's Compen-sation	Distribu-tion Expenses	Total Costs	Agents' Fees	Distribu-tion Expenses	Total Costs
$0.3	—	—	—	.15	.12	.27
$0.3–$0.4	—	—	—	.13	.09	.22
$0.5–$0.9	.63	.38	1.01	.10	.06	.16
$1.0–$1.9	.48	.21	.69	.08	.05	.13
$2.0–$4.9	.19	.12	.31	.06	.03	.09
$5.0–$9.9	.08	.07	.15	.04	.03	.07
$10.0–$19.9	.07	.05	.12	.02	.03	.05
$20.0–$49.9	.07	.04	.11	.01*	.02	.03
$50.0	.07	.02	.09	—	—	—

[1] Distribution costs reported in Table 4–8.

[2] The calculation assumes that the issue is paid off at maturity rather than retired through periodic sinking fund payments.

* $20 million or more.

---

[17] In Table 4–10, for example, if a 6% coupon is used, the increase in interest cost on a 20-year bond in the $0.5–$0.9 million category which is publicly offered increases from 1.01% to 1.09%. Because this category has the greatest discount from par, the differences for all other size categories would be less than this.

interest cost of 6.01% over the life of the issue. This issuer would fare considerably better in the private placement market assuming that he experienced representative costs. The same issue sold with the help of an investment banker acting as an agent would cost 1.31% of the gross proceeds in fees and an additional 0.83% in other expenses, or a total of 2.14%. In effect, the issue would have sold at 97.86% of par. The cost to the issuer over the life of the issue would have been 5.16%. Thus, the difference in the cost to the issuer of this small issue would be 0.85% in favor of the private placement. If the issuer could avoid the agent's fee, the differential increases to 0.95%.

Contrast these results with the hypothetical experience of an issue ten times as large. If an issue of $8 million with the same maturity and coupon was floated in the public market, compensation and other costs would absorb 1.83% of the gross proceeds. The cost of the issue would be 5.15% over its life. The same issue floated privately, with the aid of an investment banker, would pay out 0.83% of the gross proceeds in costs and the issuer's net cost is 5.07% on the issue over its life. This is a saving of only 0.08% in net interest expense over the public flotation.

The actual results will vary somewhat as a function of the maturity and the coupon of the issue and if the average life rather than the final maturity of the issue is used, but the lesson of this illustration is clear.[18] Even if no other advantages accrued to the private placement method of sale, the interest cost savings in going private on small issues is substantial enough to justify the private placement on this basis alone. Even assuming that the issue could have been sold publicly, the costs of public and private sales for lower quality borrowers (Table 2–1) indicate that it is doubtful whether the interest cost on the loan to smaller and presumably less financially secure borrowers would have been lower at all, let alone by almost 1%.

In larger issues the distribution cost savings of a private placement largely evaporate. If a large issue is sold privately, it usually must depend on other advantages of the private placement method of sale—such as timing advantages and the opportunity to tailor and renegotiate terms. If the nonprice advantages of the private placement remain relatively constant over time, then the large borrower's choice of the distribution channels depends on the spread

---

[18] If a bond has a 10-year as opposed to a 20-year maturity, for example, total distribution costs on a public offering decrease from 1.59% for $0.5–$0.9 million size issues to 0.15% for issues of $50 million or more. If the issue has a 30-year maturity, total costs decrease from 0.81% to 0.08% over the same size range of issues. Comparable relationships occur for the total costs of private placements. If the bond has a 6% coupon, for example, the interest costs on a 20-year bond in the $0.5–$0.9 million category which is offered publicly increases to 1.09% from 1.01% in the case of the 5% coupon. Because this size category experienced the largest discount from par as a result of distribution expenses, the differences for all other issue size categories is less than this.

in net interest costs between the public and the private markets. As this spread changes we can expect the borrower to change his channel of distribution.

The Secondary Market for Private Placements

An organized secondary market in privately placed corporate bonds is virtually nonexistent. This is in part because of legal restrictions on the resale of such issues. Issues sold privately were exempted from the SEC registration requirement because the buyers of such issues presumably were sophisticated enough to get as much information about an issue as was provided by the prospectus of a public offering. But an adequate flow of information cannot be assured if a privately sold issue was resold in the secondary market. Resales would make it possible to achieve the equivalent of a public distribution without appropriate restrictions and while avoiding the registration requirement.

The question of whether a sale in the secondary market is exempted from registration has been reduced to a question of the investor's original intent in buying the issue. If his intent was to hold the issue for investment purposes, the sale in the secondary market was exempt from registration. If his motive was to resell the issue, then the investor was considered to be an underwriter and the transaction was not exempt.[19]

The question of an investor's original intent in buying a private issue has been the subject of considerable discussion.[20] Most of this has centered around issues containing incentive features. The most recent major decision in this area involved the private sale of $3 million convertible debentures and $1 million straight-debt debentures by the Crowell-Collier Publishing Company in 1955 and 1956.[21] In the SEC's eyes this sale represented a clear violation of the intent of the Securities Act. The first issue was sold to 83 individual investors including several investment houses. The conversion price was set below the price of the common stock at the time of sale. Conversion and subsequent resale of the common stock in the secondary market began six months after the original sale just when the long-term capital gains tax rate became effective. The violation of the law in this case was so flagrant that the decision by the SEC was of limited value in indicating the circumstances under which straight-debt issues normally might be sold by institutional investors.

In the absence of a more precise ruling, the law has been interpreted by the investment community in the following way. If there has been a change of

---

[19] Securities Act of 1933. Section 4(1) of the act exempts from registration "Transactions by any person other than an issuer, underwriter or dealer" while Section (4)2 exempts "Transactions by an issuer not involving any public offering."

[20] See, for example, Loss, *Securities Regulation,* Vol. 1, pp. 653–689.

[21] Crowell-Collier Publishing Co., Securities Act Rel. 3825 (1957). For a discussion of this case see Loss, *op. cit.,* pp. 667–671, 674–677.

circumstances between the time the issue was bought and the time it was sold, then a decision to sell the issue would be consistent with the original intent to hold for investment purposes; the sale of the issue in the secondary market would be exempted from the registration requirement. The only change in circumstances which presumably is allowed is one occurring within the investing company itself—such as a change in investment objectives. Changes in the circumstances of the borrower or in the conditions of the capital markets would be insufficient evidence in reconciling the investor's initial intention to hold a security for investment purposes and his subsequent decision to sell.

In practice the problem of verifying an investor's original intent has been avoided; instead, intent is assessed by the length of time an investor owns an issue before selling it. As one market observer explains: "It is clear that if a sufficient period of time has elapsed, a sale by virtue of the passage of time is consistent with original investment intent." If a sufficient period of time has not elapsed, then presumably evidence of a change in internal circumstances must be provided at the time of sale.

What makes up a "sufficient period of time" is, of course, subject to interpretation. In 1938 the SEC's General Counsel said that the retention of an issue for as long as a year "would create a strong presumption that (it) had been purchased for investment."[22] Despite this opinion, however, most lawyers and investment bankers who sell issues privately consider that one year is too short a period to establish *prima facie* evidence of investment intent. One investment banker, who frequently acts as an agent, considers eighteen months to be a minimum holding period; another thought that any period shorter than three years was insufficient.

In view of these interpretations of the law, it is not surprising that the volume of secondary market transactions has been limited. Investment bankers estimate that approximately one-half of the secondary market sales of a publicly offered issue occur as part of the underwriting process—in the first few months of the issue's life. If we assume that the activity patterns in the public and private markets would be similar in the absence of legal restrictions on the resale of privately placed issues, the presence of such restrictions probably reduces the volume of secondary market transactions by at least 50%.

Even in the absence of legal restrictions, however, the volume of secondary market transactions in the private placement market would be limited. The large majority of issues sold privately are small, nonstandard contracts held by a small number of investors. Owners of these issues would incur substantial transactions costs if they attempted to sell them. Investors are aware

22 Opinion, General Counsel, Securities Act Release 1862 (1938). See Loss, *op. cit.,* p. 668, for a discussion of this ruling.

of this and acquire privately placed issues with the intent of holding them to maturity.

Sales in the secondary market do occur, however. There appear to be two situations which motivate them. One arises when an investing institution acquires another institution and changes the portfolio policy to conform with its own preferences for risk and return. The other situation arises when an institution actually seeks to increase the return on its portfolio. The motives for increasing portfolio return may be to take advantage of higher market rates or to increase the risk-return characteristics of its portfolio. But by itself, a sale to take advantage of higher interest rates is inconsistent with an investor's original intent to hold the issue for investment purposes. Typically, however, investors increase the risk-return configurations of their portfolios at the same time. This then establishes a change in circumstances which is consistent with original investment intent. Moreover, if the institution has owned the issue for a sufficient length of time, its original investment intent is established on the basis of the holding period criterion as well.

According to industry observers, most sales in the secondary market result from investors attempting to improve portfolio returns. The issues that reach the market are usually large, high quality bonds which were sold initially to a large number of investors. Issues contributing to secondary market activity during the early 1960s, for instance, included the Westinghouse Electric 3½'s of 1981 (a $300 million issue sold in 1951) and the Ford Motor 4's of 1976 (a $250 million issue sold in 1956). Various issues of the General Motors Acceptance Corporation also were frequently traded. All of these issues were sold initially during the 1950s when interest rates were lower than the levels prevailing in the early 1960s. A number of similar issues—all at least $100 million in size—which were initially sold during 1964–1965, including Dow Chemical 4½'s of 1990, Republic Steel 4⅝'s of 1989, Shell Oil 4½'s of 1990, Texaco 4½'s of 1989, and Union Carbide 4½'s of 1994, undoubtedly appeared in the secondary market during subsequent years when yields rose substantially above the levels prevailing during 1964–1965.

The major buyers of these issues in the secondary market appear to be other owners of the issues. Since these institutions already are familiar with the issues, sellers find it easy to solicit these investors first.[23] A second group of buyers includes investors who prefer lower risk-return portfolio configurations than the sellers. During the 1950s, for instance, private pension funds were the major buyers of issues sold by life insurance companies. During the 1960s

---

[23] It should be noted that the natural process of redistributing outstanding privately placed issues conforms with the spirit of the law, discussed on p. 104, which seeks to prevent the redistribution of securities to investors who have an inadequate knowledge of the issues. This is avoided when issues are sold to existing owners.

state and local retirement systems have acquired the issues sold by life insurance companies and, more recently, by private pension funds. Finally, a third group of buyers is composed of the borrowers themselves who meet sinking fund requirements by acquiring their issues at a price below par in the event that market yields have risen above the coupon rates on their issues. In such cases, the seller and borrower typically agree on a price between the market price and the par value of the issues at which to complete the trade. When the loan contract specifies sinking fund payments at par, obviously this is precluded.

When an issue is narrowly distributed, sale of the bonds in the secondary market might be difficult, time consuming, and costly, particularly if the initial owners are not interested in increasing their participation in the issue. For larger issues, initially sold to a large number of buyers, secondary sales are much easier to complete. Sellers can contact buyers directly since these buyers are listed in the loan agreement, but they typically use an intermediary for convenience. This intermediary might be the agent who originally distributed the issues. If the agent has not displayed a continuing interest in the issue, however, sellers usually favor one of the larger investment banking houses, such as Salomon Brothers or the First Boston Corporation; these major underwriters of corporate securities "make it extremely easy to sell these issues," according to one insurance company executive. If the issue is widely held, these investment banking houses will take the issue into inventory on a temporary basis as a convenience to the seller.

There are few data available on secondary market transactions in privately placed issues. The only published data report the sales of privately placed issues by life insurance companies during 1934–1951. Of a total of $19.9 billion of corporate long-term debt acquired directly by 16 major life insurance companies during this period, $234 million or slightly more than 1% was resold in the secondary market.[24] The largest volume of resales occurred in public utility issues ($111 million) perhaps because these standardized, high quality issues are more acceptable to other institutional investors.

Unpublished data on the secondary sales of private placements during the mid-1960s, provided by a few major banks which manage corporate pension fund portfolios, reveal a somewhat higher percentage of sales than that made by life insurance companies in earlier years. Secondary market sales by one bank, for example, represented over 13% of more than $400 million of new private placement issues purchased between 1964 and 1967. In 1967 alone

---

[24] "Memorandum on Resales of Direct Placements by Life Insurance Companies, 1934–1951," *Hearings* Before a Subcommittee of the Committee on Interstate and Foreign Commerce, U.S. Congress, House, May 20 and 21, 1952, p. 1134.

secondary market sales by this bank represented over 80% of new issues purchases. These percentages undoubtedly overstate the extent of secondary market activity for investors as a whole, however. First, a substantial fraction of the sales of this bank probably involved issues acquired before 1964. Thus, a more meaningful activity figure could be obtained only by determining the percentage of sales to private placements owned by the bank. On the basis of some rough calculations, it seems unlikely that this exceeded 2% or 3% of private issues owned at the time. Secondly, and perhaps more importantly, during the mid-1960s private pension funds were beginning to shift the composition of their corporate bond portfolios from privately placed to publicly offered issues, as discussed in Chapter 3; and this contributed both to a reduction in new issues purchased and to an increase in secondary market sales.

Rough estimates of activity in the secondary market for privately placed issues dramatized the limited amount of trading in this market. One observer estimates that even for a more widely distributed private issue, only around 10% of an issue was resold during its lifetime.[25] For an issue with a 20-year maturity—quite average for a private placement—this is equivalent to average annual sales of 0.5% of the outstanding amount of the issue per year. Since there were about $87 billion privately placed corporate bonds outstanding at the end of 1970, this estimate suggests that secondary market sales were around $450 million in 1970.[26] This figure overstates secondary market activity to the extent that smaller, less widely distributed issues are traded less frequently.

A second observer estimates that in his firm—a major dealer servicing institutional investors—secondary market sales of privately placed issues average around 5% of secondary market transactions in the over-the-counter market for publicly offered issues. To translate this percentage into a volume figure for 1970, it first is necessary to estimate activity in the over-the-counter market for publicly offered issues.[27] In a survey conducted during January-

---

[25] Another observer estimated that up to 7% of the outstanding amount of widely distributed issues sold during the mid-1960s, identified above, were traded in the secondary market in 1970. He also noted that this level of activity was the result of portfolio rearrangements by a few major holders of these issues and was unlikely to be repeated in future years.

[26] The $87 billion estimate was obtained by multiplying $206 billion, the total volume of corporate (and foreign) bonds outstanding at the end of 1970, as reported in the Federal Reserve's *Flow-of-Funds Accounts*, by .42, the fraction of corporate bonds sold in the private market during the postwar period (shown in Table 5–1). If it is assumed that corporate bonds have a weighted average maturity of 20 years and only those issues sold since 1951 are counted, the fraction of issues sold privately would change by only .005. This calculation assumes that the weighted average lives of public offerings and private placements are the same, whereas in fact the average life of public offerings is probably somewhat longer. At the same time, it overestimates public offerings to the extent that convertible bonds, 86% of which have been sold in the public market, were converted prior to maturity.

[27] Corporate bond transactions of $5.1 billion on the New York and the American Stock

March 1962, over-the-counter transactions in corporate bonds totaled $2,190 million or about $8.8 billion on an annualized basis.[28] Estimated outstanding publicly offered issues rose from around $54 billion at the end of 1961 to about $119 billion by the end of 1970.[29] If we assume that the fraction of transactions to outstanding issues remained constant between 1962 and 1970 at around 16%, this suggests that over-the-counter transactions approximated $20 billion in the latter year. If we assume further that the 5% fraction of private to public secondary market sales experienced by the reporting dealer was representative of the market, then about $1 billion private placements were traded in the secondary market during 1970.

Although this estimate is over twice as large as the first estimate of $450 million, it represents only a small fraction of the $20 billion of transactions in the secondary market for publicly offered corporate issues. The insignificant volume of trading in the secondary market for private issues is even more strikingly illustrated when it is compared with trading in the U.S. Government securities market. On average, daily transactions during 1970 amounted to almost $2.5 billion or between two and a half and five times the entire year's transactions in the private placement market.

Moreover, it seems unlikely that activity in the secondary market for private placements will increase significantly at least in the near future. With corporate long-term borrowing reaching record levels during the latter half of the 1960s, there has been little incentive for large, financially secure corporations to sell their issues privately. Thus, since 1965 there has been little replenishment of the issues which account for most of the activity in the secondary market for private placements. Private pension funds, for instance, have been relatively active sellers of private placements in recent years, chiefly to state and local retirement systems. Such activity eventually will diminish, however, once private pension funds achieve the desired proportion of public and private issues in their corporate bond portfolios and/or they exhaust their supply of salable private issues.

Exchanges during 1970 (as reported in the New York Stock Exchange's *Fact Book* (1971) and the American Stock Exchange's *Amex Data Book* (1971)) are excluded from the following calculation. Transactions on the two exchanges, mostly in convertible and short-term issues, for the most part involve trades between individual investors.

[28] Friend et al., *op. cit.,* Table 3–1, pp. 182–183.

[29] These estimates are derived from calculations similar to the one used to estimate outstanding private placements at the end of 1970. For the period 1937–1961, 57% of corporate bond issues were sold publicly and $96 billion corporate bonds were outstanding at the end of 1961 (as reported by the Federal Reserve in the *Flow-of-Funds Accounts*). For the period 1946–1970, 58% of corporate bonds were sold publicly and $205 billion were outstanding at the end of 1970.

CHAPTER 5

Private Placements and Public Offerings in the Postwar Period

IN THIS CHAPTER we explain postwar changes in the division of long-term corporate borrowing between the public and private markets through an analysis of the structure of supply and demand. First, we describe the major trends in corporate borrowing and the division of financing between the public and private markets during the postwar period. Next the character of the supply of funds to the public and private markets is examined. In the following sections we focus on the character of the demand for funds in the two markets. Specifically, we start by considering the distribution decision from the viewpoint of the individual borrower and examine the cyclical behavior of the variables which appear to exert an important influence on this decision. Then we examine the distribution patterns of the major borrower categories, first, to determine the comparative ability of these groups to borrow in both markets and, second, to ascertain their contribution to the pattern of total corporate borrowing in the public and private markets, described at the beginning. Finally we summarize the discussion.

Corporate Borrowing in the Public and Private Markets

During the postwar period (1946–1970) sales of new corporate bond issues totaled $266.1 billion. Of this amount $109.6 billion or 42.0% was sold in the private placement market. The proportion of debt sold privately fluctuated quite widely from year to year, however, chiefly as a result of wide fluctuations in total corporate borrowing (Figure 5–1). On only one occasion in the postwar period—in the later 1960s and 1970—did the volume of private financing decline substantially. The pattern has been: whenever corporate borrowing grows rapidly (slowly) the percentage of debt sold in the private

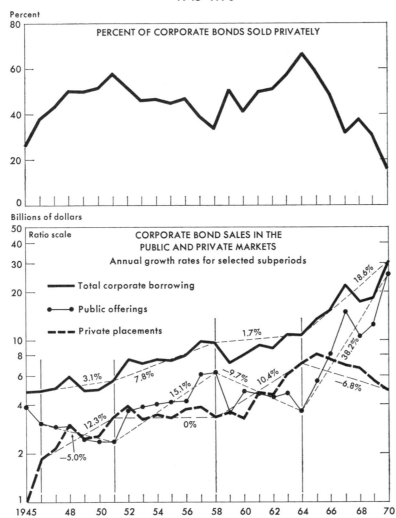

FIGURE 5–1
Corporate Bond Financing
1945–1970

SOURCE: Table 5–1.

market tends to decrease (increase). In effect, the public market serves as a buffer supplying funds to borrowers whenever demand accelerates.

During the postwar period, four major trends in the growth in corporate borrowing and in the percentage of debt sold privately are evident. Total corporate borrowing increased slowly during the early postwar years from $4.9 billion in 1946 to $5.7 billion in 1951 (Figure 5–1 and Table 5–1). The average annual rate of increase was 3.1%. Private financing grew at an annual rate

TABLE 5–1
Corporate Bond Financing
Public Offerings and Private Placements
1946–1970
(Dollar amounts in billions)

Year	Public	Private	Total	% Private
1946	$3,019	$1,863	$4,882	38.2%
1947	2,889	2,147	5,036	42.6
1948	2,965	3,008	5,973	50.4
1949	2,437	2,453	4,890	50.2
1950	2,360	2,560	4,920	52.0
1951	2,364	3,326	5,691	58.4
1952	3,645	3,957	7,601	52.1
1953	3,856	3,228	7,083	45.6
1954	4,003	3,484	7,488	46.5
1955	4,119	3,301	7,420	44.5
1956	4,225	3,777	8,002	47.2
1957	6,118	3,839	9,957	38.6
1958	6,332	3,320	9,653	34.4
1959	3,557	3,632	7,190	50.5
1960	4,806	3,275	8,081	40.5
1961	4,700	4,720	9,420	50.1
1962	4,440	4,529	8,969	50.5
1963	4,714	6,158	10,872	56.6
1964	3,623	7,243	10,865	66.7
1965	5,570	8,150	13,720	59.4
1966	8,018	7,543	15,561	48.5
1967	14,991	6,964	21,954	31.7
1968	10,731	6,651	17,383	38.3
1969	12,735	5,613	18,348	30.6
1970	25,385	4,880	30,264	16.1

NOTE: Components may not add to totals due to rounding.
SOURCE: Securities and Exchange Commission.

of 12.3% during the same period. As a result, the percentage of debt sold privately increased from 38.2% of total financing in 1946 to 58.4% of the total in 1951.

Between 1951 and 1958 the growth in corporate borrowing accelerated to a 7.8% annual rate. Borrowing in the private market failed to increase. As a consequence, the percentage of debt sold privately declined to 34.4% of the total in 1958.

The period 1958–1964 was marked by a sharp decline in the growth of corporate borrowing to a 1.7% annual rate. During this period the percentage of debt sold privately increased to 66.7% as a result of the accelerated growth of private financing to a 10.4% annual rate. Finally, in 1965–1970 the growth in corporate borrowing once again accelerated to an 18.6% annual rate; and private financing declined at a 6.8% annual rate. This led to a sharp decline in the percentage of debt sold privately to only 16.1% of total borrowing in 1970.

Quarterly fluctuations in the volume of public and private financing were somewhat wider than the annual fluctuations, but the major trends in corporate borrowing and the percentage of debt sold in the private market are still evident (Figure 5–2).[1] What becomes more evident in the quarterly data is the sharp rise in new commitments in 1964–1965. This sharp increase stemmed from the heavy use of the private market by large corporations capable of borrowing in either market and from the entry of state and local retirement funds into the private market. The subsequent decline in 1966 and 1967 is explained by the departure of corporate pension funds from the private market. Commitment data from life insurance companies, reported by the Life Insurance Association of America, also reveal that this group accelerated their new commitments in 1965 but reduced them in the last half of 1966 in response to an unexpected outflow of funds caused by an increase in loans to policyholders.

The Supply of Funds to the Corporate Bond Market

The distinctive feature of the supply of funds to the private market is its limited ability to respond to cyclical changes in demand and in interest rates. In contrast, the supply of funds to the public markets appears to be quite sensitive to changes in interest rates.

The unresponsiveness of the supply of funds in the private market to changes in demand and in interest rates stems from two factors. Investors who normally lend in this market are either unable or unwilling to change their investment of funds in the private market significantly in the short run. Furthermore, investors who do not normally lend in this market are discouraged by various institutional factors from entering it in the short run and for brief periods.

Life insurance companies, corporate pension funds, and state and local retirement systems cannot materially influence the growth rate of their contractual liabilities in the short run because the funds available in any year are almost completely independent of decisions made during the year. The relatively steady growth of reserves of these institutions is evident (Figure 5–3). Even if sales of policies were substantially increased in a particular year, the short-term incremental cash inflow would still represent an insignificant fraction of all premium inflows. Payments into state and local retirement systems also depend on commitments made in previous years. Payments into corporate pension funds depend on previous union bargaining contracts and other pre-

---

[1] See Note to Figure 5–2.

FIGURE 5–2
Corporate Bond Sales in the Public and Private Markets
1953–1967, Adjusted Quarterly

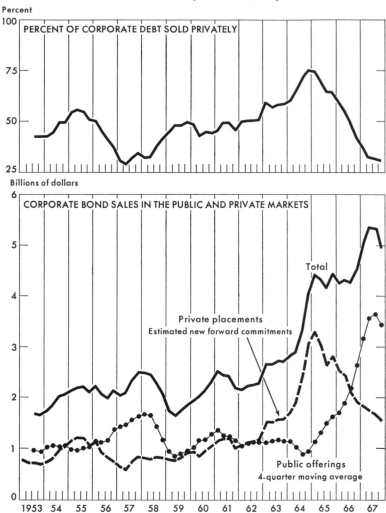

NOTE: These series represent modifications of data reported by the SEC. First, the series on public offerings has been converted to a four-quarter moving average series in order to eliminate the wide, possibly random fluctuations evident in the quarterly data. (See Appendix A.) Second, the SEC series on private placements has been converted from a takedown to a commitment series. The SEC reports private placements at the time of deliveries. These deliveries, however, are the result of commitments made at earlier points in time and possibly under quite different circumstances from those prevailing at the times of deliveries. The commitment series provides a more meaningful picture of the actual financing taking place in the private market and is essential for any accurate statistical analysis of developments in the corporate market for long-term debt. The conversion of the SEC series to a commitment series was accomplished by adjusting the SEC data on the basis of the commitment-delivery experience

FIGURE 5–3

Net Increase in Reserves
Life Insurance Companies, Private Pension Funds, and State and
Local Retirement Systems
1946–1970

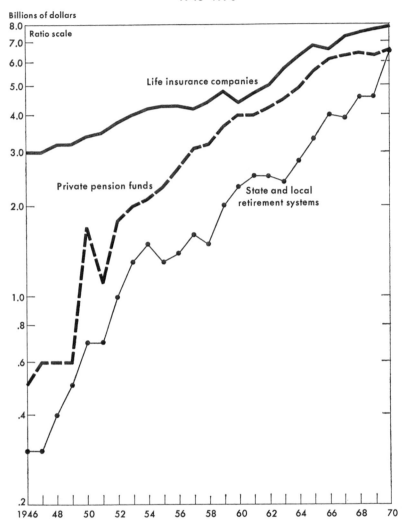

SOURCE: Board of Governors, Federal Reserve System, *Flow-of-Funds Accounts, 1945–1968*, March 1970; *Flow-of-Funds Accounts,* Second Quarter 1971.

of two groups of corporate borrowers. The method used to accomplish this along with the supporting data and the resulting series are presented in Appendix B. Because of the long time lag between the commitment and deliveries of funds in recent years, the commitment series is reliable only through 1967. Commitments in subsequent years are underestimated to the extent that the takedowns of commitments made during 1968–1970 had not occurred by the end of 1970.

dictable variables such as the composition of the work force and cost of living changes. Corporations can, and do, exercise some control over their annual contributions to the pension fund, but variations in contributions typically result from changes in the company's earnings rather than changes in the attractiveness of the pension fund's investment opportunities.

Institutions lending in the private market generally have been unwilling to augment the growth in their contractual liabilities by borrowing. Where borrowing has occurred, the amounts have been insignificant. One large life insurance company sold a $100 million long-term debt issue in 1970, and a few large life insurance companies have borrowed from banks for longer than seasonal periods. In the Life Insurance Association of America's sample of major life insurance companies, the largest annual increase in borrowing, which occurred in 1969, amounted to only $70 million. This represented less than 1% of the total cash inflow of these companies for the year.[2]

Given their steady growth of liabilities, life insurance companies and pension funds historically have invested a relatively steady amount of funds in the corporate bond market. This is evident in the small annual changes in the net amount of corporate bonds acquired by these investors (Table 3–1). Longer run changes in the acquisition of corporate bonds have occurred quite frequently, however, chiefly as a result of changes in portfolio investment policies. These institutions have been reluctant to vary their allocation of funds in the new issues market substantially in response to changes in demand and interest rates.

In life insurance companies, for example, major allocation decisions are made at infrequent intervals—often for an entire year. These companies are restricted in their ability to change the fractions of available funds allocated to competing instruments unless a major change in portfolio composition is being undertaken. The presence of personnel and facilities to administer a private placement portfolio discourages the reduction of new investments in the corporate bond market. In order to maintain their mortgage correspondent network for acquiring new mortgages, life insurance companies believe it to be necessary to invest a substantial fraction of their funds in the mortgage market regardless of the short-term attractiveness of mortgage rates. Life insurance companies' short-run flexibility to alter their investments is further reduced by the use of forward commitments which encourages these companies to commit an important fraction of the funds available for investment during a year, before the year begins.[3]

---

[2] For a discussion of borrowing by life insurance companies, see Bishop, *The Response of Life Insurance Investments to Changes in Monetary Policy, 1965–1970,* p. 17.

[3] Jones, *Investment Policies of Life Insurance Companies,* pp. 518–519. Using a regression analysis, Jones found little evidence that insurance companies responded to short-run

State and local retirement systems also have had limited flexibility to rearrange their portfolios. With the progressive relaxation of investment restrictions in the latter half of the 1950s, they began to shift out of Government securities and invest almost all of their net inflows in corporate bonds. This eliminated any opportunity to vary their allocations among competing instruments in the short run, at least. In principle, private pension funds might have been expected to vary their allocation of funds to the corporate stock and bond markets on the basis of available and anticipated returns in the two markets. Until quite recently, however, private funds have tended to minimize even short-run deviations from their longer-run objective of increased participation in the stock market.

The second aspect of the portfolio policies of life insurance companies and pension funds which contributed to their steady acquisition of corporate bonds was their limited reliance on secondary market sales to augment investible funds. This is well documented in the case of life insurance companies. Sales of long-term debt and equity by the companies in the LIAA sample accounted for only 8% to 13% of their annual cash inflows between 1957 and 1970 with the exception of 1966. In that year, such sales represented 18% of cash inflows, undoubtedly in response to a substantial and unexpected increase in loans to policyholders. Of course, by investing a major portion of their portfolios in mortgages and private placements, life insurance companies have limited ability to sell securities in the secondary market.

It seems unlikely that secondary market activity on the part of state and local retirement funds differed from that of life insurance companies, although data on such activity are not available. The managers of these funds have been relatively inexperienced; as a consequence they probably have pursued "buy-and-hold" portfolio management strategies. Secondary market sales of corporate bonds on the part of private pension funds no doubt have exceeded those of either life insurance companies or public funds. Sales by two major bank pension fund departments (discussed on pp. 107–108) during 1964–1970, for example, amounted to $1.8 billion or 59% of their gross purchases of corporate bonds during this period. In 1968–1970 when these departments were more actively engaged in switching from corporate bonds to corporate stocks, secondary market sales of $0.8 billion represented 87% of their gross purchases. The (annual) fractions of the corporate bond portfolios of these departments which were traded in the secondary market cannot be determined since data on their ownership of corporate bonds are not available.

Institutions normally lending in the private market also have the option

---

changes in yield differentials between corporate bonds and mortgages once they liquidated most of the U.S. Governments accumulated during World War II.

of buying publicly offered issues and thus can vary their purchases of public and private issues in response to changes in yield differentials. Switching between the two markets by these institutions over the course of the business cycle has been limited, however. Large life insurance companies, for example, have invested almost exclusively in private placements. This has resulted from their limited concern for marketability and the fact that private issues have provided higher returns than public issues. Their modest acquisitions of publicly offered issues in recent years have occurred in periods, such as 1970, when yields in the public market were comparatively high.[4] Although the yield differential between the public and private markets was relatively wide at such times, it was small in comparison with the differential between public offering yields and life insurance companies' contract rates: that is, the assumed compounded earnings rates written into life insurance companies' contracts with policyholders. Because they could cover their cost of funds by a wide margin in the public market, life insurance companies felt a less compelling need to acquire private placements despite the attractive yields available in this market.

The relative amounts of public and private issues acquired by public retirement systems probably have been influenced more by the relative amounts of public and private issues sold by corporations with high credit ratings than yield differentials between the two markets. There are no data which measure the extent of such shifts, but data on the sales of issues by large corporations (see pages 149–152) indicate that in the last half of the 1960s and in 1970, these corporations have sold a major fraction of their issues in the public market. This, in turn, suggests not only that shifts between the public and private markets by state and local funds have been modest but that purchases in the public market were also directly rather than inversely related to the yield differential between the two markets (see page 77).

The supply of funds to the private placement market by life insurance companies and pension funds has been relatively interest-inelastic in the short run, but major shifts in the supply of funds to this market have occurred quite frequently during the postwar period. The shifts which occurred (Tables 3–2, 3–10, and 3–12) resulted chiefly from changes in portfolio investment policies. The immediate factor underlying these shifts usually was a relaxation of the legal restrictions on the ownership of securities. The changes in portfolio regulations, in turn, resulted from the lobbying efforts of the institutions themselves which sought to improve portfolio returns by taking advantage of longer-

---

[4] Data on the purchase of publicly offered corporate bonds by life insurance companies are not available. Such purchases are reflected in the volume of commitments which are taken down by insurance companies within one month. In the fourth quarter of 1970, these amounted to 17% This percentage is quite high historically. See Bishop, *op. cit.,* pp. 48–49.

run yield relationships in the financial markets. In the early 1950s noninsured private pension funds began to actively shift their portfolios into corporate stock and private placements. This resulted from a liberalized interpretation of banks' fiduciary responsibility as managers to the trustees of the pension funds. Beginning in the late 1950s, as investment restrictions were progressively relaxed, state and local retirement funds liquidated municipal bonds to buy publicly offered corporate bonds and, subsequently, privately placed corporate issues. In response to increased competition in the management of accounts from life insurance companies and investment advisory services, bank-administered private pension funds virtually stopped buying private placements in the late 1960s in order to acquire corporate stocks and, to a lesser extent, publicly offered corporate bonds. In 1967–1970 life insurance companies shifted their mix of investments from corporate bonds and mortgages to corporate stocks, reflecting the growth of separate accounts for the management of private pension fund assets.

One shift in the supply function to the private market did occur which did not reflect a change in portfolio investment policy. As a result of a sharp and involuntary increase in life insurance companies' loans to policyholders in 1969–1970 there was a decrease in their net corporate bond purchases from $3.9 billion in 1968 to only $1.5 billion in both 1969 and 1970. As shown in Table 3–7, authorizations of private placements also declined dramatically in these years, although the deliveries of outstanding forward commitments remained close to levels reached in earlier years, as shown in Table 3–6.

Recent changes in the portfolio investment policies of life insurance companies and pension funds—in particular the substitution of common stocks for less marketable debt instruments—suggest that these institutions may be more responsive in their portfolio choices to short-run changes in actual and anticipated yield differentials than they have been in the past. Whether this will materially increase the interest elasticity of the supply of funds to the private market is uncertain, however. Private pension funds appear to have shown the greatest flexibility in their choice of competing instruments. This is evidenced, for example, by their shift from common stocks to bonds in 1970 (Table 3–10). This group also increased their activity in the secondary market for corporate stocks during the 1960s. The activity rate of private noninsured pension funds—that is, the average of their purchases and sales divided by the average market value of their common stock portfolios—increased from 9.7% in 1962 to 18.7% in 1970.[5] As institutions increase their activity in the secondary markets, it seems reasonable to suppose that they will become more alert and responsive to opportunities to improve portfolio return by varying

---

[5] Securities and Exchange Commission, "Stock Transactions of Financial Institutions in 1970."

their acquisitions of competing financial market instruments. In the case of private pension funds, however, more flexible investment strategies led them to withdraw from the private placement market because of the limited marketability offered here.

Life insurance companies are likely to continue to concentrate their acquisitions of corporate bonds in the private market, but there is little evidence to date that they have responded to short-run changes in bond and stock yield differentials in their portfolio choices. Secondary market sales of stocks and bonds accounted for less than 1% of the insurance companies' cash inflow. Within the common stock portfolio itself, however, life insurance companies recorded an activity rate of 24.9% in 1970, somewhat higher than that recorded by private pension funds. The activity rate of life insurance companies has grown rapidly during the 1960s—increasing from 9.5% in 1962 to a high of 29.0% in 1969. In 1970 the cash flows into separate accounts represented 14% of the total cash inflows of the companies in the LIAA sample of major life insurance companies' reserves. Whether the increased activity of life insurance companies in the secondary market will lead to greater flexibility in their purchases of corporate stocks and bonds—and in particular, private placements—will be revealed only through their future activities.

State and local retirement funds are likely to continue to respond to the demand for funds on the part of large corporations in their acquisitions of issues in the public and private markets. It seems unlikely, however, that their increased purchases of corporate stock will increase the interest elasticity of the supply of funds to the private market even if public funds should become more flexible in their purchases of stocks and bonds. As noted previously, this is because the opportunities to acquire corporate bonds at attractive rates, such as in 1970, are likely to coincide with periods when yield differentials between the public and private markets are wide and financially secure corporations are selling most of their debt issues in the public market.

Cyclical changes in the supply of funds to the private placement market are further hindered by institutional factors which discourage the entry of temporary investors into the market. Smaller financial institutions and most individuals do not possess sufficient financial resources to participate in the market. Those institutions which have the funds are unlikely to enter the market on a temporary basis because to invest in lower quality, higher return issues would entail start-up expenses in training personnel which these institutions would be reluctant to incur. Of course, new or temporary investors could enter the private market in that segment which supplies funds to corporations that sell issues with standard contracts. Again, however, at times when the private yields on such issues are attractive, the majority of financially secure corporations have sold their issues in the public market.

In contrast with the private market, the supply of funds to the public market is much more responsive to cyclical changes in demand. Both permanent and temporary investors in the public market vary their acquisitions in response to changes in yield differentials. As an example, mutual savings banks were consistent net liquidators of corporate bonds between 1961 and 1965, selling a total of $856 million. When the demand for funds on the part of corporations accelerated in the second half of the 1960s, interest rates on corporate bonds became more attractive in relation to the rates on mortgages. During the peak corporate financing years of 1967 and 1970, mutual savings banks responded by acquiring $2 billion and $1.4 billion of corporate bonds respectively.

Investors with limited buying capacity, such as smaller financial institutions and individuals, can participate in the public market because there are no restrictions on the number of investors in an issue. In reflection of this, corporations usually sell convertible bonds in the public market because of their strong appeal to individual investors.

In summary, although the supply of funds to the private market has periodically shifted chiefly in response to changes in the investment programs of participants in this market, it has exhibited little flexibility to effect cyclical adjustments in response to changes in the demand for funds and yield differentials. Institutions permanently investing in the private market experience a relatively steady inflow of funds, and they have not sought to change this pattern by borrowing or by selling securities in the secondary market, with the possible exception of private pension funds. They are also limited in their ability to vary their allocation of available funds between competing instruments. Only public retirement systems appear to possess sufficient flexibility to vary their purchases of high quality issues between the public and private markets. The extent of their shifting appears to have been limited. In addition, investors not normally buying private placements cannot easily enter the market in the short run except perhaps to acquire issues which contain standard contracts, but it seems doubtful that such acquisitions have been significant. In contrast, the supply of funds to the public market appears to be quite interest-elastic. This is chiefly because there are no barriers to entering the market in the short run in the form of required investment expertise or a minimum level of financial resources.

The Cyclical Behavior of Variables Influencing the Distribution Decisions of Borrowers

In the following discussion we assume that a corporation has determined the amount of long-term debt it wishes to sell and that it has only to choose the market in which to sell its issues.[6]

---

[6] This assumption appears to be realistic in the case of a public offering but, as discussed below, issue size sometimes is an item of negotiation in a private placement.

In his negotiations with lenders, a borrower presumably can effect a trade-off between the operating flexibility provided in the loan agreement and the issue's nominal interest rate. The borrower might accept a more restrictive contract, for example, to provide lenders with greater protection in exchange for a lower nominal interest rate. Of course, a more restrictive contract could reduce the borrower's operating flexibility and, in turn, adversely affect the expected level, if not the variability, of future earnings.

To decide on his preferred distribution channel, a borrower should first determine the optimum loan package he can obtain on a public offering and on a private placement and then choose the channel which meets his needs. In determining the optimum loan package in each market, the borrower must be able to measure the effects of terms and provisions of the contract—including the opportunity to reneogiate them—on the level and variability of future earnings. The borrower must assess the probability distributions of the specified relationships. To simplify our description of the problem and the following discussion, we can view the borrower as assigning a certainty equivalent, expressed as an incremental interest cost, to the effects of the loan contract on his operating flexibility. This incremental interest cost would have the same (depressing) effect on the estimated price of his common shares as the loss in operating flexibility resulting from the terms and provisions of the loan contract. In other words, it would serve to equate (1) the stock price associated with a loan with that incremental cost as well as the nominal interest rate but with no restrictions on operating flexibility and (2) the stock price associated with a loan bearing only the nominal interest rate, but with the specified restrictions on operating flexibility resulting from the contract.

The borrower's distribution decision, then, may be stated as follows: The borrower should select a public offering or a private placement to minimize $(\hat{C}_p, \hat{C}_u)$

where $\hat{C}_p = (\hat{r}_{1p} + \hat{r}_{2p} + \hat{r}_{3p})$ is the optimum loan package in the private market,

$\hat{C}_u = (\hat{r}_{1u} + \hat{r}_{2u} + \hat{r}_{3u})$ is the optimum loan package in the public market,

r_1 is the nominal interest rate on the loan,

r_2 is the interest cost equivalent of the selling expenses,

r_3 is the certainty equivalent, expressed as an incremental interest cost, which is assigned to the loss of operating flexibility resulting from the provisions of the loan contract,

$\wedge$ indicates the values of r_1, r_2, and r_3 in the optimum loan package,

the subscript p indicates a private placement, and
the subscript u indicates a public offering.

To specify and assess the effects of alternative loan contracts on operating flexibility is indeed so difficult that borrowers attempt it, at best, on an informal basis. Fortunately, the mechanics of the distribution process in the public and private markets help to simplify this task. Investors as well as underwriters in the public market prefer issues with standard contracts unless the issues are convertible into equity. A standard contract enhances the marketability of an issue in both the primary and secondary markets by enabling the issue to be traded solely on the basis of its credit rating and the issuing company's name.

The incremental nominal interest cost of selling a straight-debt issue with a nonstandard contract in the public market has not been measured because the sales of such issues have occurred infrequently. This, itself, implies that either (1) the penalties imposed for nonstandard provisions in the form of a higher nominal interest rate must be substantially larger in the public market than in the private market and/or (2) the indirect (r_3) cost to the issuer in standardizing the contract is sufficiently large as to offset any savings in interest expenses that would result from standardizing the contract and selling the issue in the public market; that is,

$$(r_{3u} - r_{3p}) > (r_{1p} + r_{2p}) - (r_{1u} + r_{2u}).$$

Although issues with nonstandard contracts are seldom sold in the public market, issues with standard contracts at times have represented a substantial fraction of the volume of private placements. Since the indirect expenses (r_{3p} and r_{3u}) are approximately equal in these instances, this implies that a private placement is less costly than a public offering on the basis of its nominal interest rate and selling expenses.

A borrower's distribution decision in practice, then, is simplified by the structure of the distribution mechanisms in the public and private markets. If the indirect costs in providing a standard contract are substantial, the borrower will choose a private placement. If the indirect costs are small or nonexistent, the borrower will choose the market which offers the lower interest cost after selling expenses. Of course, if greater call protection is demanded in the private market, the borrower must add the expected interest cost equivalent of the more restrictive call feature to the nominal rate of the private placement.

The preceding comments suggest that borrowers may be divided into two groups: those who find it prohibitively expensive to sell straight-debt issues in the public market and those who do not. Moreover, as discussed in the following section, within the second category there is a group of companies that are encouraged to sell their issues in the public market through various legal and marketing constraints. There, the distribution patterns of different borrower categories are examined to determine (1) their comparative ability to shift their financing between the public and private markets and (2) their relative contribution to changes in the percentage of corporate debt sold privately. In the remainder of this section we examine the cyclical behavior of interest rate differentials between the public and private markets and a number of other variables which influence the values of r_1, r_2, and r_3 and, in turn, the distribution decisions of borrowers.

Of the three variables a potential borrower has to assess (r_1, r_2 and r_3), only interest rates in the public and private markets have been measured over time. The nominal yield differentials between the public and private markets should widen during periods when the demand for funds on the part of corporations is relatively large and should narrow at other times. This is because the supply of funds to the private market is less interest-elastic than the supply of funds to the public market. In addition, shifts in the supply function in the private market have been quite modest in comparison with shifts in the demand function for corporate bonds during the postwar period. At the same time, the magnitude of changes in yield differentials between the public and private markets should be limited by the presence of an important group of borrowers who can easily borrow in either market (see pages 147–152). In response to an increase in yield differentials, for example, these borrowers shift their financing to the public market and limit the potential increase in yield differentials.

In terms of the pattern of borrowing in the corporate bond market, the above analysis suggests that interest rate differentials should have widened between 1953 and 1958, narrowed through 1964, and widened thereafter through 1970 with the possible exception of 1968–1969 when corporate borrowing fell slightly from the level reached in 1967. In addition, reductions in the supply of funds to the private market in 1966 and in 1969–1970, chiefly as a result of an increase in policy loans in insurance companies, should have contributed to a widening of yield differentials during these periods.

Two factors serve to disturb the hypothesized relation between the demand for funds in the corporate bond market and yield differentials between the public and private markets. On the one hand, there are imperfections in the rate-setting process in the private placement market. On the other hand, there are deficiencies in the reported public and private yield series in that they do not measure the yields on comparable issues in the two markets at identical points in time.

Nominal yields in the private market fail to measure underlying market conditions accurately because of institutional factors present in this market. The private market has a less organized system for distributing new issues than the public market. In particular, there is no underwriting system which serves to inform investors immediately whether issues have been correctly priced. Moreover, most borrowers have limited access to alternative sources of funds. As a result, both lenders and borrowers in the private market are less aware of and responsive to changes in market conditions than participants in the public market.[7] Nominal interest rates in the private market also fail to measure current market conditions accurately because lenders vary the effective interest rate to the borrower by varying the terms and provisions of the loan agreement as well as the nominal rate (see pages 131–135).

The relation between the aggregate demand by corporations for long-term funds and yield differentials between the public and private markets is also obscured because the reported yield series on public offerings and private placements are not comparable. One exception is an unpublished yield differential series compiled from data provided by the Bankers Trust Company.

Reported interest rates in the private market are provided by two sources. One set of yield series, compiled by Avery Cohan for 1951–1961, reports industrial, public utility, and finance company yields at the time of commitment.[8] The other set of yield series has been compiled by the Life Insurance Association of America on a quarterly basis since 1960 for industrial, public utility, and finance companies.[9] Yields on these series are recorded at the time of commitment and the series is derived as a size-weighted average of each issue.

Interest rates on publicly offered issues are compiled by Moody's Investor Service for industrial and public utility issues. These series also represent size-weighted averages of the yields on issues sold during a quarter. In addition, Salomon Brothers publishes a five-year deferred call, new issues public utility series. Quarterly observations for these series were derived by averaging the first-of-the-month observations which comprise the Salomon Brothers series.

The yield differentials series, comparing Cohan's (1953–1959) LIAA's

---

[7] As discussed below, lenders appear to respond to changes in the volume of uncommitted funds rather than yield changes on comparable publicly offered issues in their pricing decisions. As a result, the time lag between the application and approval of loans—a period of a few weeks to a few months—may also contribute to a lag in interest rate changes in the private market.

[8] Cohan, *Yields on Corporate Debt Directly Placed*. These series are based on the yields of 2,400 privately placed issues, representing 27% of all estimated private issues sold during Cohan's period of study. Cohan also constructs quality yield series for the industrial and public utility categories.

[9] The LIAA series are based on yield data supplied by their sample of major life insurance companies. The LIAA also publishes quality yield series for the three borrower categories.

(1960–1970) yields for privately placed public utility issues with Moody's publicly offered public utility series, fluctuates quite erratically from quarter to quarter and displays no well-defined cyclical patterns (Figure 5–4). Before drawing any conclusions from these data, it is useful to mention a number of deficiencies in this series.

To begin with, the series used to construct it were obtained from different sources and lack the consistency in construction that a series compiled by a single source would achieve. For example, the yield differential series undoubtedly is influenced by changes in the level of yields within a quarter since the issues comprising the public and private yield series were sold on different dates. In addition, the public utility issues sold in the public market receive higher credit ratings than public utility issues sold privately. Thus, the yield differentials between public and private issues also are influenced by changes in yield differentials between different quality categories.[10] Finally, some error in the yield differential series results from differences in the degree of call protection between issues sold publicly and privately. Public issues tend to provide less call protection than private issues. The yield differentials between issues providing different call protection tend to increase during periods of relatively high interest rates (Figure 1–1). Between the end of 1965 and the middle of 1967, for example, the spread in yields between public utility issues providing no call protection and public utility issues providing five years of call protection increased about 20 basis points. The differential between 5-year and 10-year deferred call issues likewise increased between 10 and 15 basis points during the same period.[11] Such increases contributed to a narrowing of nominal yield differentials between the public and private markets during periods of relatively high interest rates. At the same time, the amount of call protection provided in both the public and private markets undoubtedly increased during the 1965–1967 period (see Chapter 1) and this served to offset a portion of the narrowing of yield differentials attributable to differences in call protection in the two markets. Indeed, one factor contributing to the increase in yield differentials during 1968-3/1970-3 (Figure 5–4) was a relative increase in the call protection provided in the public market relative to the private market. The SEC first allowed public utilities falling under its jurisdiction to provide five years of call protection beginning in 1969.

The Salomon Brothers 5-year deferred call yield series partially corrects for differences in call protection in the public and private markets. In the

---

[10] For a discussion of these differentials, see Van Horne, *Function and Analysis of Capital Market Rates,* pp. 100–115.

[11] Salomon Brothers, "Comments on Values," September 2, 1969, and "Bond Market Review," September 30, 1970.

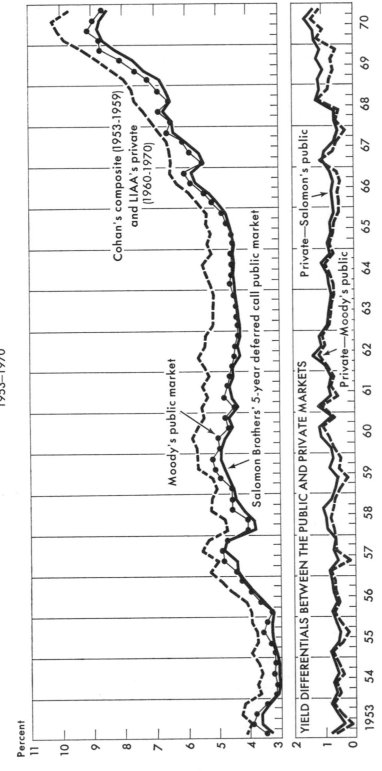

FIGURE 5–4

Interest Rates in the Public and Private Markets
Public Utilities
1953–1970

private market, most issues have provided 10 years of call protection during the last half of the 1960s and in 1970. When the Salomon Brothers series is substituted for Moody's public utility series, also shown in Figure 5–4, yield differentials still follow the same pattern although the magnitude of the differentials are somewhat larger.[12]

The second set of yield series on private placements was compiled from the 325 issues acquired in the private market by the pension department of Bankers Trust Company between 1956 and 1967. As part of its recommendation to purchase an issue, the department estimated the rate at which the issue would have sold in the public market. A yield differential series based on such estimates provides a more accurate measure of market conditions than the yield differentials series derived from reported data. The issues being compared are sold on the same date, thus eliminating the potential influence of varying interest rate levels on the yield differentials. In addition, the issues are of the same quality and presumably contain identical terms and provisions. Of course, the estimated yields on comparable publicly offered issues are subject to judgmental errors, but these should be small since the estimators are in continuous contact with the market. They are small in comparison with the errors which arise in the reported yield series.

The Bankers Trust yield differential series exhibited relatively small fluctuations from quarter to quarter in contrast with the reported yield differential series (Figure 5–5). Moreover, the series also displays well-defined patterns. After reaching a high of 36 basis points in 1958-1, yield differentials declined to 18 basis points in 1958-3 and then gradually rose to a second peak of 35 basis points in 1961-1. They then drifted to a low of 8 basis points in 1965-2. From there they progressively increased to 39 basis points in 1967-4, the last quarter for which data are available.[13]

There appears to be little relation between the volume of corporate long-term financing and the yield differentials between the Cohan/LIAA private placement yield series and the Salomon Brothers public offering yield series between the public and private markets (Figure 5–6). However, the highs

---

[12] It should be noted that the increase in the average call protection provided in the private market during 1965–1967 limited the increase in private yields and in turn contributed to a narrowing of yield differentials between the Salomon Brothers and the LIAA series during this period.

[13] Subsequent data on the yield differentials between Aa railroad conditional sales agreements sold privately and Aa railroad publicly offered equipment trust certificates which were collected by Salomon Brothers show that differentials narrowed in 1968 but widened thereafter. The average annual yield differentials were as follows: 1966, 0.44%; 1967, 0.56%; 1968, 0.50%; 1969, 0.69%; 1970, 0.75%. For additional comments on yield differentials between public and private issues, see Salomon Brothers, "Comments on Values," September 30, 1971.

FIGURE 5–5
Interest Rates in the Public and Private Markets
All Corporate Bond Issues Acquired by the Bankers Trust
Pension Department
1956–1967

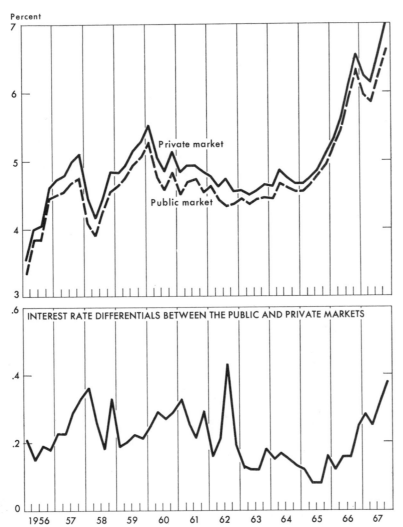

and lows of the Bankers Trust series are quite close to the peaks and troughs of corporate financing. For example, the Bankers Trust series reached relative highs in both 1957 and 1958, years of relatively heavy corporate financing, and a low in 1965 following a period of comparatively modest corporate borrowing.

A regression of yield differentials on corporate long-term borrowing

FIGURE 5–6

Interest Rate Differentials Between the Public and Private Markets
Corporate Bond Sales
1953–1970

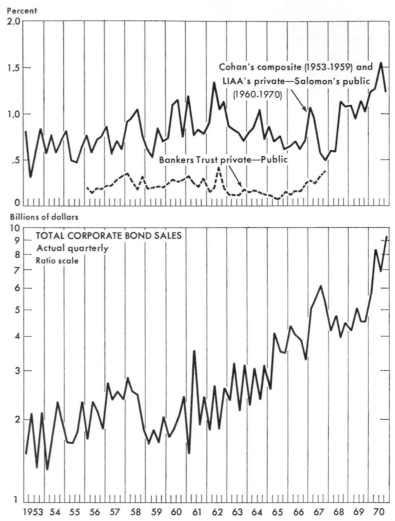

SOURCE: Securities and Exchange Commission.

tends to confirm this. The correlation coefficient between the Cohan/LIAA-Salomon Brothers yield differential series and the volume of corporate borrowing was only —.07.[14] In comparison, the regression of the Bankers Trust

---

[14] The regression results were:

$$(r_p - r_u) = .829 - .065(X - \hat{X}) \quad \text{for the period} \quad 1953\text{-}1/1970\text{-}4$$
$$(.56)$$
$$(r_p - r_u)' = .215 + .074(X - \hat{X}) \quad \text{for the period} \quad 1956\text{-}1/1967\text{-}4$$
$$(1.71)$$

yield differential series on corporate long-term borrowing produced a correlation coefficient of .25. The latter value is still quite low, but this is in part explained by the imperfections in the rate-setting process in the private market. Moreover, a number of variables in addition to the demand for corporate financing also appear to influence yield differentials.

Although distribution expenses (r_2) have not been measured over time, market participants indicate that these expenses have not changed materially during the postwar period.

A number of other variables influence the distribution choices of borrowers and the percentage of corporate debt sold privately. These include:

(1) the availability of funds in the private market, or equivalently, the terms and conditions upon which funds are made available in the private market,

(2) the fraction of debt issues which are convertible into equity,

(3) the fraction of debt issues earmarked for the retirement of short-term debt,

(4) the size of issues sold in the corporate bond market, and

(5) the desirability of a quickly consummated sale.[15]

We discuss each variable in turn.

In the private placement market, lenders frequently tighten the terms and provisions of the loan contract or allocate funds on the basis of non-(nominal) interest rate criteria during periods when the supply of funds to the private market is limited. Such procedures are commonly referred to as rationing—although strictly speaking, rationing describes the situation where borrowers demand more funds at the prevailing interest rate than lenders are willing to supply. Lenders' ability to ration funds in the private market stems from the fact that issues frequently contain nonstandard contracts and issuers have limited access to alternative sources of funds.

Rationing is triggered by an increase in the volume of loan requests and/or by a reduction in funds available for investment. The reduction in available funds typically results from an increase in the volume of outstanding

---

The t-statistics are shown in parentheses below the coefficients.

where $(r_p - r_u)$ is the Cohan/LIAA-Salomon Brothers yield differential series

$(r_p - r_u)'$ is the Bankers Trust yield differential series

X is the logarithm of actual long-term corporate borrowing

$\hat{X}$ is the logarithm of the trend value of long-term corporate borrowing, computed by regressing the logarithm of X on time

[15] In addition to these variables, the maturity of issues became an important factor in borrowers' distribution decisions in 1970. During this year, around 25% of the Fortune 500 sales of debt issues had maturities of around five years. These issues were distributed publicly since their maturity was too short for lenders in the private markets but appealed to individual investors.

forward commitments, but it can also result from reductions in cash inflows. In life insurance companies the ratio of outstanding security forward commitments against cash flows—a measure of the availability of funds in the private market—exhibits a strong cyclical pattern (Figure 5–7). The ratio increased to 1957, declined to 1964, then rose once again to 1967, and remained at a comparatively high level through 1970. The percentage of corporate debt sold privately varied inversely with this ratio.

Lenders tighten the terms and provisions of the loan contract chiefly to reduce the risk of loss at the prevailing level of interest rates or to change the cash flow characteristics of the loan. Their ability to employ such techniques reflects their superior bargaining position during periods when the supply of funds in the private market is limited. In terms of the distribution decision of the individual borrower, what this development implies is that borrowers prefer to accept a more restrictive contract at the prevailing nominal interest rate than to bargain for a less restrictive contract at a higher nominal rate.[16]

Lenders in the private market employ a variety of procedures to allocate funds on the basis of noninterest rate criteria. They frequently establish preferred customer categories and, in effect, accept lower returns when a loan request falls in a preferred category—e.g., old customers. Requests from this group are likely to represent a fairly constant proportion of total demand, so this means that such requests will represent a larger fraction of available funds during periods of rising demand—leaving a smaller portion available for other borrowers. Another selection category is the borrower's credit rating. When the supply of funds is limited, lenders often provide preferential treatment to the requests of borrowers with higher credit ratings. Since higher interest rates usually prevail at such times, lenders are able to upgrade the quality of their portfolios without sacrificing return.

Lenders also allocate funds on a noninterest rate basis by reducing the size of individual commitments and/or postponing the delivery of funds.[17] These techniques accommodate the loan requests of a larger number of borrowers. A reduction in the size of individual commitments appears to have the strongest impact on the supply of funds to large corporate borrowers. If lenders reduce their positions in individual issues, the number of potential buyers of an issue might have to be increased to where it exceeds the maximum number generally acceptable for a private placement. The maximum number of buyers has not been defined absolutely, but agents hesitate to distribute issues of $100 million to substantially more than 100 buyers.

---

[16] For an analytic treatment of this procedure, see Guttentag, "Credit Availability, Interest Rates and Monetary Policy."

[17] Bishop, op. cit., p. 32.

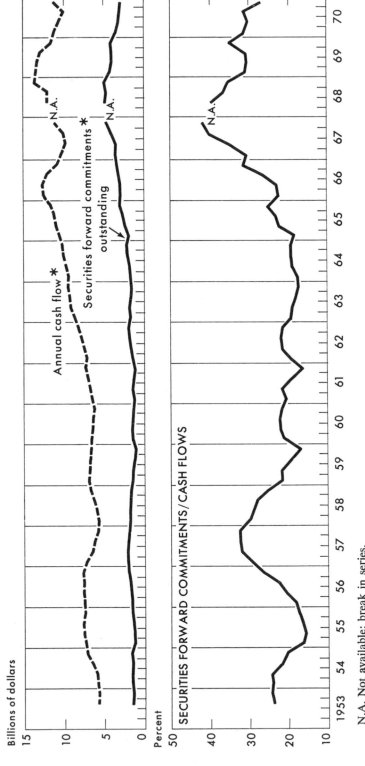

FIGURE 5–7

Securities Forward Commitments Outstanding and Cash Flows

Major Life Insurance Companies

1953–1970

N.A. Not available; break in series.

* Each observation represents the sum of the current quarter and the three preceding quarters' cash flows.

SOURCE: LIAA Sample of Major Insurance Companies.

FIGURE 5–8
Average Monthly Lags
Commitment to Takedown Dates
1953–1967

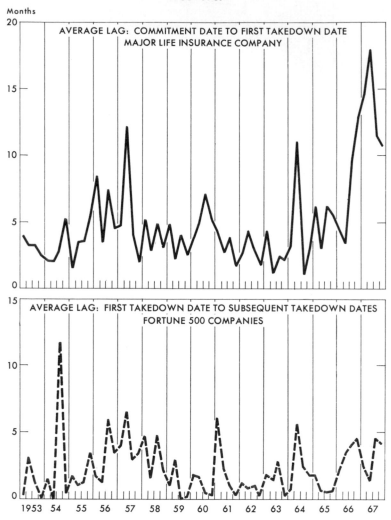

Lenders can delay the delivery of funds by increasing the average time lag between commitment and the first takedown date.[18] This average lag exhibits a strong cyclical pattern, rising in 1957, 1964, and again in 1967 by several months above previous levels (Figure 5–8). Delivery delays can have an important effect on the distribution choices of borrowers. Delays might interfere with the completion of capital projects. If the borrower plans to use

18 *Ibid.,* p. 47.

the proceeds to retire short-term debt, such delays would prohibit a private sale.

The allocation of funds on the basis of variables other than the nominal interest rate occurs throughout the capital markets, of course. In the commercial loan market, for example, banks favor old customers because of deposit relationships and attempt to accommodate a larger number of borrowers by limiting the amounts loaned to individual customers. Both actions are designed to maximize longer-run profits.[19] In markets where the new issues' distribution process is better organized, such as the market for publicly offered corporate bonds, investors pursue portfolio strategies such as those employed in the private market. They frequently upgrade the quality of their portfolios during periods of high interest rates and invest smaller fractions of available funds in individual issues.

Theoretically, borrowers in the private market could negotiate with lenders for less restrictive contracts or for more funds by offering to pay higher nominal rates. These borrowers have limited access to alternative sources of funds, however. What seems likely is that the effective interest rate structure in the private market (the nominal interest rate + the interest cost equivalent of indirect expenses) increases disproportionally in relation to the interest rates that prevail in a market where the distribution of new issues is well organized and where borrowers have access to a wide range of buyers. Borrowers in the private market are unable or unwilling to pay the higher effective rates. They either turn to the public or to other financial markets for funds or postpone their financing.

The impact of these allocation procedures on the financing decisions of corporations has not been measured systematically. However, two surveys of the effects of financial factors on 1966 and 1967 plant and equipment expenditures indicate that such expenditures were not affected significantly.[20] In the *Survey of Current Business* study, for example, only 228 of 4,275 replying companies indicated a reduction of expenditures in 1966. Of these 288, 95 companies cited difficulties in raising funds from financial institutions as one cause, but most likely the majority of these involved term loans at

---

[19] For a review of the literature on rationing in the commercial loan market, see Jaffe, *Credit Rationing and the Commercial Loan Market*, pp. 15–68. Jaffe argues that strict credit rationing (the inability of borrowers to obtain all the funds they desire at the prevailing interest rate) results from profit-maximizing behavior on the part of lenders in a market where it is in the collective best interests of the lenders to limit the number of interest rates charged customers. Borrowers whose credit ratings lie between two of the rates set by banks will be subject to rationing during periods when banks have a limited supply of funds.

[20] Crockett, et al., "The Impact of Monetary Stringency on Business Investment," and Donaldson, Lufkin and Jenrette, Inc., *Timely Review of 1966 Credit Shortage Effects on Business Financing and Spending Decisions*.

commercial banks. Only 10 of the 228 companies attributed their reductions in part to unattractive terms in the capital markets. The effects of financial factors on 1967 plant and equipment expenditures were approximately the same. The observation that financial factors had but a minor aggregate influence on plant and equipment expenditures may reflect the fact that large corporations which account for a major fraction of these capital expenditures were able to switch from the private to the public market to secure their financing. This is strongly evident in the distribution patterns of the Fortune 500 companies. Thus the major impact of financial constraints was felt by smaller companies that were restricted to the private placement market.

A second variable which influences borrowers' choice of distribution methods is the sale of convertible bond issues. Convertible issues usually are sold in the public market. During the period 1956–1970, $20.4 billion or 86% of $28.3 billion convertible issues were sold publicly (Table 5–2). This figure does not include issues with warrants, however, which usually are sold in the private market. Sales of convertible bond issues followed a cyclical pattern, increasing during periods when the demand for long-term funds on the part of corporations was strong. Convertible issues represented around 12% of corporate borrowing in the late 1950s, fell to around 4% in the early 1960s, and then rose to around 20% in 1967–1969. The decline in 1970 at a time of heavy corporate financing resulted from a major decline in stock prices which substantially increased the cost of selling convertible issues. If we assume, however, that all convertible issues were sold in the public market, then it can be seen (Table 5–3) that convertible issues were an important fraction of bond sales in the public market for both Fortune 500 and other industrial companies. For the smaller industrial companies, convertible issues represented over 91% of their total bond sales in the public market during 1956–1970.

Cyclical changes in the sale of convertible issues have contributed significantly to an increase in the percentage of corporate debt sold publicly during periods of heavy financing demands and in turn to the pattern of corporate borrowing in the public and private markets. Undoubtedly most companies sold convertible issues to improve their debt/equity ratios. A smaller, but undeterminable, number of companies which were unable to locate funds in the private market undoubtedly sold convertible issues because it was the only way they could borrow in the public market. Because convertible issues usually have short lives (in comparison with straight-debt issues) investors in the public market do not penalize the issue for nonstandard provisions as they would in the case of straight-debt issues.

A third variable which fluctuates in a cyclical manner to influence the division of financing between the public and private markets is the sale of

TABLE 5–2
Total Corporate Convertible Bond Sales
1956–1970
(Dollar amounts in millions)

Year	Industrial & Miscellaneous		Public Utilities		Real Estate & Financial		Total Corporate Convertible Bond Sales			% of Total[2] Bond Sales
	Amt.	% of Total[1] Bond Sales	Amt.	% of Total[1] Bond Sales	Amt.	% of Total[1] Bond Sales	Public	Private	Total	
1956	$ 745	21.7%	$ 161	5.0%	$ 18	1.3	$ 763	$ 163	$ 925	11.6%
1957	770	23.2	288	5.5	6	.4	995	69	1,064	10.7
1958	332	8.5	804	16.1	11	1.4	1,071	77	1,147	11.9
1959	378	18.6	218	5.7	31	2.3	536	92	628	8.7
1960	294	14.0	96	2.4	71	3.5	356	105	462	5.7
1961	577	14.0	70	1.9	62	4.0	625	84	710	7.5
1962	377	10.9	10	.2	58	4.1	346	99	445	5.0
1963	263	6.7	79	1.9	15	.5	234	122	357	3.3
1964	259	7.0	89	2.4	77	2.3	366	59	425	3.9
1965	697	11.9	211	5.2	355	9.4	1,181	83	1,264	9.2
1966	1,196	17.0	641	9.4	34	1.9	1,764	109	1,872	12.0
1967	3,643	31.3	733	9.2	100	4.4	4,108	367	4,475	20.4
1968	2,228	30.4	455	5.8	598	27.7	2,663	619	3,281	18.9
1969	2,714	42.8	547	5.9	779	28.4	3,099	942	4,041	22.0
1970	1,484	13.3	441	2.9	729	18.9	2,264	392	2,656	8.8
Total	$15,957	20.1%	$4,843	5.5%	$2,944	9.0%	$20,371	$3,382	$23,752	11.9%

[1] Total bond sales shown in Table 5–4.
[2] Total bond sales shown in Table 5–1.
SOURCE: Securities and Exchange Commission.

TABLE 5-3
Convertible Bond Sales
Industrial and Miscellaneous Companies
1953–1970

(Dollar amounts in millions)

| | Fortune 500 Companies | | | | | | Other Industrial and Miscellaneous Companies | | |
| | Publicly Offered | | Privately Placed | | | | | % Publicly | |
Year	Amount	% of Total[1] Public Sales	Amount	% of Total[1] Private Sales	Total	% of Total[1] Bond Sales	Amount	Offered[1] Issues	% of Total[1] Bond Sales
1953	$ 274	30.3%	$ 48	6.5%	$ 322	19.6%			
1954	15	2.3	98	14.3	113	8.4			
1955	323	38.7	116	13.9	439	26.3			
1956	501	38.4	230	21.5	731	30.8	$ 14	5.3%	1.3%
1957	576	53.7	116	10.7	692	32.2	78	23.4	6.6
1958	243	12.3	4	.5	247	8.8	85	30.0	7.8
1959	154	33.3	24	4.7	178	18.2	200	64.5	18.9
1960	26	5.5	0	0	26	2.6	268	91.8	24.4
1961	329	20.8	13	1.5	342	13.8	235	103.5	14.2
1962	127	22.2	10	1.0	137	8.7	240	71.4	12.7
1963	99	11.6	11	.8	110	5.1	153	61.4	8.8
1964	139	54.1	8	.6	147	8.9	112	53.8	5.4
1965	514	37.5	8	.4	522	16.3	175	104.8	6.6
1966	678	31.6	21	1.2	699	17.8	497	98.0	16.1
1967	2,143	33.7	153	7.3	2,296	27.2	1,347	112.3	42.1
1968	691	31.3	66	3.4	757	18.2	1,471	85.4	46.4
1969	1,003	38.5	106	13.9	1,109	32.9	1,605	135.3	54.0
1970	716	8.7	49	5.2	765	8.4	719	121.5	36.1 ·
Total	$8,551	25.3%	$1,081	5.3%	$9,632	17.8%	$7,199	91.4%	24.1%

[1] Total sales shown in Table 5-6.
Source: Securities and Exchange Commission.

long-term debt issues to restore short-term liquidity. If the proceeds of an issue are earmarked for plant and equipment expenditures, the borrower prefers to receive funds at the times payments are scheduled. If the proceeds are used to retire short-term debt, however, the borrower usually prefers the immediate delivery of funds—and would favor a public sale when funds can be obtained in the private market only by accepting a delayed delivery schedule.

Participants in the corporate market have noted a strong cyclical pattern in the sales of debt issues to retire short-term liabilities. Such sales appear to concentrate in periods such as 1958, 1960, 1967, and 1970 after cyclical expansions have peaked. During the expansion phase, corporations typically rely on short-term borrowing to finance a portion of their acquisitions of long-term assets. At the peak of business cycles, corporations apparently experience some difficulty in obtaining all the funds they desire from commercial banks. Corporations' funding of short-term debt is motivated both by a desire to restore short-term liquidity and by the expectation of high long-term interest rates in the future.

A fourth variable which influences the distribution choices of borrowers is the size of issues sold in the corporate bond market. The interest cost equivalent of differences in selling costs in the two markets is substantial for smaller issues but decreases rapidly as issue size increases. The percentage of corporate debt sold privately should be inversely related to a measure of issue size such as average issue size or the percentage of sales represented by issues of less than some amount such as $10 million.

Data on issue size for all issues sold in the corporate bond market have not been compiled over time. However, we did compile the average issue size of issues sold by the Fortune 500 companies on a quarterly basis for 1953–1970 (Figure 5–9). Issues sold privately were assigned to the quarter in which their first takedown occurred. Since the companies represented in the Fortune 500 sample were growing during this period, we would expect a secular increase in average issue size. To some extent this increase would be modified by the tendency of the largest corporations to limit the size of individual issues as a way of containing the risks of distribution and to sell new issues more frequently. Since average issue size fluctuated quite widely from one quarter to the next, we also computed the four-quarter moving average of this series.

Average issue size for this group of companies was relatively high in periods such as 1958, 1966–1967, and 1970 when the percentage of debt sold publicly was high. Issue size was not noticeably smaller, however, in years such as 1964 when the percentage of debt sold publicly was low. This

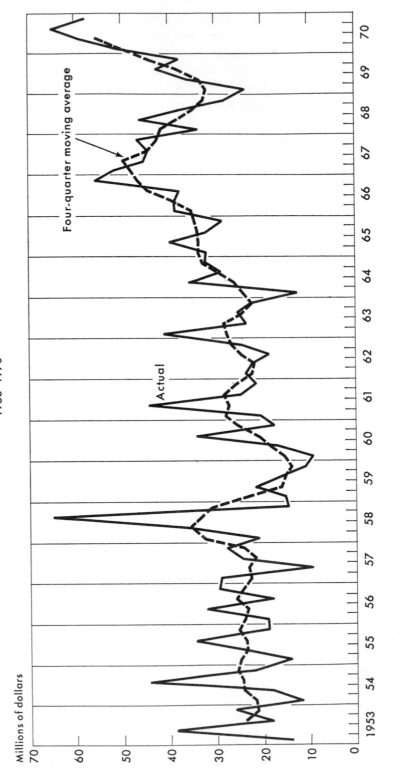

FIGURE 5–9
Average Issue Size
Fortune 500 Companies
1953–1970

reflects the sale of large issues in the private market by corporations which can borrow in either market.

A final variable which historically has influenced the distribution decisions of borrowers is the desirability of a quickly consummated sale. Presumably, when borrowers anticipate a near-term increase in interest rates or are simply uncertain as to the direction of interest rate changes, they will favor a private placement because the sale can be consummated more quickly in this market. Time differences in the completion of sales in the two markets have been substantially reduced in recent years—at least for large corporations—from a streamlining of the registration process by the Securities and Exchange Commission. This variable is probably a much less important consideration in the distribution decisions of major borrowers than it once was.

The Distribution of Issues in the Public and Private Markets by Borrower Category

Against a background of comparatively steady growth in the volume of private placements during the postwar period, changes in the volume of corporate long-term borrowing have been absorbed chiefly by changes in the volume of borrowing in the public market. Since the supply of funds to the private placement market is relatively interest-inelastic, this postwar pattern implies that the demand for funds in the public and private markets is relatively elastic as a function of the interest rate differentials between the public and private markets. In the aggregate, corporations are capable of shifting their financing from one market to the other. As a result the volume of private financing has been largely determined by shifts in the supply function of the private market.

The Demand for Funds in the Corporate Bond Market by Major Borrower Category

A strong component of a corporation's ability to borrow in the public and private markets is whether it can provide standard terms and provisions on its issues. This ability can be identified along industry lines. The industry of a company is an important determinant of that company's business risk and, in turn, its ability to provide a standard contract. Various marketing and legal constraints on selling issues in one market or the other are frequently defined along industry lines. In the discussion in Chapter 2, corporate borrowers were divided into three major categories—industrial and miscellaneous companies, public utilities, and real estate and financial companies; we retain this classification in the following discussion. Within such broad groups, it is impossible to combine industries all of which are homogeneous in their distribution behavior on debt issues; where it is possible, we identify industries within a catagory which differ in this respect.

With respect to business risk, the most notable difference is found between public utilities and other industries. As a regulated industry, public utilites are protected from the full impact of changes in economic activity and are characterized by relatively stable earnings. Even though they maintain comparatively high debt/equity ratios, their issues generally receive ratings and contain standard terms and provisions. A major exception is the airline industry. Companies in nonregulated industries generally experience much greater fluctuations and hence uncertainty in their earnings stream. Consequently, they are less able to provide standard contracts.

The incentive of public utilities to borrow in the private market is reduced further by various marketing requirements. Public utility holding companies, for example, are legally required to sell their issues through competitive biddings; so are utilities located in states which require competitive bidding. In addition, some utilities simply prefer to sell issues through competitive bidding in the public market where there are no limits on the number of buyers of an issue. If the issue were sold privately, the increased risks to the bidding syndicate imposed by limited distribution opportunities would substantially increase the interest cost.

A second constraint on the use of the private market results from the limited ability of certain public utilities in providing adequate call protection. Until quite recently, the Securities and Exchange Commission did not permit companies falling under its jurisdiction to sell issues with deferred call terms. Since lenders in the private market have demanded from five to ten years of call protection depending on market conditions, this requirement effectively restricted the sale of the issues of these companies to the public market.

Virtually all real estate issues, on the other hand, are sold privately. Finance companies, whose borrowing requirements are substantial, distribute issues in both markets in order to avoid saturating either. These companies typically sell senior debt issues publicly and subordinated debt issues privately in reflection of the different risk-return preferences of investors in the two markets. These companies are usually successful in postponing long-term borrowing during periods of high interest rates, and it is doubtful whether they ever borrow privately when market conditions favor a public issue because of a concern for minimizing interest costs. Finance companies' net sales of long-term debt accounted for 41% of their net borrowing (net increase in liabilities less net increase in taxes payable) during 1963–1965, a period of stable interest rates, but only 25% in 1966, a year of relatively high rates. During 1967, a recession year, long-term financing represented 125% of finance companies' total borrowing. In contrast, during 1968–1969, a period

TABLE 5-4
Corporate Bond Financing
Public Offerings and Private Placements
by Borrower Category
1948–1970

(Dollar amounts in thousands)

	Public Utilities				Industrial & Miscellaneous				Real Estate & Finance			
	Public	Private	Total	% Priv.	Public	Private	Total	% Priv.	Public	Private	Total	% Priv.
1948	$ 2,694	$ 745	$ 3,439	21.6%	$ 258	$ 1,820	$ 2,079	87.5%	$ 13	$ 443	$ 455	97.4%
1949	1,976	959	2,935	32.6	382	1,093	1,474	74.2	77	400	479	83.5
1950	2,196	880	3,076	28.6	153	1,154	1,307	88.3	12	525	536	97.9
1951	1,906	825	2,731	30.2	395	2,281	2,677	85.2	63	221	284	77.8
1952	2,426	1,069	3,495	30.6	1,159	2,579	3,739	69.0	59	307	366	83.9
1953	2,316	977	3,293	29.6	1,046	1,367	2,413	56.7	493	883	1,375	64.2
1954	3,036	1,208	4,244	28.4	784	1,757	2,541	69.1	184	518	702	73.8
1955	2,496	975	3,471	28.0	1,003	1,578	2,582	61.1	619	748	1,368	54.7
1956	2,301	902	3,203	28.1	1,571	1,864	3,435	54.3	354	1,011	1,364	74.1
1957	4,041	1,209	5,250	23.0	1,406	1,921	3,326	57.8	672	709	1,381	51.3
1958	3,790	1,192	4,982	23.9	2,257	1,636	3,892	42.0	287	494	781	63.3
1959	2,406	1,399	3,805	36.7	773	1,261	2,035	62.0	377	972	1,349	72.1
1960	3,082	880	3,962	22.2	765	1,332	2,097	63.5	959	1,063	2,023	52.5
1961	2,452	1,267	3,719	34.0	1,809	2,322	4,132	56.2	438	1,131	1,569	72.1
1962	3,264	818	4,082	20.0	908	2,547	3,454	73.7	268	1,164	1,431	81.3
1963	2,863	1,286	4,149	30.9	1,100	2,816	3,915	71.9	755	2,056	2,810	73.2
1964	2,405	1,348	3,753	35.9	465	3,256	3,721	87.5	752	2,639	3,391	77.8
1965	2,628	1,466	4,094	35.8	1,536	4,328	5,863	73.8	1,406	2,357	3,762	62.7
1966	5,102	1,685	6,787	24.8	2,654	4,374	7,027	62.2	263	1,485	1,748	85.0
1967	6,421	1,531	7,952	19.3	7,555	4,099	11,654	35.2	915	1,334	2,249	59.3
1968	5,922	1,966	7,888	24.9	3,934	3,399	7,333	46.4	874	1,284	2,160	59.4
1969	7,473	1,800	9,273	19.4	3,790	2,549	6,338	40.2	1,474	1,264	2,739	46.1
1970	13,695	1,570	15,265	10.3	8,810	2,332	11,143	20.9	2,879	979	3,859	25.4
Total	$86,891	$27,957	$114,848	24.3%	$44,513	$53,665	$98,177	54.7%	$14,193	$23,987	$38,181	62.8%

FIGURE 5–10
Bond Sales in the Public and Private Markets
Industrial and Miscellaneous Companies
1948–1970

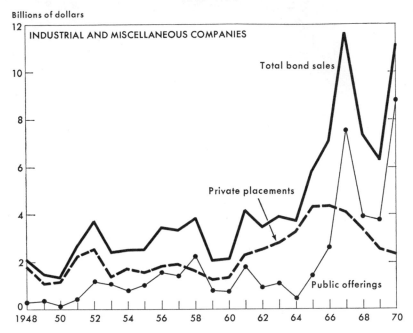

of rising rates, long-term financing represented only 20% of total borrowing.
Finally, in 1970 when interest rates fell through part of the year, long-term
borrowing by finance companies accounted for 139% of their total borrowing. The industry of an issuer then exerts an important influence on its ability
to borrow in both the public and private markets. The only group not encumbered by such restrictions is that of the industrial and miscellaneous companies.

The relative ability of the major industry categories to borrow in both
the public and private markets is demonstrated by their long-run use of the
two markets as well as in the annual changes in the percentage of debt sold
privately. Public utilities sold only 24% of their debt issues in the private
market between 1948 (the first year borrowing in the public and private markets by borrower category is available) and 1970 (Table 5–4). The percentage of debt sold privately ranged between a high of 37% and a low of
10% with changes averaging 6.5 percentage points from one year to the next.
In comparison, industrial and miscellaneous companies sold 55% of their
debt issues privately during the same period. The annual percentage of debt
sold privately varied between 88% and 20%; year-to-year changes averaged
11.3 percentage points. Real estate and financial companies displayed a pat-

FIGURE 5–10 (continued)
Real Estate and Financial Companies and Public Utilities

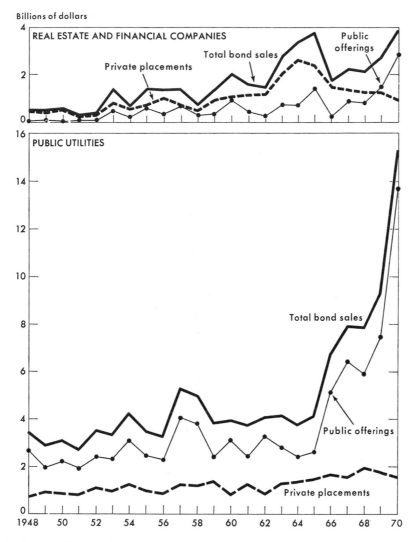

Billions of dollars

tern similar to industrial and miscellaneous companies. They sold 63% of their debt privately. The percentage of debt sold privately by this group varied between 98% and 25%; year-to-year change averaged 15.2 percentage points.

Year-to-year changes in borrowing in the private market were relatively more stable than comparable activity in the public market for industrial and miscellaneous companies and for public utilities (Figure 5–10). At the same time, the greater flexibility on the part of industrial and miscellaneous companies to vary their sales of debt issues between the public and private

FIGURE 5–11

Percentage of Debt Sold Privately
by Borrower Category and
by All Corporations
1948–1970

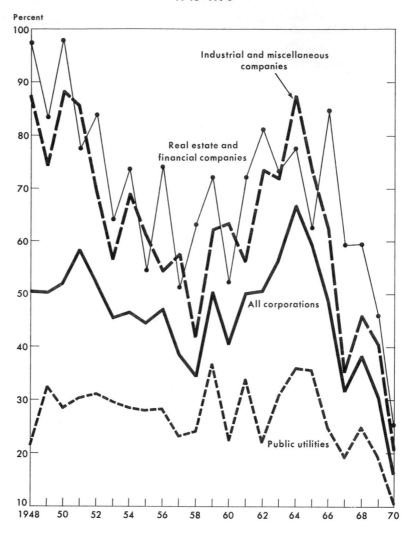

markets is also evident. During the early 1960s, for example, when total borrowing by this group was relatively stable, companies shifted a substantial portion of financing from the public to the private market. In the late 1960s and 1970, when their total borrowing was substantially increasing, they reversed the trend. No similar shifts are evident in the case of public utilities. Borrowing in the private market by real estate and financial companies fluctuated widely, but sales of issues in the public market also evidenced considerable movement, particularly during the early 1960s. Fragmentary data available from the SEC indicate that this resulted from a change in the composition of borrowers in this category; namely, a rise in financing by real estate and finance companies, both heavy users of the private market, and then a subsequent decline beginning in 1965.

The question remains whether changes in the division of corporate borrowing between the public and private markets by the three borrower categories coincided with the pattern for all corporate borrowers. If the observation that the volume of private financing is determined chiefly by supply factors is correct, then the coincidence of the patterns of individual categories and all corporate borrowers need not occur. Borrowers would compete with one another for available funds in the private market and one group could increase its share of supply only at the expense of the others. The only borrower category displaying reasonably well-defined trends in the percentage of debt sold privately during 1953–1970 was industrial and miscellaneous companies (Figure 5–11). The major trends in the percentage of corporate debt sold privately coincide most closely with the trends experienced by the industrial and miscellaneous group. For both industrial and miscellaneous companies and all corporate borrowers, the percentage of debt placed privately reached a low in 1958, a high in 1964, and a second low in 1970. This similarity might be the coincidental result of offsetting movements in the percentage of debt sold privately among all three categories. What seems more plausible, however, is that the similarity in movements stemmed from the fact that only industrial and miscellaneous companies displayed discernible trends in the use of the two markets during the study period.

The Demand for Funds in the Corporate Bond Market by Large and Small Industrial and Miscellaneous Companies

Within an industry, large companies typically possess greater financial strength than small companies by virtue of their survival and growth. As a result, they receive higher credit ratings and are in a better position to offer standard contracts. Moreover, large companies tend to sell larger issues. Thus, the incremental distribution expenses in selling their issues publicly increase their net interest costs by only a few basis points.

To measure the effect of company size on the security distribution decisions of borrowers we selected the industrial and miscellaneous category for study. These companies are not protected from the impact of the business cycle as public utilities are, and they do not face marketing constraints on their security distribution choices as the other categories do. As a result, differences in company size presumably should have more impact on distribution choice. Furthermore, the distribution patterns of the industrial and miscellaneous group coincided most closely with the pattern for all corporate borrowers.

In dividing industrial companies by size, we took as our sample the Fortune 500 companies. Borrowing by small companies was then obtained by subtracting the Fortune 500 totals from industrial and miscellaneous company borrowing.[21]

The financial strength of the Fortune 500 group is evident in the credit ratings of their issues in comparison with the ratings of issues sold by other industrial companies (Table 5–5). On the basis of a zero (Caa rating) to 6 (Aaa rating) ranking scale, the Fortune 500 group averaged 4.01, equivalent to an A rating. Straight debt issues sold by all other industrial companies averaged only 2.66—between a Ba and a Baa rating. For convertible bonds, the issues of Fortune 500 companies averaged 2.42 compared with 1.47 for other industrial companies.

The Fortune group shifted their financing between the public and private markets quite readily. Of the 498 companies appearing on the Fortune lists during the period of study which sold two or more debt issues between 1953–1970, 138 or 28% sold straight-debt issues in both the public and private markets. In addition, 139 other companies which sold issues in the private market also sold convertible issues in the public market. Thus 277, or 56% of the Fortune companies which sold more than one issue, used both markets to distribute their debt.

Additional evidence of the Fortune group's ability to borrow in the public and private markets is indicated by the percentage of debt placed privately in comparison with other industrial companies. For the 18-year period 1953–1970, Fortune companies sold 63% of their issues publicly; other industrial companies sold only 25% of their issues there. The percentage of debt placed privately by the Fortune group fluctuated between a high of 84% in 1964 and a low of 10% in 1970; year-to-year changes averaged 14.8 percentage points (Table 5–6). The percentage of debt sold privately by small industrial companies fluctuated within the much narrower range; 90% in 1964 and

---

[21] It should be noted that occasionally there were differences between the SEC's and Fortune's classification of industry of a company. In 1970, for example, Fortune included Greyhound Corporation and General American Transportation in its list of 500 companies, but the SEC assigned these companies to the other transportation group in the public utility category. As a result of these differences, the financing of small industrial companies is occasionally distorted to the extent that companies classified differently in a particular year sold issues during that year.

TABLE 5–5

Moody's Ratings of Issues Sold in the Public Market by
Fortune 500 Companies and by Other Industrial and
Miscellaneous Companies
Outstanding Issues, Year-End 1968

Rating	Straight-Debt			Convertible		
	FFH	Other	Total	FFH	Other	Total
Aaa	24	0	24	1	0	1
Aa	66	5	71	2	0	2
A	140	40	180	5	1	6
Baa	59	32	91	29	10	39
Ba	16	26	42	70	91	161
B	7	31	38	20	129	149
Caa	0	3	3	0	4	4
Total	312	137	449	127	235	362
Weighted Average	4.01	2.66		2.42	1.47	

SOURCE: *Moody's Industrial Manual*, 1969.

46% in 1968. The average annual change was only 7.8 percentage points. Borrowing by the Fortune companies in the private market was comparatively steady; changes in the percentage of debt sold privately by these companies resulted chiefly from fluctuations in the volume of public financing. This was the same pattern observed in the case of all corporate borrowers.[22]

The major trends in the percentage of debt sold privately by Fortune 500 and by other industrial companies were quite similar until 1968 (Figure 5–12). For both groups a low was reached in 1958–1959 and a high in 1964–1965. Although the percentage of debt sold privately by the Fortune 500 group declined almost continuously from 1965 through 1970, the percentage placed privately by other industrial companies reached a low in 1968 but rebounded in 1969–1970.

Changes in the percentage of debt sold privately by the Fortune group exerted much more influence on the direction of change in the percentage sold privately by all industrial and miscellaneous borrowers than did changes in the division of financing by small industrial companies (Figure 5–12). In only one year, 1960 (and then by an insignificant percentage), did the percentage of debt sold privately by all industrial and miscellaneous borrowers change in a direction opposite to that of the percentage sold privately by Fortune 500 companies. In 10 of the 17 years, on the other hand, the percentage placed privately by the industrial and miscellaneous category changed

---

[22] Adjusted quarterly figures for the two groups are shown in Appendix B.

TABLE 5-6

Corporate Bond Financing

Public Offerings and Private Placements

Fortune 500 and Other Industrial and Miscellaneous Companies

1953–1970

(Dollar amounts in thousands)

Year	Fortune 500 Companies				Other Industrial & Misc. Companies				Total Industrial & Misc. Companies				Fortune 500 as % of Total I & M		
	Pub.	Priv.	Total	% Priv.	Pub.	Priv.	Total	% Priv.	Pub.	Priv.	Total	% Priv.	Pub.	Priv.	Total
1953	$ 906	$ 734	$ 1,640	44.8%	$ 140	$ 633	$ 773	81.9%	$ 1,046	$ 1,367	$ 2,413	56.7%	86.6%	53.7%	68.0%
1954	653	684	1,337	51.2	131	1,073	1,204	89.1	784	1,757	2,541	69.1	83.3	38.9	52.6
1955	835	833	1,668	49.9	168	745	914	81.5	1,003	1,578	2,582	61.1	83.3	52.8	64.6
1956	1,305	1,067	2,372	45.0	266	797	1,063	75.0	1,571	1,864	3,435	54.3	83.1	57.2	69.1
1957	1,072	1,080	2,152	50.2	334	841	1,174	71.6	1,406	1,921	3,326	57.8	76.2	56.2	64.7
1958	1,974	823	2,797	29.4	283	813	1,095	74.2	2,257	1,636	3,892	42.0	87.5	50.3	71.9
1959	463	516	979	52.7	310	745	1,056	70.5	773	1,261	2,035	62.0	59.9	40.9	48.1
1960	473	529	1,002	52.8	292	803	1,095	73.3	765	1,332	2,097	63.5	61.8	39.7	47.8
1961	1,582	894	2,476	36.1	227	1,428	1,656	86.2	1,809	2,322	4,132	56.2	87.5	38.5	59.9
1962	572	995	1,567	63.5	336	1,552	1,887	82.2	908	2,547	3,454	73.7	63.0	39.1	45.4
1963	851	1,316	2,167	60.7	249	1,500	1,748	85.8	1,100	2,816	3,915	71.9	77.4	46.7	55.4
1964	257	1,393	1,650	84.4	208	1,863	2,071	90.0	465	3,256	3,721	87.5	55.2	42.8	44.3
1965	1,369	1,828	3,197	57.2	167	2,500	2,666	93.8	1,536	4,328	5,863	73.8	89.1	42.2	54.5
1966	2,147	1,789	3,936	45.5	507	2,585	3,091	83.6	2,654	4,374	7,027	62.2	80.9	40.9	56.0
1967	6,355	2,098	8,453	24.8	1,200	2,001	3,201	62.5	7,555	4,099	11,654	35.2	84.1	51.2	72.5
1968	2,211	1,953	4,164	46.9	1,723	1,446	3,169	45.6	3,934	3,399	7,333	46.4	56.2	57.5	56.8
1969	2,604	764	3,368	22.7	1,186	1,785	2,970	60.1	3,790	2,549	6,338	40.2	68.7	30.0	53.1
1970	8,218	935	9,153	10.2	592	1,397	1,990	70.2	8,810	2,332	11,143	20.9	81.6	40.1	82.1
Total	$33,847	$20,231	$54,078	37.4%	$8,319	$24,507	$32,823	74.7%	$42,166	$44,738	$86,901	54.9%	80.3%	42.4%	62.2%

FIGURE 5–12
Bond Sales in the Public and Private Markets
Fortune 500 and Other Industrial Companies
Percentage of Debt Sold Privately
1953–1970

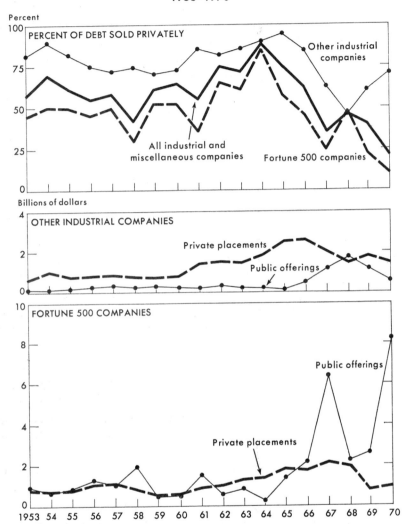

in a direction opposite to the change in the percentage placed privately by small industrial companies. The strong influence of the Fortune group on the pattern of financing for the group stems from the fact that the Fortune companies not only accounted for a major fraction of the category's financing but also varied their financing between the two markets to a greater extent than did other industrial companies.

It has been noted previously that large corporations, such as the Fortune

500 group, which are capable of borrowing in both the public and private markets respond chiefly to the magnitude of yield differentials between the two markets in their distribution choices. This was evidenced in a survey of large borrowers, discussed on pages 45–46. A regression of the percentage of debt sold privately by the Fortune 500 group (shown in Appendix Figure B–3) against the Bankers Trust yield differential series (shown in Figure 5–5) also tends to confirm this. The regression produced a correlation coefficient of —.66 and a t-statistic of 5.93.[23] The elasticity of the percentage of debt sold privately with respect to yield differentials was .67. A reliable measure of the influence of yield differentials on the distribution decisions of borrowers, how-ever, can only be determined within the context of a more fully specified model of the corporate bond market. The problems in specifying and testing such a model are considered on pages 156–157.

Effects of Changes in the Composition of Borrowers on the Percentage of Corporate Debt Sold Privately

A significant shift in the composition of borrowers who sell their issues chiefly in one market or the other market might also affect the division of corporate borrowing between the public and private markets. Such changes in composition could lead to shifts in the demand for funds in the two markets. But, if the volume of private financing is determined by supply factors, as argued previously, then changes in borrower composition would have little im-pact on the volume of private financing and, in turn, the percentage of cor-porate debt sold privately.

The composition of financing exhibited considerable variation during 1948–1967 (Figure 5–13). The annual proportion of corporate debt issues accounted for by industrial and miscellaneous companies, for example, fluc-tuated between 26% and 54%. Public utilities' share varied between 30% and 62% while real estate and financial company sales ranged between 5% and 31%.

The one apparent cyclical pattern (Figure 5–13) is that industrial and miscellaneous company debt issues tended to account for a relatively high portion of borrowing during periods of heavy demand such as 1956–1958 and 1965–1967. Industrial companies apparently experience a greater need for long-term financing than other corporate borrowers during periods of ex-

---

[23] The regression results were:

$$x_p/(x_p + x_u) = .84 - 1.58 \ (r_p - r_u) \quad \text{for the period, 1956-1/1967-4}$$
$$(5.93)$$

where x_p is the estimated volume of new commitments of the Fortune 500 companies
   x_u is the 4-quarter moving average of public offerings of the Fortune 500 com-panies and
   $(r_p - r_u)$ is the Bankers Trust yield differential series.

FIGURE 5–13
Borrower Composition of Corporate Bond Financing
Percentage Share of Corporate Bond Sales
1948–1970

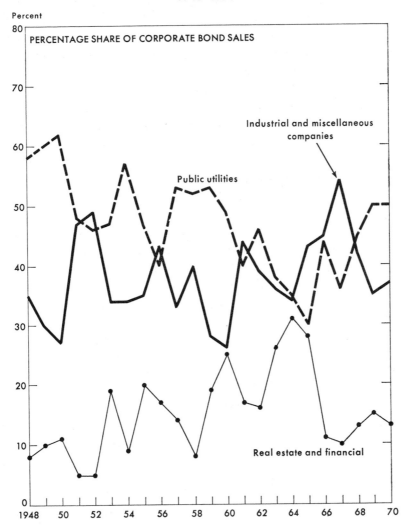

pansion. Finance companies attempt to postpone long-term borrowing during such periods. The decline in real estate and financial company borrowing in 1966–1969 from the levels reached in 1964–1965 was also the result of reduced sales of debentures by commercial banks which by then had largely satisfied their initial needs for long-term funds.

Within the industrial and miscellaneous category itself, the fraction of total borrowing accounted for by the Fortune 500 group tended to increase during periods of peak demand such as 1956–1958, 1967, and 1970 and to decline at other times (Table 5–6). If we assume that the increase in the demand for funds experienced by small borrowers is approximately the same as that for large borrowers, then the evidence suggests that small industrial companies might find it relatively more difficult to obtain funds during periods of peak demand. This observation is explained by the ability of large borrowers to tap the public market to secure additional financing—an option not as readily available to small borrowers.

To ascertain the effects of changes in the composition of borrowers on the percentage of corporate debt placed privately, we recalculated these annual percentages holding borrower composition constant. We assumed that in each year of the 1948–1970 period, the fraction of corporate borrowing accounted for by each category equaled the average fraction accounted for by that category over the entire period: 39.1% for industrial and miscellaneous companies; 45.7% for public utilities; and 15.2% for real estate and financial companies. We also assumed that the annual percentages of debt sold privately by each group as well as total corporate borrowing were the same as that actually observed. The latter assumption is of questionable validity if the volume of private financing is largely determined by supply factors. If the supply function is the chief determinate, the hypothetical volume of private placements would not increase (or decrease) with a shift in borrower composition but remain approximately the same with the percentage of debt sold privately by the individual categories undergoing compensating adjustments.

Even with this questionable assumption, differences between the hypothetical and actual percentages of debt sold privately were quite modest (Figure 5–14). Moreover, the major trends in the two series were virtually identical.

The data suggest, therefore, that changes in the division of financing between the public and private markets cannot be attributed to changes in the composition of borrowers using the corporate market.

Summary

We have attempted to identify those borrowers that were responsible for changes in the percentage of corporate debt sold privately. We argued that this group should consist of companies which are capable of borrowing in either market. Identifying this group is difficult, however, because of the heterogeneous character of the readily definable borrower categories. Only the industrial category evidenced an identifiable pattern in its use of the public and private markets during the postwar period; and this pattern coincided with the cyclical changes in the percentage of debt sold privately by all cor-

FIGURE 5–14
Percentage of Corporate Debt Sold Privately
Actual and Hypothetical with Borrower Category Composition Held Constant
1948–1970

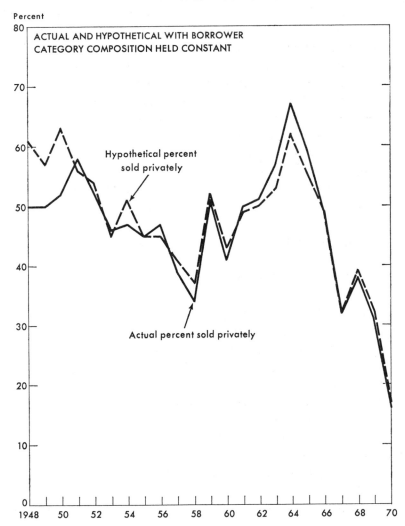

porate borrowers. We discovered that within the industrial and miscellaneous category, the distribution pattern of public and private financing by large companies (represented by the Fortune 500 group) determined the pattern for this category. Moreover, changes in the relative shares of public and private financing by the Fortune group also coincided with the pattern of public and private financing characteristic of all corporate borrowers.

The Use of Statistical Analysis to Explain the Division of Corporate Financing Between the Public and Private Markets

It is apparent that a more precise measurement of the influence of factors determining changes in the division of financing between the public and private markets must await an econometric analysis where supply and demand equations are formulated and estimated simultaneously. This is because a number of variables are determined simultaneously with the amounts borrowed in the two markets. Yield differentials between the two markets, for example, not only influence the distribution and lending decisions of borrowers and lenders in the corporate market, but are themselves influenced by these decisions. Indeed, a number of other variables which influence the distribution decisions of borrowers—such as the availability of funds in the private market and sales of convertible issues—are in turn influenced by both the supply of and the demand for funds in the two markets. Our major reason for not undertaking such an analysis was the unavailability of a number of essential data series.

It would not be difficult to formulate demand functions for borrowers. The demand for private placements and for public offerings would be a function of yield differentials between the public and private markets and measures of the availability of funds in the private market, issue size, issues sold to retire short-term debt, convertible bond issues, and the desirability of a quickly consummated sale. To gain insight into the structure of the demand for funds in the two markets, it would be desirable to separate corporations on the basis of their ability to sell debt issues in both markets and to test equations for each group. Data on the sales of long-term debt by different groups are available assuming the estimated commitment series are reasonably accurate. However, separate data series for most of the other variables, including yield differentials, the availability of funds, and the volume of issues sold to retire short-term debt, are not available.

On the supply side of the corporate bond markets there are problems not only in obtaining the necessary data series, but also in formulating appropriate supply equations. Previous econometric studies of the financial markets have utilized supply equations composed chiefly of the yields in different financial markets.[24] These models not only ignore the widely accepted portfolio management concept of maximizing a combination of expected return and risk, first formulated by Markowitz, but they also are of limited value in explaining the acquisition of private placements.[25] Since lenders

---

[24] See, for example, Silber, *Portfolio Behavior of Financial Institutions,* and Hendershott, "Recent Development of the Financial Sector of Econometric Models."

[25] Markowitz, *Portfolio Selection.*

commit funds in advance of delivery in the private market, multi-period models incorporating dynamic programming techniques or sequential decision analysis appear to offer a more realistic description of the investment process.[26]

As in the case of borrowers, it would be desirable to estimate supply equations separately for those lenders which participate only in the public and private markets and those lenders which participate only in the public market. To accomplish this the gross purchases of private placements and public offerings for the specified categories would be required. The only acquisition data available by lender category, however, are the net purchases of corporate bonds, as reported in the Federal Reserve's *Flow-of-Funds Accounts*. In addition, for those variables, such as private market interest rates, which appear in the supply as well as the demand equations, the data deficiencies noted previously also would be present in the supply equations.

A number of data as well as equation formulation problems, then, must be solved before an econometric analysis of the supply and demand for public and private financing can be successfully undertaken. Certainly such a study would represent a contribution to our understanding of the structure of the corporate bond market. In all likelihood, however, it would refine rather than change the major conclusions of our analysis in this chapter.[27]

Summary

During the postwar period, the percentage of corporate debt sold in the private market has declined during periods of rapid growth in corporate borrowing and increased during periods of modest growth. This pattern can be attributed to a number of factors. In comparison with the supply of funds to the public market, the supply of funds to the private market is relatively insensitive to changes in yield differentials between the private and other capital markets. In addition, shifts in the private supply function have been quite modest in comparison with shifts in the joint demand function for funds in the public and private markets. As a result, cyclical fluctuations in corporate borrowing have been absorbed largely by changes in the volume of public offerings. On the demand side of the corporate market, an important segment

---

[26] See, for example, Kaufman, *Statistical Decision and Related Techniques in Oil and Gas Exploration,* pp. 209–259. In his book Kaufman develops a model of oil and gas exploration which is quite similar to the forward commitment problem.

[27] To test our understanding of the variables influencing the distribution decisions of borrowers, we attempted to explain changes in the percentage of debt sold privately by the Fortune 500 group through an ordinary least squares regression analysis. All of the explanatory variables influencing the percentage of debt sold privately, which were discussed earlier on pp. 131–141, entered the equation with the anticipated sign and most of these were significant at the 5% level or higher. Moreover, the equation explained around 75% of the variations in the percentage of debt sold privately by the Fortune 500 group.

of borrowers have the ability to shift their financing between the public and private markets. During periods of rising demand, this has served to limit the increase in interest rate differentials between the two markets.

The interest insensitivity of the supply of funds in the private market stems from the character of the financial institutions normally lending in this market as well as from the costs experienced by other lenders in entering it. The major lenders in the private market—life insurance companies and pension funds—experience relatively steady growth in their contractual liabilities which they are reluctant to augment through short-term and long-term borrowing. They also are limited in their ability to rearrange their portfolios in the short run because of institutional constraints; they frequently have rearranged their portfolios on a more permanent basis, however, during the postwar period.

Lenders which do not normally supply funds to the private market are discouraged from entering it in the short run because of the start-up expenses involved in acquiring privately placed issues. Moreover, since private issues are nonmarketable, the decision to acquire them involves a long-term commitment to participate in this market which temporary investors are reluctant to make.

In response to an increase in loan requests, lenders in the private market initially might increase new commitments. As outstanding forward commitments come to represent a larger fraction of anticipated cash inflows, however, they become increasingly selective—raising nominal yields in relation to those in the public market but relying more frequently on noninterest rate allocation devices. Both measures increase the effective yield differential between the public and private markets and in turn reduce the demand for funds in the private market.

The use of noninterest rate or rationing procedures to allocate funds during periods when the supply of funds in the private market is limited results from the absence of an underwriting structure for distributing new issues. This limits borrowers' access to alternative sources of funds in this market. The presence of issues with nonstandard contracts enabels lenders to increase the effective return on a loan by tightening its terms and provisions as well as increasing the nominal rate. Under these circumstances the interest rate structure in the private market can become distorted in relation to the yields prevailing in the public market. Borrowers who are unwilling either to meet the lenders' conditions for obtaining funds or to pay a higher nominal rate to obtain funds on a more desirable basis borrow in the public market or postpone their financing.

An examination of the demand for funds in the corporate market indicates a three-fold division of borrowers on the basis of their ability to borrow in both the public and private markets. One group, including a substantial fraction of public utilities, invariably borrows in the public market because of various marketing constraints on their use of the private market and their ability to provide standard contracts, a prerequisite for the sale of straight-debt issues in the public market. A second group, consisting of smaller, less financially secure companies, finds it too costly to provide standard contracts and thus almost always borrows in the private market except when selling convertible issues. In between is a third group of corporations which can offer standard contracts but which is not prevented from borrowing in the private market by marketing constraints. Since this group realizes no special advantage in borrowing in the private market, it is quite sensitive to changes in interest cost differences between the two markets whether these changes are manifested through changes in nominal yields spreads or the conditions on which funds can be obtained.

An analysis of financing by borrower category reveals that shifts in the composition of borrowers relying on one market or another to distribute their issues has had virtually no effect on the division of total corporate borrowing between the private and public markets. Against a background of a relatively interest-inelastic private supply function, changes in the division of financing between the two markets have reflected shifts between the two markets by companies capable of borrowing in both markets. This movement has been reinforced by increased sales of both convertible issues and issues used to retire short-term debt during periods of peak demand for long-term financing. Borrowers prefer to sell both types of issues in the public market. In addition, issue size also appears to have increased during such periods, lending further impetus to the use of the public market.

Although it is difficult to identify all of the corporations which can borrow in both the public and private markets, the Fortune 500 companies, an important segment of this group, have been considerably more flexible in their use of the two markets than other corporations. Moreover, during the postwar period, the distribution patterns of the Fortune 500 companies not only accounted for the patterns evidenced by all industrial and miscellaneous borrowers but also coincided with the patterns displayed by all corporate borrowers. More convincing evidence of the role of companies, which are capable of borrowing in either market in influencing the distribution patterns of all corporate borrowers would be provided if this group could be expanded to include the public utilities and real estate and financial companies which also can borrow in either market.

The Securities Act of 1933 exempted borrowers from registering their issues with the SEC if these issues were sold to a limited number of informed investors. Because of the contract standardization requirement of sales in the public market, the private market soon evolved into one whose major function was to supply funds to financially less secure companies which were unable or unwilling to meet these requirements. Although the percentage of corporate debt sold privately has fluctuated quite widely during the postwar period, these fluctuations appear to have limited significance when assessing the performance of the private market in fulfilling its traditional role. This is because they have resulted chiefly from shifts in financing between the public and private markets by companies which realize no special advantage in selling their issues in the private market. Less financially secure companies have continued to rely on the private market as their primary source of long-term funds.

ABSTRACT

The Role of Private Placements in Corporate Finance

Private placements accounted for over $100 billion or almost half of corporate bond financing during the years since World War II. Despite the importance of the private placement market as a source of long-term funds for corporations, the literature on the financial market during the past 20 years has been sparse. In large part, this paucity of written material can be attributed to the structure of the market itself in which new issues are distributed with little, if any, publicity. Only the small group involved in the purchase and distribution of private placements have possessed detailed knowledge of the nature of this market.

The major purpose of this study is to redress this deficiency in the financial literature. Relying chiefly on interviews with participants in the market, on surveys, and on the compilation of new data series, the authors attempt to provide an integrated view of the private placement market. They examine the unique features of the private placement loan agreement, the changing composition of borrowers and lenders in the market, and the distribution of new and/or outstanding issues. They also analyze the economic factors which have contributed to the secular and cyclical changes in the division of corporate borrowing between the public and private markets. In particular, attention is focused on the sharp decline in the fraction of long-term debt sold privately from over two-thirds in 1964 to one-sixth in 1970.

The authors are Eli Shapiro, Sylvan C. Coleman Professor of Financial Management at the Harvard Business School, presently on leave and serving as Chairman of the Finance Committee, Travelers Insurance Companies, and Charles R. Wolf, Associate Professor of Business, Graduate School of Business, Columbia University.

The most important characteristic of the private placement market is that it serves as the major source of long-term debt financing for smaller, less financially secure companies. The distribution costs for privately placed issues are significantly less as a percentage of the proceeds than for publicly offered issues—especially for small issues. The underwriting fees and other expenses incurred in preparing a registration statement are eliminated. Borrowers in the private market are able to tailor the terms and provisions of the loan agreement to meet their specific needs. Lenders in this market are willing to accept unusual contract features because they typically obtain fairly close control over the operations of a borrowing company. Furthermore, these lenders are not disturbed by the fact that unusual contract provisions reduce marketability; private placements have limited marketability anyway.

In contrast, the terms and provisions of the loan contracts of publicly offered issues typically are standardized along the dimensions of the industry and credit rating of the borrower. Underwriters insist on a standard contract because it increases an issue's marketability in both the new issues and secondary markets. Less financially secure companies find such requirements prohibitively expensive since they can substantially reduce their financial and operating flexibility. Financially secure companies can provide these terms quite easily, however. As a result, they have the option to borrow in either the public or the private market. Since the private market offers no special advantages to these larger companies, their distribution choices depend chiefly on the costs of borrowing in the two markets.

Private placement loan agreements are far more heterogeneous than publicly offered loan agreements. In general, a private placement agreement is more restrictive than a public offering agreement, especially with respect to the call protection afforded the lender. At the same time, the contract can be renegotiated with relative ease in the private market whereas it is quite difficult to renegotiate the contract of a publicly offered issue. Another distinguishing feature of the private placement agreement is the use of the forward commitment; that is, the commitment of funds for future deliveries at an interest rate set at the time of commitment. In the public market, funds usually are delivered to the borrower at the time of sale. Forward commitments enable the lender to schedule his disbursements of funds to match his cash inflows; borrowers embarking on capital projects where expenditures are scheduled over an extended period also find the forward commitment advantageous. For this privilege, borrowers pay the lender a commitment fee depending on the duration of the commitment and the size of the borrower. The rationale underlying this fee has been explained in a variety of ways. Perhaps, most importantly, the payment of the fee reflects the inferior bargaining position of most borrowers in the private market who typically have limited access to alternative sources of funds.

The major borrower categories—public utilities, real estate and financial companies, and industrial and miscellaneous companies—have exhibited quite different patterns in their reliance on the public and private markets during the postwar period. Public utilities, with the exception of airlines, have sold their debt almost exclusively in the public market. Because they are a regulated industry, public utilities tend to possess greater financial security than other borrower categories and thus can satisfy the standard contract requirements of a public offering. In addition, they frequently are prevented from selling private issues by various regulatory constraints. Within the real estate and financial category, the virtually exclusive reliance of real estate companies on the private market to distribute their debt has resulted from the complicated terms and provisions that characterize their issues. In contrast, commercial banks have sold almost all their debt in the public market. Large finance companies have distributed the major fraction of their debt in the public market, selling senior issues in the public market and subordinated issues in the private market. On the other hand, smaller finance companies predominantly have sold their issues in the private market. As a group, industrial and miscellaneous companies have the greatest freedom to vary their distribution choices in response to changes in the yield differentials between the public and private markets and to changes in other economic variables. Substantial differences in the use of the two markets occur chiefly on the basis of company size. In the period, 1953-1970, large industrial companies, represented by the Fortune 500 companies, sold 37% of their debt privately whereas all other industrial and miscellaneous companies sold 75% of their debt privately. This difference reflects the greater financial security of large companies and their consequent ability to meet the standard contract requirements of a public offering.

In the early history of the private placement market, the supply side was completely dominated by life insurance companies. During the past two decades both private pension funds and state and local retirement systems at times have been active lenders in the private market. Life insurance companies have concentrated their investments in lower quality, higher return issues which require the negotiation of specialized terms and provisions. The larger private pension funds, managed in most cases by commercial banks, likewise pursued a similar investment policy until the last half of the 1960s. At that time, they ceased buying private placements altogether except for a few issues with equity options. In contrast, state and local retirement systems have limited their purchases of private placements to higher quality issues. This investment policy reflected in part legislative restrictions on the quality of investments and in part the lack of personnel capable of evaluating issues with nonstandard features. Purchases of private placements by state and local retirement systems have depended to a large extent on the sale of these issues in the private market by large, financially secure companies.

The distinctive feature of the distribution of new issues in the private market is that they are sold directly by borrowers to lenders, frequently with the aid of an investment banker who acts as an agent for the borrower. Although larger private placements have been distributed to as many as 100 buyers, in most cases an issue is purchased by one or, at most, a handful of institutions. In contrast, publicly offered issues have been sold to over 1,000 investors. By eliminating registration fees and underwriting costs, the expenses of distributing issues in the private market are less than in the public market, particularly for smaller issues. For issues of $1 million, for example, these savings can reduce the effective interest cost of a loan by as much as .85%. There is no organized secondary market in private placements. The infrequent sales in this market are limited chiefly to higher quality issues which were initially distributed to a comparatively large number of investors.

During the postwar period, the percentage of corporate debt sold privately fluctuated between a high of 67% in 1964 and a low of 16% in 1970. Since the volume of private placements grew at a relatively steady rate—at least until 1967—changes in the percentage of debt sold privately resulted chiefly from changes in total corporate borrowing. These changes were absorbed by changes in the volume of public offerings.

The steady growth in the supply of funds to the private market stemmed from the steady growth of the institutions supplying funds to this market. Moreover, in their investment choices, these institutions have been relatively insensitive to cyclical changes in yield differentials between the private and other financial markets, although all of them have undertaken major portfolio rearrangements at one time or another during the postwar period. Other lenders have been discouraged from entering the private market even when yields in this market were attractive because they lacked the expertise to acquire issues with nonstandard features. They were also reluctant to make a permanent commitment to the corporate bond market; the limited marketability of private placements results in little opportunity for portfolio turnover. The only significant reduction in the supply of funds to the private market occurred in a few of the most recent years which were characterized by rapid monetary expansion followed by severe monetary restraint, which produced a substantial curtailment of funds available for investment on the part of life insurance companies.

During periods when the demand for long-term funds on the part of corporations has been modest in comparison with the supply available in the private market, many large, financially secure corporations have sold their debt privately. Such companies were attracted to the private market chiefly by the narrow interest rate differentials between the two markets. The major buyers of these issues were state and local retirement systems who were attracted because the issues featured standard contracts and carried high credit ratings. The high percentage of corporate bonds sold privately in 1964 largely reflected the sale of private placements by these larger companies.

During periods of heavy financing, such as 1967 and 1970, larger corporations shifted their financing to the public market in response to an increase in yield differentials between the public and private markets and to a deterioration of the terms on which funds were available in the private market. Regardless of market conditions, however, smaller, less financially secure companies have satisfied the major fraction of their long-term financing needs in the private market. Many of these companies, however, have been able to obtain private financing only by providing incentive features or "equity kickers." They have also obtained funds in the public market by selling convertible bond issues for which the standard contract requirements are less onerous and/or through the use of special financing arrangements such as equipment trust certificates.

The percentage of corporate debt sold privately appears to have limited significance in assessing the performance of the private placement market in fulfilling its traditional function of supplying funds to financially less secure companies. Recent changes in the investment policies of life insurance companies and pension funds toward greater participation in the stock market have not as yet signaled any significant reduction in the volume of private financing available to small borrowers. If these institutions continue to expand their portfolios of equities, however, there may be smaller sums available in the private market relative to the demand for such funds by these smaller corporations. Although this could raise the cost of borrowing in the private market for smaller, less financially secure companies, its major impact would be to reduce the volume of private issues sold by financially secure corporations.

(Published by Division of Research, Harvard Business School, Soldiers Field, Boston, Mass. 02163. LC 72–87769; ISBN 0–87584–099–X. xiii + 187 pp. $10.00. 1972)

Appendixes

APPENDIX A

Public Offerings: Quarterly Series

APPENDIX A presents quarterly series on public offerings sold by four categories of borrowers: Fortune 500 companies (a proxy for large industrial companies), other industrial and miscellaneous companies, public utilities, and real estate and financial companies. For each category two series are shown in Figure A–1: the actual volume of public offerings in the quarter as reported by the Securities and Exchange Commission and a four-quarter moving average of the quarterly data.[1]

The four-quarter moving average series is intended chiefly to reduce the impact of random elements on the quarterly observations. The volume of public offerings in a particular quarter can be affected by a number of procedures surrounding the sale of an issue quite independently of the underlying demand for funds during the quarter. Most importantly, once the decision to sell an issue in the public market has been made, the particular date on which the issue is sold can vary by several weeks or months depending on the time consumed in the registration process. (Random variations in the timing of sales can also arise from differences in the decision-making structure within the issuing companies themselves. Their differences might influence the time consumed in obtaining formal approval of the decision to sell the issue.) Finally, shorter variations in timing might result from underwriters' attempts to pinpoint the time of sale within a relatively short interval to achieve optimum market reception. In addition, the four-quarter moving average serves to reduce any seasonal variation percentage in the unadjusted public offerings series.

---

[1] Since 1966 an increasing number of public offerings have featured the delayed delivery of a portion of the issue. In contrast with their practice of recording the deliveries of private placements at the times of deliveries, the SEC records the entire amount of public offerings with delayed deliveries at the time of sale.

FIGURE A–1
Publicly Offered Corporate Bonds
Actual and 4-Quarter Moving Average
Fortune 500 and Other Industrial and Miscellaneous Companies
1953–1970

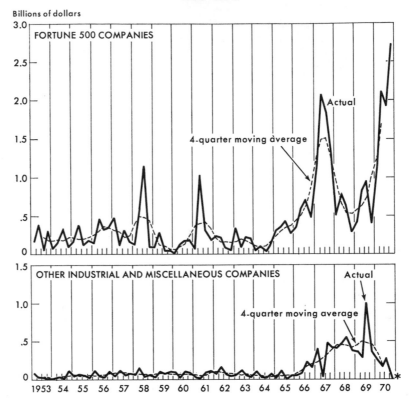

* Figure less than zero; see footnote 21, p. 146.

As is evident in Figure A–1, the use of a four-quarter moving average series tends to minimize shorter-run and smaller fluctuations in the volume of public offerings but leaves the major fluctuations relatively unchanged. Since the moving average series reflects more accurately the influence of underlying market conditions on the distribution choices of borrowers, it would be preferable to actual quarterly observations as the dependent variable in any statistical analysis which attempts to explain changes in the division of corporate financing between the public and private markets.

Figure A–1 (continued)
Public Utilities and Real Estate and Financial Companies
1953–1970

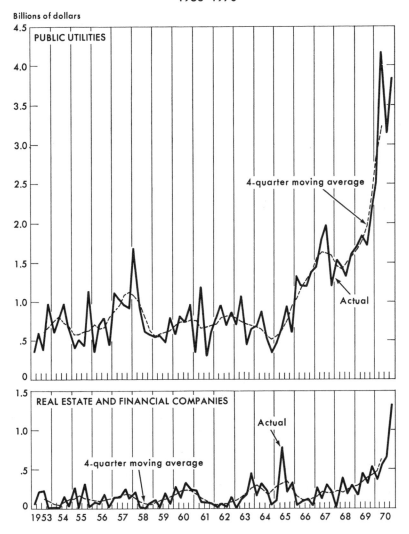

APPENDIX B

The Conversion of SEC Data on Private Placements from a Delivery to a Commitment Basis

A COMMITMENT SERIES of private placements is necessary for any statistical analysis of the corporate bond market which attempts to explain changes in the division of financing between the public and private markets. The decision to borrow in the private market is made at the time of commitment on the basis of market conditions prevailing at that time. Furthermore, virtually all other data series of the variables which may influence the debt distribution decisions of borrowers are measured at the time of *commitment*.

The SEC data on sales of private placements, unfortunately, are collected on a delivery basis. Conditions prevailing at the time of delivery are completely irrelevant to the corporate debt distribution decisions. This appendix explains the method used to convert the SEC data to a commitment basis. It also presents the resulting series for public utilities, real estate and financial companies, Fortune 500 industrial companies (i.e., the largest firms), and other industrial and miscellaneous companies (i.e., the smaller firms). The percentage of debt sold privately for these categories has also been recalculated, using the private placement commitment series and a four-quarter moving average of public offerings (Appendix A).

The SEC delivery series on private placements was converted to a commitment series in two stages. In the first, reported takedowns were converted to a first takedown series; that is, a series which assumed that all takedowns of an issue occurred at the time of the first delivery. To determine this series, the second and subsequent takedowns of an issue were assigned to the quarter in which the first takedown occurred. In the second stage of the conversion process, the resulting first takedown series was converted to a commitment series by assigning the first takedowns in each quarter (determined in the first stage of the process) to the quarters in which their corresponding commitments occurred. This two-stage procedure for converting the takedown data into a commitment series was necessitated by the absence of reliable data which reported the commitment and all takedown dates of an issue. The SEC, for example, did not begin to collect commitment dates from issuers until 1970. Reliable sample data were available however, which permitted the conversion of takedowns to commitments to be accomplished in two separate steps.

To convert the SEC takedown data to a first takedown series, borrowing by the 500 largest industrial and 50 largest commercial companies ranked by *Fortune* magazine was used. These data were recorded in the files of the SEC by delivery date and amount. For each quarter between 1953-1 and 1970-4, each delivery of an issue which occurred during a quarter was assigned to the quarter in which the first takedown of the issue occurred. In 1965-4, for example, there were $300 million takedowns of issues by Fortune 500 companies. Of these, $252 million represented portions of issues whose first deliveries occurred in 1965-4, $26 million whose first deliveries occurred in 1965-3, and the remaining $21 million whose first deliveries occurred in 1965-2. Thus, $252 million were assigned as first deliveries to 1965-4, $26 million to 1965-3, and $21 million to 1965-2. This procedure was repeated for each quarter; and the sums of the amounts assigned to each quarter exactly determined the first takedown series for the Fortune 500 group.

To determine the first delivery series for the other borrower categories, two alternative procedures were available. One simply was to allocate the takedowns in a quarter to previous quarters using the distribution of first takedowns for that quarter recorded by the Fortune 500 group. This procedure assumes, however, that the delivery schedules of Fortune 500 companies represents exactly the delivery schedules of other corporate borrowers. This is a questionable assumption, particularly for short intervals such as a quarter, since the actual takedowns of companies in the Fortune 500 sample may be affected by random factors connected with the delivery requests of a relatively small number of borrowers. Over a long interval, however, such factors should tend to offset one another and the average delivery schedule should be influenced chiefly by underlying supply conditions (i.e., the availability of funds) in the private market. Consequently, over a longer interval we might expect the takedown experience of the Fortune 500 group to become more representative of the takedown schedules of other corporate borrowers.

To determine the appropriate intervals for measuring the distribution of first takedowns of Fortune 500 companies, the (takedown-size weighted) average lag from the month of an issue's takedown to the month of its first takedown was calculated for each quarter. On the basis of this series (Figure B–1) the study period was divided into seven subperiods. In each, the average lag appeared to be sufficiently different from the lag in the preceding subperiod, indicating perhaps a change in the supply conditions in the private market.

The quarterly distribution of first takedowns of the Fortune group in a subperiod then was used to assign the takedowns of the other categories during the subperiod to their first takedown quarters. Specifically, the average delivery schedule (quarterly distribution of first takedowns) of a subperiod was determined by assigning the takedowns in a quarter to the quarters in which the first takedown occurred. The one modification of the procedure described above was that the first takedown quarter of an issue was identified, not by its actual date but by the number of quarters it preceded the takedown quarter. In the case of our previous example, $252 million of the Fortune 500's takedowns in 1965-4 were assigned a zero-quarter backward lag, $26 million, a one-quarter backward lag, and $21 million, a two-quarter backward lag. This procedure was repeated for all quarters in the study period.

To obtain the quarterly distribution of first takedowns during a subperiod, the amounts allocated to each quarter on the basis of the modified classification scheme; e.g., the current quarter (a zero-quarter backward lag), the previous quarter (a one-quarter backward lag), etc. were added and a percentage distribution of backward lags for the subperiod was calculated. In the subperiod from 1965-3 through 1967-4, for example, there were $4,579 million takedowns by Fortune 500 companies. Of these $3,015 million or 65.8% were the sum of takedowns assigned a zero-quarter lag to first takedown quarter, $534 million or 11.7% were the sum of takedowns assigned a one-quarter backward lag, $449 million or 9.8%, the sum of takedowns assigned a two-quarter backward lag, and the remaining $581 million or 12.7% the sum of takedowns assigned longer backward lags. This percentage distribution calculated for a subperiod then was used to allocate the actual takedowns in each quarter of the subperiod for the other borrower categories. Of the $412 million takedowns by public utilities in 1965-4, for example, 65.8% were assigned to 1965-4, 11.7% to 1965-3, etc. The sums of the amounts assigned to each quarter provided the first takedown series. The quarterly distribution of first takedowns for each of the subperiods used in this calculation is shown in Table B–1.

The conversion of the first takedown series to a commitment series for the four borrower categories employed the same procedure. In this instance, the sample financing data consisted of 880 issues acquired by the John Hancock Life Insurance Company between 1953 and 1969. These issues were recorded by amount, commitment date, and first takedown date.

Briefly, the (issue-size weighted) average monthly lag from the first delivery to commitment dates first was determined for each quarter; and on the basis of the

TABLE B–1

Percentage Distribution of First Delivery Dates

Quarter of First Delivery, 53-1/70-4

Subperiod	0	−1	−2	−3	−4	−5	−6	−7	−8	−9	−10	−11	−12
53-1/54-4	71.2	1.3	4.6	5.0	3.8	5.6	.9	3.2	.3	.6	1.0	2.5	—
55-1/56-2	85.9	2.9	1.8	2.4	5.7	.1	.1	—	—	—	—	1.1	—
56-3/57-3	44.1	15.6	15.0	7.9	5.6	.9	1.2	—	4.8	—	.1	4.8	—
57-4/59-4	68.1	7.9	3.3	6.9	8.4	2.2	.9	1.6	.7	—	—	—	—
60-1/65-2	85.1	5.0	4.1	1.2	1.5	.8	.9	.6	.1	.2	—	.5	—
65-3/67-4	65.8	11.7	9.8	6.9	2.4	1.9	1.5	—	—	—	—	—	—
68-1/70-4	49.0	6.9	7.5	17.3	7.1	4.8	4.2	.8	.7	.1	—	1.6	—

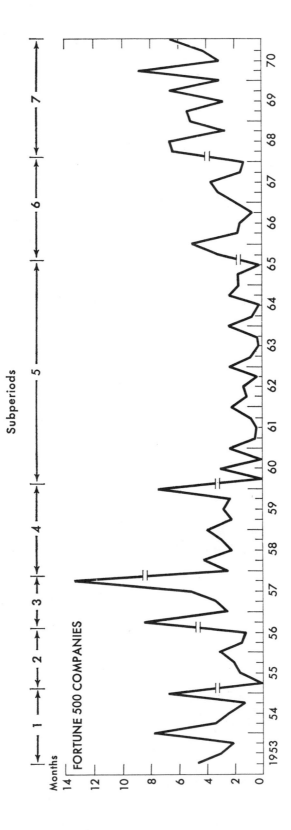

FIGURE B–1
Average Monthly Lag
Subsequent Takedown Dates to First Takedown Date
Fortune 500 Companies
1953–1970

pattern of average lags, the study period was divided into seven subperiods, as shown in Figure B–2. The first deliveries in a quarter then were assigned to their corresponding commitment quarters; the commitment quarters were identified by the number of quarters they preceded the first delivery quarter. In 1965-2, for example, John Hancock made first deliveries of $62.9 million. Of these, $14.6 million resulted from commitments made in the same quarter and thus were assigned a zero-quarter backward lag, $27.6 million resulted from commitments made in 1965-1 and were assigned a one-quarter backward lag, while $20.7 million resulted from commitments made in 1964-4 and were assigned a two-quarter backward lag. The quarterly distributions of commitments were accumulated for each subperiod (Table B–2). These distributions in turn were used to allocate the first takedowns of the other categories (obtained in the first stage of the conversion procedure) to their respective commitment quarters. Of the estimated $557 million of first takedowns of issues by public utilities in 1966-1, for example (using the distribution of first commitments shown in Table B–2 for the subperiod 1965-3/1966-3), 22.3% ($124 million) were assigned to 1966-1, 35.3% ($197 million) to 1965-4, 11.5% ($64 million) to 1965-3, and the remaining 30.9% ($172 million) to earlier quarters. Finally, the amounts assigned to each quarter were added to obtain the commitment series.

Before reviewing the resulting series, a few comments concerning the quality of the two samples used to represent the experience of all corporate borrowers seem necessary. The experience of the Fortune 500 group, used to determine the first takedown series, is probably quite representative of all corporate groups. To begin with, the $20 billion issues used to compile the series amounted to 22% of all corporate issues sold privately during the period. Moreover, there is little reason to believe that once the first takedown of an issue has occurred, the time pattern of subsequent deliveries should differ markedly among borrowers. Consequently, the Fortune 500 sample appears large enough to provide a reasonably accurate estimate of the takedown experience of other corporate groups.

Less confidence can be placed in the representative quality of the John Hancock commitment-delivery data although the sample size itself is quite large. Before choosing the Hancock sample, two other samples of similar data were analyzed

TABLE B–2
Percentage Distribution of Commitment Dates
Quarter of Commitment, 53-1/69-4

Subperiod	0	−1	−2	−3	−4	−5	−6	−7	−8
53-1/55-3	31.4	54.2	10.1	4.3	—	—	—	—	—
55-4/57-3	16.9	40.4	9.8	21.2	3.7	8.0	—	—	—
57-4/60-1	31.0	47.8	10.2	4.9	1.9	1.5	.4	2.3	—
60-2/62-4	19.6	49.1	20.2	3.2	1.2	3.2	.8	1.5	1.2
63-1/65-2	35.5	51.8	9.5	2.1	.1	.3	—	.7	—
65-3/66-3	22.3	35.3	11.5	22.1	3.8	1.2	1.4	2.4	—
66-4/69-4	8.1	20.2	14.6	13.7	13.4	9.2	5.5	5.3	10.0

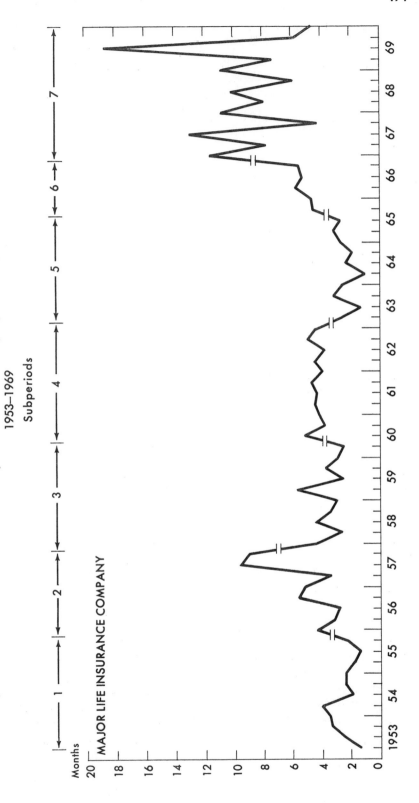

FIGURE B–2
Average Monthly Lag
First Takedown Date to Commitment Date
Major Life Insurance Company
1953–1969

thoroughly. One, based on a questionnaire sent to all Fortune 500 companies which had sold private placements during the period of study, proved to be totally unreliable. The respondents frequently were unaware of or in error on the date when a commitment actually occurred. The other sample, the private issues acquired by the Prudential Life Insurance Company, suffered from an unacceptably large number of missing observations.

Despite the acceptable size of the Hancock sample, however, it seems possible that the time intervals between the commitment and first delivery dates of issues acquired by this company are longer than those for issues acquired by other lenders. Life insurance companies tend to lend to smaller borrowers who have limited access to alternative sources of funds. As a consequence, insurance companies are in a superior bargaining position in negotiating the delivery schedules of issues, and they can delay initial deliveries without risking the loss of customers. In addition, life insurance companies undoubtedly employ more sophisticated cash planning procedures than other lenders and thus can commit funds for delivery at more distant dates in the future. Of course, in the absence of additional data, it is not possible to estimate the reliability of the Hancock sample. In view of the fact, however, that the average monthly lag between the first delivery and commitment dates was usually less than five months, a substantial percentage reduction in this lag would have been required before the commitment series was materially affected.

Figures B–3 through B–6 show the volume of actual takedowns and estimated commitments on a quarterly basis for the period 1953–1967 for the four borrower categories, the Fortune 500 companies, other industrial and miscellaneous companies, public utilities, and real estate and financial companies. It also compares the actual percentage of debt sold privately with the estimated percentage after the public offering data are adjusted to a four-quarter moving average (as described in Appendix A) and the private placement data are converted to an estimated commitment series.

As we would expect, given the mechanics of the adjustment process, the commitment series leads the takedown series for the four borrower categories, particularly during periods of rising commitments, such as 1955–1956 and 1964–1965. During these periods, lenders extended delivery schedules in response to the rising demand for funds and as a way to accommodate a larger number of borrowers. During periods of modest demand, such as 1959–1963, differences in the commitment and takedown series are quite modest.

For the period as a whole, the commitment series evidenced much smaller quarterly fluctuations than the takedowns series. This likewise results from the mechanics of the adjustment process which serves to smooth out short-run fluctuations in the takedown data.

The major difference between the actual and the adjusted percentages of debt sold privately for the four borrower categories is that the adjusted percentages present much smaller quarterly fluctuations than the actual percentages. The cyclical peaks and troughs of the two series coincide quite closely, however. This

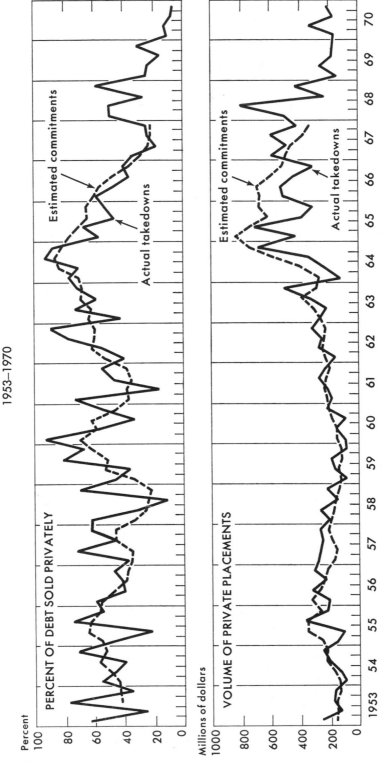

FIGURE B–3

Borrowing by Fortune 500 Companies by Takedown and
Estimated Commitment Dates

1953–1970

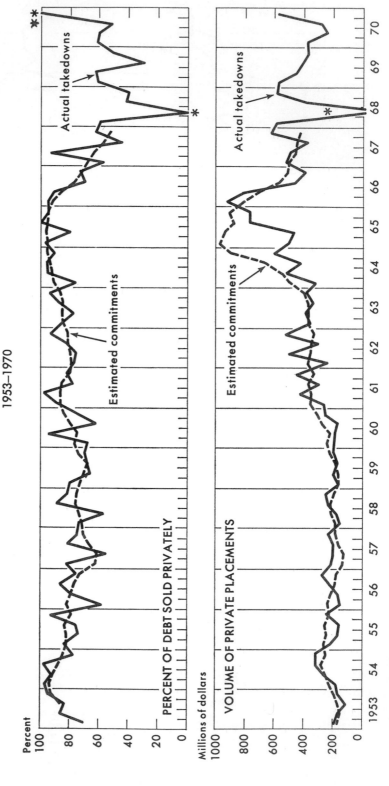

FIGURE B–4

Borrowing by Other Industrial and Miscellaneous Companies by Takedown and
Estimated Commitment Dates
1953–1970

* Number less than zero; see footnote 21, p. 146.
** Figure more than 100; see Figure A-1 (industrial and miscellaneous companies) and footnote 21.

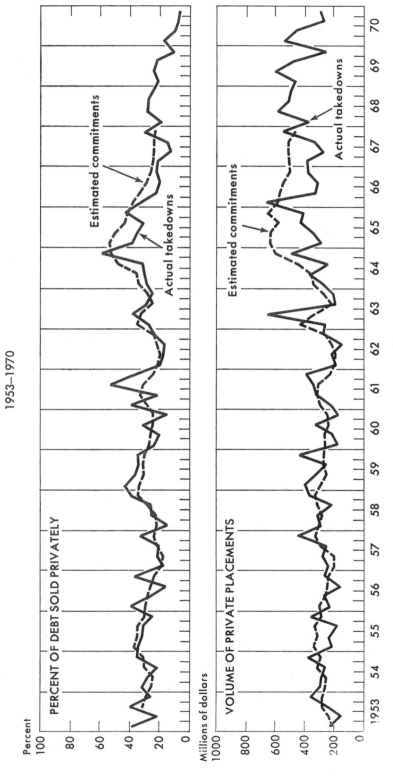

FIGURE B–5

Borrowing by Public Utilities by Takedown and Estimated
Commitment Dates
1953–1970

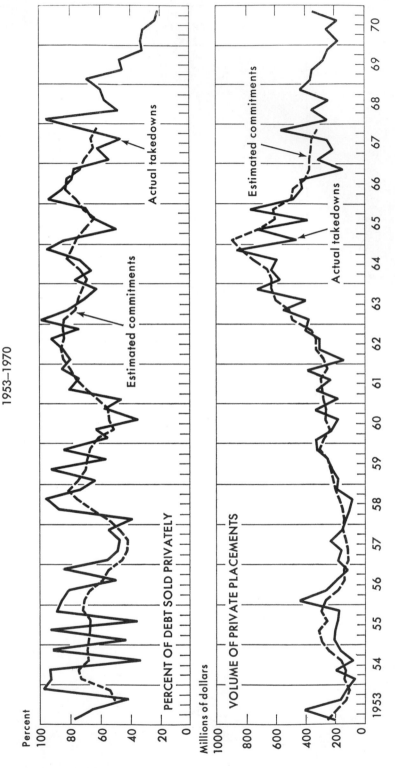

FIGURE B–6

Borrowing by Financial and Real Estate Companies by Takedown
and Estimated Commitment Dates
1953–1970

stems from the fact (Figures 5–1 and A–1) that cyclical fluctuations in the volume of public offerings were much wider than cyclical fluctuations in the volume of private financings. As a result, changes in the volume of public offerings tended to exert a dominating influence on changes in the percentage of debt sold privately.

To determine the sensitivity of the series on the percentage of corporate debt sold privately to the method used to estimate commitments from takedowns, the first takedowns series was recalculated for all corporate borrowers in two different ways. In the first, the actual quarter-by-quarter (quarterly) lags from the subsequent to the first takedown dates of the Fortune 500 companies were used to determine the first takedown series. In the second, the average period (1953-1/ 1970-4) lag from the subsequent to the first takedown dates of the Fortune group was used to determine the first takedown series. The corresponding commitment series then was obtained by multiplying the first takedown series by the appropriate subperiod lags between the first takedown and commitment dates (Table B–2). The two resulting series on the percentage of corporate debt sold privately are shown in Figure B–7 along with the original series, which was computed from the subperiod lags between the subsequent and first takedown dates, shown in Table B–1. It can be seen that with the exception of a few early observations, the three series vary by, at most, a few percentage points. This indicates that the series on the percentage of corporate debt sold privately which incorporates estimated commitments is quite insensitive to the method used to construct the first takedown series from takedown data. A similar analysis of the first takedown-to-commitment data provides similar results.

It is evident that considerable effort would be required to keep the commitment series up to date.[1] Thus, it would be convenient if the takedown data reported by the SEC could be used in place of the commitment series in studies of the corporate bond market. Through the method of construction, the commitment series leads the takedown series. It was observed above, however, that changes in the percentage of corporate debt sold privately chiefly reflected changes in the volume of public offerings rather than private placements. Thus, if the changes in the private financing series that result from the conversion of private placements to a commitment basis are small in comparison with the cyclical fluctuations in public offerings, the percentage of corporate debt sold privately may be influenced only modestly by this conversion.

To assess the effect of the conversion of private placements to a commitment series on the percentage of corporate debt sold privately, two series were computed. In one, seasonally adjusted takedowns served as the numerator of the fraction (private placements/total corporate borrowing). In the other, estimated commitments, determined by the subperiod lags between takedowns and commitments

---

[1] Beginning in 1970 the SEC began to collect commitment dates from borrowers as part of a voluntary questionnaire on the characteristics of privately placed issues and issuers. Although the SEC has not calculated the fraction of respondents who have provided commitment dates, they estimate that about three-fourths of all the questionnaires have been at least partially completed.

FIGURE B–7
Percentage of Corporate Debt Sold Privately
First Takedowns of Private Placements Determined by Quarterly,
Subperiod, and Average Period Lags Between Subsequent and
First Takedown Dates of Fortune 500 Companies
Public Offerings, 4-Quarter Moving Average
1953–1967

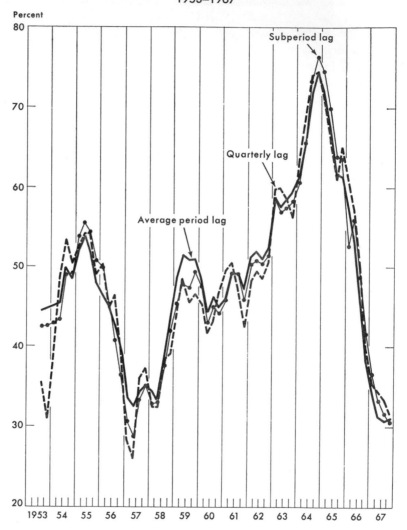

(Tables B–1 and B–2), served as the numerator.[2] In both, the four-quarter moving average of public offerings was used in calculating total corporate borrowing.

---

[2] Private placements were seasonally adjusted by the moving average method, described in Yamane, *Statistics, An Introductory Analysis,* pp. 357–363. The seasonal adjustment of

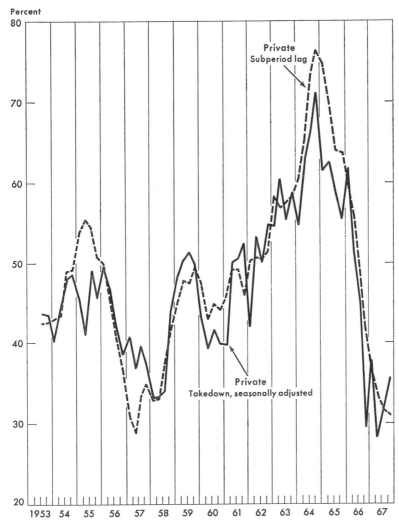

FIGURE B–8
Percentage of Corporate Debt Sold Privately
Private Placements, Takedowns, and Estimated Commitments
Public Offerings, 4-Quarter Moving Average
1953–1967

The two series on the percentage of corporate debt sold privately are within five percentage points of one another in the majority of quarters in the study

takedowns was undertaken in response to the fact that takedowns of private placements tend to be concentrated in the second and fourth quarters of a year, reflecting a concentration of policy premium payments to life insurance companies during these quarters. The four seasonal adjustment ratios were 1.071, 0.969, 1.105, and 0.894 respectively.

period (Figure B–8). The correlation coefficient between the two series is .89. However, the series derived from takedown data fails to reach the highs in 1955-2 and 1964-4, recorded by the series based on commitment data, as well as the low reached in 1957-2. The largest difference between the two series, in 1955-2, was about 15 percentage points. In view of these differences it would seem preferable to use commitment data in regression studies attempting to explain changes in the percentage of corporate debt sold privately, despite the difficulties in obtaining these data. Whether the choice of a takedown or a commitment private placement series substantially affects the coefficients of the explanatory variables in such studies, however, must await subsequent analysis.

Bibliography

American Stock Exchange, *Amex Data Book* (New York, 1971)

Andrews, Victor L., "Noninsured Corporate and State and Local Government Retirement Funds in the Financial Structure" in *Private Capital Markets,* Commission on Money and Credit Monograph (Englewood Cliffs, Prentice-Hall, 1964)

Atamian, Elliot, "Modifying Direct Placement Agreements," *Financial Executive,* February 1967

Bishop, George A., *The Response of Life Insurance Investments to Changes in Monetary Policy, 1965–1970* (New York: Life Insurance Association of America, 1971)

Board of Governors, Federal Reserve System, *Flow-of-Funds Accounts: 1945–1968* (Washington, Government Printing Office, 1969) Also quarterly

Brimmer, Andrew R., *Life Insurance Companies in the Capital Market* (East Lansing, Michigan State University, Business Studies, 1962)

Cates, David, "Are Debentures Still a Luxury?" Address delivered before the 26th Annual Bank Study Conference of the Michigan Bankers Association, Ann Arbor, December 3, 1964

Chapman, John M. and Frederick W. Jones, *Finance Companies: How and Where They Obtain Their Funds,* Studies in Consumer Credit No. 1 (New York: Graduate School of Business, Columbia University, 1959)

Christenson, Charles, *Strategic Aspects of Competitive Bidding for Corporate Securities* (Boston, Division of Research, Harvard Business School, 1965)

Cohan, Avery B., *Yields on Corporate Debt Directly Placed* (New York, National Bureau of Economic Research, distributed by Columbia University Press, 1967)

Conklin, George T., Jr., "Direct Placements," *Journal of Finance,* Vol. VI, June 1951

"Corporate Financing Directory," *Investment Dealers' Digest,* semiannually

Crockett, Jean, et al., "The Impact of Monetary Stringency on Business Investment," *Survey of Current Business,* Vol. 47, August 1967

Donaldson, Lufkin and Jenrette, Inc., *Timely Review of 1966 Credit Shortage Effects on Business Financing and Spending Decisions,* July 1967

Freitas, Lewis P., "Private Placements and Their Role in the Growth of Selected Industries," unpublished doctoral dissertation, Columbia University, 1966

Friend, Irwin, et al., *Investment Banking and the New Issues Market* (Cleveland, World Publishing Company, 1967)

Guttentag, Jack, "Credit Availability, Interest Rates, and Monetary Policy," *Southern Economic Journal,* Vol. 26, January 1960

Hardy, C. Colburn, "New Jersey's State Pension Fund: 866 Bonds, 75 Stocks, and 1 Generation Behind," *The Institutional Investor,* Vol. 1, November 1967

Hayes, Samuel L., III, "Investment Banking: Power Structure in Flux," *Harvard Business Review,* Vol. 49, March–April 1971

————, and Henry B. Reiling, "Sophisticated Financing Tool: The Warrant," *Harvard Business Review,* Vol. 47, January–February 1969

Hendershott, Patric, "Recent Development of the Financial Sector of Econometric Models," *Journal of Finance,* Vol. 23, March 1968

Hess, Arleigh P., and Willis J. Winn, *The Value of the Call Privilege* (Philadelphia, University of Pennsylvania, 1962)

Institute of Life Insurance, *Life Insurance Fact Book,* 1970

Investment Bankers Association of America, *State and Local Pension Funds* (Washington, 1968)

————, "Today's Challenge to Investment Bankers: Report of the Securities Study Committee," November 30, 1964

Jacobs, Donald, "Sources and Costs of Funds of Large Sales Finance Companies," in *Consumer Installment, Conference on Regulation,* Part II, Vol. 1 (New York, National Bureau of Economic Research, 1956)

Jaffe, Dwight, *Credit Rationing and the Commercial Loan Market* (New York, John Wiley and Son, 1971)

Jen, Frank, and Jean Wert, "The Value of the Deferred Call Privilege," *National Banking Review,* Vol. 4, March 1966

Jessup, Paul, "Bank Debt Capital: Urchin of Adversity to Child of Prosperity," *The Bankers Magazine,* Vol. 148, Summer 1965

Jones, Lawrence D., *Investment Policies of Life Insurance Companies* (Boston, Division of Research, Harvard Business School, 1968)

Kaufman, Gordon, *Statistical Decision and Related Techniques in Oil and Gas Exploration* (Englewood Cliffs, Prentice-Hall, 1963)

Lenzer, Robert, "Private Placements—The Hinges Are Turning," *Corporate Financing,* Vol. 3, September/October 1971

Life Insurance Association of America, "Average Yields on Directly Placed Corporate Bond Authorizations," various reports

————, "Record of Life Insurance Investments," various issues

————, "Sample of Major Life Insurance Companies," various issues

————, "Survey of Life Insurance Company Investment Policies Toward Refunding Protection on Company Bonds," 1958

Loomis, Carol, "The Lesson of the Credit Crisis," *Fortune,* May 1971

Loss, Louis, *Securities Regulation* (Boston, Little Brown and Company, Vol. I, 1961)

Markowitz, Harry M., *Portfolio Selection* (New York, John Wiley and Son, 1959)

New York Stock Exchange, *Fact Book* (New York, 1971)

"Oregon Blazes the Pension Trail," *The Institutional Investor,* Vol. 4, February 1970

Pye, Gordon, "The Value of Call Deferment on a Bond: Some Empirical Results," *Journal of Finance,* Vol. XXII, December 1967

————, "The Value of the Call Option on a Bond: Some Empirical Results," *Journal of Finance,* Vol. XXII, December 1967

Salomon Brothers, "An Analytic Record of Yields and Yield Spreads," various issues

————, "Bond Market Review," September 30, 1970

————, "Comments on Values," September 2, 1969; September 30, 1971

Securities and Exchange Commission, Cases:
Arkansas Louisiana Gas Company (35 SEC 313) (1953)
Crowell-Collier Publishing Co., Securities Act Release 3825 (1957)
Holding Company Act Release 16369 (1969)
Indiana and Michigan Electric Company (35 SEC 321, 326) (1953)
SEC vs. Ralston Purina Co., 346 US 126 (1953)

Securities and Exchange Commission, *Cost of Flotation of Directly Placed Corporate Securities, 1951–1955* (Washington, Government Printing Office, 1957)

————, *Institutional Investor Study, Report* (Washington, Government Printing Office, 1971)

————, "Stock Transactions of Financial Institutions in 1970," Statistical Series Release No. 2514, Washington, April 21, 1971

Silber, William, *Portfolio Behavior of Financial Institutions* (New York, Holt, Rinehart and Winston, 1970)

Thackray, John, "Investment Banking Breaks Formation," *Corporate Financing,* May/June 1971

U.S. Congress, House, *Hearings* Before a Subcommittee of the Committee on Interstate and Foreign Commerce, "Memorandum on Resales of Direct Placements by Life Insurance Companies, 1923–1951"

Van Horne, James G., *Financial Management and Policy*, second edition (Englewood Cliffs, Prentice-Hall, 1971)

Van Horne, James G., *The Function and Analysis of Capital Market Rates* (Englewood Cliffs, Prentice-Hall, 1970)

Walter, James E., *The Investment Process as Characterized by Leading Life Insurance Companies* (Boston, Division of Research, Harvard Business School, 1962)

Weingartner, Martin, "Optimal Timing of Bond Refunding," *Management Science,* Vol. 13, March 1967

Yamane, Taro, Statistics, *An Introductory Analysis* (New York, Harper and Row, 2nd ed., 1967)

INDEX